JOURNAL FOR THE STUDY OF THE PSEUDEPIGRAPHA SUPPLEMENT SERIES
17

Executive Editor
James H. Charlesworth

Associate Editors
Philip R. Davies
James R. Mueller
James C. VanderKam

The Ladies and the Cities

Transformation and Apocalyptic
Identity in Joseph and Aseneth,
4 Ezra, the Apocalypse and
The Shepherd of Hermas

Edith McEwan Humphrey

Journal for the Study of the Pseudepigrapha
Supplement Series 17

t&t clark

LONDON · NEW YORK · OXFORD · NEW DELHI · SYDNEY

For my parents, Bessie and Andrew, who read to me whenever
'the sun did not shine; it was too wet to play', and who opened
to me the wonder of words and the Word.

T&T CLARK
Bloomsbury Publishing Plc
50 Bedford Square, London, WC1B 3DP, UK
1385 Broadway, New York, NY 10018, USA

BLOOMSBURY, T&T CLARK and the T&T Clark logo are
trademarks of Bloomsbury Publishing Plc

First published by Sheffield Academic Press 1995
Paperback edition first published by Bloomsbury Academic 2018

Bloomsbury Publishing Plc does not have any control over,
or responsibility for, any third-party websites referred to or in this book.
All internet addresses given in this book were correct at the time of
going to press. The author and publisher regret any inconvenience
caused if addresses have changed or sites have ceased to exist,
but can accept no responsibility for any such changes.

A catalogue record for this book is available from the British Library.

PB: 978-0-56768-680-0
ePDF: 978-0-56768-526-1

To find out more about our authors and books visit
www.bloomsbury.com and sign up for our newsletters.

CONTENTS

My interest in transformation and things apocalyptic was first whetted during a graduate seminar on Jesus, in which we were encouraged to do 'background' studies on the synoptic Transfiguration passages. The background was transformed into foreground as I entered the intriguing world of apocalypses. I would like to express my thanks to Dr N.T. Wright and Dr D. Runnalls for their questions and guidance in my study of this genre, which led to the initial form of this study as a dissertation at the Faculty of Religious Studies of McGill University. Thanks is also due to the Canadian government for the funds made available through the Social Sciences and Humanities Research Council during my graduate studies.

My appreciation goes also to numerous colleagues of the Canadian Society of Biblical Studies and Society of Biblical Literature's Reading the Apocalypse Seminar, who have both challenged and inspired me in my research and thinking during and since that time. I am especially grateful for the probing questions and expertise of Dr John J. Collins, and for the wit and welcome of Dr David Barr, chair of the SBL Seminar, who has been encouraging to a younger colleague. I was tempted, in my revision, to reflect my recent turn towards a rhetorical analysis of vision, but realized that the original project was so moulded by a literary approach that such a change would necessitate an entirely different book. Moreover, although rhetorical analysis is perhaps a more timely endeavour, it should not be seen as supplanting, but complementing literary studies. In the preparation of this manuscript, I have thus left the original argument of the 1991 thesis relatively untouched, but have endeavoured to respond to the pertinent research that has been done on the four texts in the last three years. While labouring on the 'transformation' of the thesis to book, I have been guided by the helpful comments and suggestions of Dr Philip R. Davies, co-director of Sheffield Academic Press. Any infelicitous expressions or opinions that remain are, of course, my own responsibility.

Finally, it is certain that this study has been noticeably improved by the support, suggestions and painstaking original editing of my colleague and husband Christopher W. Humphrey. Without his grace, and the forebearance and humour of my three daughters, my own study would have been far less engaging, and this book might never have come to birth.

ABBREVIATIONS

AB	Anchor Bible
ANRW	*Aufstieg und Niedergang der römischen Welt*
ATANT	Abhandlungen zur Theologie des Alten und Neuen Testaments
ATR	*Anglican Theologiacal Review*
BEvT	Beiträge zur evangelischen Theologie
BJS	Brown Judaic Studies
BZNW	Beihefte zur *ZNW*
ConBNT	Coniectanea biblica, New Testament
DBAT	*Dielheimer Blätter zum Alten Testament*
DNTT	*Dictionary of New Testament Theology*
EBib	Etudes bibliques
ETL	*Ephemerides theologicae lovanienses*
EvQ	*Evangelical Quarterly*
EvT	*Evangelische Theologie*
ExpTim	*Expository Times*
FRLANT	Forschungen zur Religion und Literatur des Alten und Neuen Testaments
GCS	Griechische christliche Schriftsteller
HDR	Harvard Dissertations in Religion
HeyJ	*Heythrop Journal*
HNT	Handbuch zum Neuen Testament
HTR	*Harvard Theological Review*
HUCA	*Hebrew Union College Annual*
ICC	International Critical Commentary
Int	*Interpretation*
JAAR	*Journal of the American Academy of Religion*
JBL	*Journal of Biblical Literature*
JewEnc	*Jewish Encyclopedia*
JSJ	*Journal for the Study of Judaism in the Persian, Hellenistic and Roman Period*
JSNT	*Journal for the Study of the New Testament*
JSNTSup	*Journal for the Study of the New Testament*, Supplement Series
JSOTSup	*Journal for the Study of the Old Testament*, Supplement Series
JSP	*Journal for the Study of the Pseudepigrapha*
JSPSup	*Journal for the Study of the Pseudepigrapha*, Supplement Series
JTS	*Journal of Theological Studies*

LCL	Loeb Classical Library
MNTC	Moffatt NT Commentary
Neot	*Neotestamentica*
NLH	*New Literary History*
NovT	*Novum Testamentum*
NTM	New Testament Message
NTS	*New Testament Studies*
OTP	*Old Testament Pseudepigrapha*
RB	*Revue biblique*
RevQ	*Revue de Qumran*
SBLDS	SBL Dissertation Series
SBLSP	SBL Seminar Papers
SEÅ	*Svensk exegetisk årsbok*
SPB	Studia postbiblica
SR	*Studies in Religion/Sciences religieuses*
TDNT	G. Kittel and G. Friedrich (eds.), *Theological Dictionary of the New Testament*
TLZ	*Theologischer Literaturzeitung*
TQ	*Theologische Quartalschrift*
VC	*Vigiliae Christianae*
WMANT	Wissenschaftliche Monographien zum Alten und Neuen Testament
WUNT	Wissenschaftliche Untersuchungen zum Neuen Testament
ZAW	*Zeitschrift für die alttestamentliche Wissenschaft*
ZNW	*Zeitschrift für die neutestamentliche Wissenschaft*

Chapter 1

INTRODUCTION: APOCALYPSES AND TRANSFORMATION

What is an Apocalypse?

Whosoever gives his mind to four things it were better for him if he had
not come into the world—what is above? what is beneath? and what was
beforetime? and what will be hereafter? And whosoever takes no thought
for the honour of his Maker, it were better for him if he had not come into
the world (*m. Hag.* 2.1).[1]

This rabbinic saying might be seen as representative of the suspicion
displayed by many ancients regarding *bereshit* or *merkavah* meditation.
Its sentiment, it seems, was paralleled by religious leaders, both Jewish
and Christian, in their general approach to apocalyptic literature, few
examples of which were canonized. Their discomfiture has been shared
until very recently by modern scholars (but for different reasons) whenever they have considered apocalypses—those visionary and complex
pieces which deal with the protological, eschatological, infernal and
celestial. Even when 'apocalyptic' came to be understood in the early
twentieth century (via Johannes Weiss and Albert Schweitzer) as a *sine
qua non* for the formation of the New Testament and Christian theology,
many shrank from the bold statements of these two, and engaged in
'agonised attempts'[2] to save at least Jesus himself from the association.
The genre 'apocalypse' therefore continued to be considered as peri-
pheral to biblical studies, and was usually treated as an ancillary concern,
with little time being given to the study of the genre *per se*. When the
question is now asked, 'What is an apocalypse?', however, the waters
are not nearly so muddy as when Klaus Koch published *Ratlos vor der
Apokalyptik* in 1970. As a first step away from perplexity, Koch's

---

1. *The Mishnah* (trans. H. Danby; London: Oxford University Press, 1933),
p. 213.
2. K. Koch, *The Rediscovery of Apocalyptic* (trans. M. Kohl; London: SCM
Press, 1972), p. 57. German original *Ratlos vor der Apokalyptik* (1970).

cogent piece traced the history of apocalyptic study through the unsym-
pathetic German school (Plöger,[3] Rössler,[4] von Rad[5]), who, for all their
differences, commonly posited a 'gulf'[6] between prophecy and
apocalyptic, with the emphasis on prophecy. In contrast, the British and
American Old Testament scholars (Rowley,[7] Frost,[8] Russell[9]) saw the
apocalyptists as successors of prophecy,[10] albeit lesser lights; British and
American critics in the field of New Testament have varied in their
assessments of these writings. Running through all these discussions,
however, have been some common elements, including the imprecise
use of the adjective 'apocalyptic', and the importance of 'apocalyptic
eschatology' for the proper definition of the genre 'apocalypse'.

Koch's study was of watershed value, in that he distinguished
between the genre, the historical movements and the theology (especially
eschatology) associated with the term 'apocalyptic'. Such precision was
of great help in a climate where 'apocalyptic' could be used interchangeably with 'eschatological', although the latter term itself had
myriad definitions.[11] Moreover, he compiled a list of characteristics
(*Rahmengattung*) which typifies at least one group of apocalypses. The
limits of Koch's scheme, however, have been illustrated by more recent
scholars, especially Christopher Rowland, who has shown that apocalypses should be understood in terms of their 'vertical dimension',[12] that
is, their vision of direct intercourse between the seer and the divine.
Without acknowledgement of this dimension, even a careful

3.   O. Plöger, *Theokratie und Eschatologie* (WMANT 2; Neukirchen-Moers:
Neukirchener Verlag, 1959).
4.   D. Rössler, *Gesetz und Geschichte* (Neukirchen–Vluyn: Neukirchener Verlag,
1960).
5.   G. von Rad, *Theologie des Alten Testaments* (2 vols.; Munich: Kaiser, 4th
edn, 1965 [1957]).
6.   Koch, *Rediscovery*, p. 36.
7.   H.H. Rowley, *The Relevance of Apocalyptic* (London: Lutterworth, 1944).
8.   S.B. Frost, *Old Testament Apocalyptic* (London: Epworth, 1952).
9.   D.S. Russell, *The Method and Message of Apocalyptic* (London: SCM Press,
1964).
10.   Koch, *Rediscovery*, pp. 49-56.
11.   G.B. Caird, in *The Language and Imagery of the Bible* (Philadelphia:
Westminster Press, 1981), pp. 241-56, makes acute observations concerning the
adventures of this slippery word.
12.   C. Rowland, 'The Visions of God in Apocalyptic Literature', *JSJ* 10 (1979),
pp. 137-54. See also *The Open Heaven* (New York: Crossroad, 1982), especially p.
199, but also throughout the entire discussion.

Rahmengattung such as that provided by Koch excludes, or at least misrepresents such apocalypses as *1 Enoch* and the *Martyrdom of Isaiah*. This is no indictment of Koch, who himself presented his framework as a 'preliminary demonstration'.[13] Despite much insight, his list still reflects a time when apocalypses, and related 'apocalyptic' literature and movements, were considered valuable material for study only insofar as they clarified New Testament issues. This was so especially because they helped to bridge the gap between the testaments, giving some insight into the mysterious years which provided the matrix for Christian thought. Because many apocalypses (although perhaps not all) contained eschatological material, they were deemed especially helpful in illuminating troublesome passages or issues such as Son of Man, 'that day', and so on. Moreover, the literature was invariably situated against the backdrop of the canonical prophetic books, some of which exhibited 'proto-apocalyptic' tendencies whenever they verged on eschatology.

While such studies suited the purposes of the day, Koch already recognized their one-sidedness. Rowland has gone further to suggest that apocalyptic literature and apocalypses ought really to be understood in the light of their visionary—rather than eschatological—heritage from prophecy. His definition of the genre runs along semantic lines (the apocalypse as an 'uncovering' or 'revelation') and continues the line of thought pursued by Gershom Scholem[14] and Ithamar Gruenwald,[15] that apocalypses are related to the later rabbinic mystical writings. Rowland's work is most helpful in that it points to a vital element of the apocalypse, that is, its visionary impulse, which has been ignored by scholars even after the gulf between prophecy and apocalypse ceased to be a credible construct.[16] Moreover, Rowland is to be applauded in that he goes

13. Koch, *Rediscovery*, p. 23.

14. G. Scholem, *Major Trends in Jewish Mysticism* (New York: Schocken, 3rd rev. edn, 1961).

15. I. Gruenwald, *Apocalyptic and Merkavah Mysticism* (Leiden: Brill, 1980).

16. The thesis of P.D. Hanson, 'Old Testament Apocalyptic Re-Examined', *Int* 25 (1979), pp. 454-79, concerning the origins of apocalyptic has been greatly qualified or rejected through the recent recognition of the genre's complex background. His view posited in apocalyptic literature the dissolution of 'realistic' and 'visionary' balance which had been found in actual prophecy. Apocalyptic was seen to gain ground when visionary sectarians rejected history as a medium of revelation and looked to a future divine breakthrough, couched in mythic terms. What emerges is 'eschatologized myth' (p. 471), and the recognition of a *bona fide* apocalyptic movement. It is now apparent that apocalypses cannot be adequately understood as degenerate prophecy, since they

beyond those apocalypses related to the canonical examples in working out the pedigree and definition of the genre. That is, he takes into account the ancient character of some portions of the Enoch corpus, and considers them to be as important as the canonical Daniel in providing early models for the genre. The very breadth of Rowland's definition, however, is troublesome, and may not in every case allow for an adequate distinction between those pieces generally deemed apocalypses and other visionary works.

The work of the Society of Biblical Literature Genres Project, published in *Semeia* 14 (1979), and headed by John J. Collins, provides a fruitful step beyond Koch's call for clarification. Rather than simply compiling a list of characteristics, as did Koch, or providing an elastic definition, as has Rowland, this study has attempted to work out a model by which individual apocalypses of various backgrounds can be classified and understood. A basic definition for the genre is given, one which includes the structure of the genre, the notion of transcendence, the temporal aspect of eschatology, and the spatial aspect of the heavenly worlds:

> 'Apocalypse' is a genre of revelatory literature with a narrative framework, in which a revelation is mediated by an otherworldly being to a human recipient, disclosing a transcendent reality which is both temporal, insofar as it envisages eschatological salvation, and spatial insofar as it involves another, supernatural world.[17]

Along with this definition, a master paradigm is suggested for the genre,[18] a paradigm which includes the literary apparatus of the apocalypse, such as manner of revelation or paraenesis, and the temporal and spatial elements often found within the works. Jewish, Christian, Gnostic, Persian and Graeco-Roman apocalypses have been analyzed by reference to the master paradigm and charted along the 'temporal' and 'spatial' axes. Collins has further classified the apocalypse genre by dividing it into two types and three sub-types:

have been informed by other traditions, notably wisdom. Nor is it at all clear that a single identifiable movement generated literature of such variety.

17. J.J. Collins, 'Introduction: Towards the Morphology of a Genre', *Semeia* 14 (1979), p. 9.

18. See the chart which is Figure 1 below, taken from J.J. Collins, 'Introduction: Towards the Morphology of a Genre', *Semeia* 14 (1979), pp. 6-8.

Ia.   'Historical' Apocalypses with No Otherworldly Journey
Ib.   Apocalypses with Cosmic and/or Political Eschatology (which have neither historical review nor otherworldly journey)
Ic.   Apocalypses with Only Personal Eschatology (and no otherworldly journey)
IIa. 'Historical' Apocalypses with an Otherworldly Journey
IIb. Otherworldly Journeys with Cosmic and/or Political Eschatology
IIc. Otherworldly Journeys with Only Personal Eschatology[19]

Type I apocalypses have no otherworldly journey, while Type II do, hence it is the spatial axis (where is the action located?) which is crucial; sub-types a, b and c are differentiated by reference to the temporal axis (what kind of eschatology and history do they contain?). A second volume of *Semeia* has adapted the suggestions of several scholars and extended the earlier definition. It adds the aspect of function to those of content and form: an apocalypse is 'intended to interpret present, earthly circumstances in light of the supernatural world and of the future, and to influence both the understanding and the behaviour of the audience by means of divine authority'.[20]

Not everyone has agreed wholly with Collins's definition or classes, some finding them too rigid,[21] while others have felt that they are too broad.[22] However, since the *Semeia* volume, it has been virtually

19. Collins, 'Morphology', pp. 14-15.
20. A. Yarbro Collins, 'Early Christian Apocalypticism: Genre and Social Setting', *Semeia* 36 (1986), p. 7.
21. Especially important here are Rowland, who insists that eschatology is not essential to the genre, but merely prominent, and E.P. Sanders, 'The Genre of Palestinian Jewish Apocalypses', in D. Hellholm (ed.), *Apocalypticism in the Mediterranean World and the Near East: Proceedings of the International Colloquium on Apocalypticism, Uppsala, August 12–17, 1979* (Tübingen: Mohr, 1983), pp. 447-59, who puts forward an essentialist definition in which the sociological function plays a key role. Collins has responded to these criticisms and alternative views on p. 8 of *The Apocalyptic Imagination: An Introduction to the Jewish Matrix of Christianity* (New York: Crossroad, 1987), and it seems that no *détente* is forthcoming. In my view, Rowland's criticism of the *Semeia* definition— that it should not imply the *necessity* of eschatology—may be worth hearing; his *ad hoc* approach, however, is by no means as fruitful as the scheme suggested by Collins. Sanders's work is simply not concerned with the genre *per se*; its inherent problems have been demonstrated by Collins.
22. D.E. Aune, *The New Testament in its Literary Environment* (Philadelphia: Westminster Press, 1987), pp. 226-52; and D. Hellholm, *Das Visionenbuch des*

impossible for scholars to refer to the term 'apocalyptic' in a careless or loose fashion,[23] and even those who have had no interest in genre analysis have had to acknowledge the important process of clarification that has begun. For those who find Collins' work congenial, the volume has provided a point of departure for the study of individual apocalypses, or for analyses of various elements of the paradigm. Such use is encouraged by Collins himself, who comments,

> these remarks on the relation of the various elements of the paradigm to each other are of the most preliminary nature. An adequate discussion of these matters can only be achieved through a detailed analysis of individual apocalypses and the examination of the precise ways in which the various elements function.[24]

The present study will adopt, for its working model, the definition of apocalypse provided by the *Semeia* project, and will proceed in the spirit of that volume.

What Kind of Transcendence?

The *Semeia* definition asserts that the vision within the apocalypse 'discloses a transcendent reality'. Even prior to the *Semeia* project, transcendence was commonly acknowledged as a key motif in apocalypses. One of the ways in which this transcendence is expressed in the documents is through 'transformation' or 'transfiguration'. Although Koch, and others preceding and following him, have seen 'glory' (δόξα or equivalents) as a 'catchword',[25] the narrative events by which divine

Hermas als Apokalypse: Formgeschichte und texttheoritische Studien zu einer literarischen Gattung. I. *Methodologische Vorüberlegungen und makrostrukturelle Textanalyse* (ConBNT 13.1; Lund: Gleerup, 1980). These critics would like to extend the definition of the genre and change its contours by reference to 'hierarchical embedment' (D. Aune, 'The Apocalypse of John and the Problem of Genre', *Semeia* 36 [1986], p. 71), first person narrative, authoritative claims and literary function. These refinements nevertheless take their point of departure from the *Semeia* discussion.

23. K. Berger, *Formgeschichte des Neuen Testaments* (Heidelberg: Quelle & Meyer, 1984), pp. 295-305, holds out for the earlier casual use of the term *Apokalyptik*, but does so only after a polemical introduction to his material. In this introduction, he points out the difficulties felt by a New Testament scholar faced by Collins's scheme, which he characterizes as having only a '(scheinbare) Weite' and as being 'nicht ohne einen Hauch von Willkür' (p. 295).

24. Collins, 'Morphology', p. 12.

25. Koch, *Rediscovery*, p. 32.

glory is transferred to humans have not been noted. Martha Himmelfarb, in a subsequent *Semeia* volume dealing with apocalypses,[26] goes beyond the generality of 'transcendence' to sample a few works which present the transformation of the seer. The experience of the apocalyptic visionary (or at least its literary facsimile) is set in the context of Graeco-Roman literature as a whole. She also discusses possible reasons for the omission of transformation in apocalypses other than the ones she has considered, and argues that this feature or its lack may be an important tool of generic description. As Himmelfarb remarks, 'If transcendence is the key to apocalypses, we still need to ask, what kind of transcendence?'[27]

Himmelfarb has called for more attention to one particular type of transcendence, that is, transformation. Her work concentrated on 'apocalypses with heavenly journey' (Type II), and the consequent change of the enraptured, glory-touched seer. There are, however, within the 'apocalypses without heavenly journey' (Type I), other types of transformation, primarily of a symbolic nature. A particularly striking example of symbolic transformation is to be found in the image of the transfigured Woman-Building. That is, in several apocalypses of the Type I variety, there is a female figure who is associated with an imposing and divinely constructed edifice, either a city or a tower, who undergoes a transformation which is central to the action of the work. The building, like the woman herself, is a symbol of the faithful as a whole, either Jewish or Christian, hence she is a figure of solidarity. In this study, we will go beyond a simple observation of transcendence and transformation in apocalypses to examine the literary function of transfiguration in four representative passages. In each case, this narrative event moves a symbolic female figure from an aspect of weakness to a picture of glory, but does this in a specific way to specific ends. We will consider, then, comparable but unique transfigurations in three apocalypses, and in one passage closely related in form to an apocalypse. The key *topoi* are *4 Ezra* 9–10, Apocalypse 12 and 21, *The Shepherd of Hermas, Vis.* 1.2.2, 2.2.3, 3.1.1-2, 10, and *Joseph and Aseneth* 18–19 (as it relates to the preceding vision, 14–17). For convenience, the latter two texts, which are less well known, shall be designated as *Hermas* (unless the entire book, not simply the *Visions*, is in view), and *Aseneth*.

26. M. Himmelfarb, 'The Experience of the Visionary and Genre in the Ascension of Isaiah 6–11 and the Apocalypse of Paul', *Semeia* 36 (1986), pp. 97-111.

27. Himmelfarb, 'The Experience of the Visionary', p. 109.

What Kind of Symbol?

It is not surprising that similar images are to be found in these works, each of which enjoyed relative popularity both in its original milieu and subsequently. The works, although separated by original language, particular *Sitz im Leben*, and even faith orientation, may be dated with all probability within a two-hundred-year period, from the first century BCE to the early second century CE. Moreover, although only the Apocalypse was actually canonized, all four works are deeply infused with Old Testament traditions and symbolism, and see themselves in direct continuity with these. As Elias Bickerman points out, Jewish works of the Hellenistic age were afforded dignity through their 'parabiblical' style.[28] The Jewish work *4 Ezra*, by its very pseudonym, calls upon its predecessors. It provided the central core for the expanded Christian version (usually called *2 Esdras*) which was appended to the Vulgate and continues to enjoy apocryphal status in the Church. *Aseneth*, although little known today, takes its point of departure from the Old Testament narrative of Gen. 41.45, and is replete with biblical images, so that it enjoyed popularity not only in its (probable) original Jewish context, but also in the early Church. The mainstream characteristics of *The Shepherd of Hermas* are well-known, and it is not surprising that such a piece was a strong contender for canonicity, despite disputes about its dating and 'Hellenistic' elements.

When such patently biblical pieces combine the image of a building (city or tower) with that of a woman, it should be clear to the reader that Zion or Jerusalem symbolism is in view. My concern in this study is to read the imagery sympathetically, with an ear for the metaphorical 'grammar' of the texts, and with an eye to the cues, or 'lures'[29] that the text itself provides. In the case of an apocalypse, we are dealing with a relatively 'open' text, a text which uses symbolism in an evocative, polyvalent, allusive and sometimes elusive manner. Certainly, an

---

28. E. Bickerman, *The Jews in the Greek Age* (Cambridge, MA: Harvard University Press, 1988), p. 204.

29. This term, which comes from process hermeneutics, seems to be an apt description of the interaction between text and reader. However, in using it, I do not intend to import all the attendant methodological and philosophical foundations of this school of interpretation. See R. Pregeant, *Christology beyond Dogma: Matthew's Christ in Process Hermeneutic* (Missoula: Scholars; Philadelphia: Fortress Press, 1978).

interpretation of this kind of text calls for a certain reconfiguration on the part of the reader; yet, to call a text 'open' is to recognize a potential range of meanings, not to accept the premise that it can mean anything and everything. The stance adopted here will be that of the active listener or involved spectator, who attempts to respond to the suggestive language of the piece at hand. Others have been concerned about the implications of female symbolism per se, and have privileged a reading of the text that concentrates upon gender codes in isolation from the other images with which these are connected. Here we will be concerned with the special configuration of Woman–Building imagery, as found in four pieces that patently employ the symbolism within a certain tradition: their pictures speak potently of the faithful people of God, drawing upon Zion imagery. Such a background is confirmed when we see that the symbolism is linked with themes of suffering, persecution or sorrow, as in each of these pieces. *Aseneth* presents us with the archetypal penitent, Aseneth, the stranger to God who is transformed into the mother of penitents, their 'City of Refuge'. *4 Ezra* depicts the lamenting woman who becomes the glorious Zion before the eyes of the prophet. The Apocalypse describes the persecuted mother in the wilderness who is really Queen of Heaven, and who becomes the Bride, the New Jerusalem. *Hermas* introduces the noble but weary woman Church who is progressively rejuvenated, and must suffer, yet who also appears as God's own tower, a stronghold against the world. In each case, the woman is transformed from weakness to strength through a remarkable event or series of events reminiscent of Zion's triumph in the closing chapters of Isaiah.

The presence of this imagery is not restricted to apocalypses alone, but is found in various forms among other pieces indebted to the earlier biblical tradition. In the Old Testament, both the land of Israel as a whole and the city Zion (as Israel's synecdoche, or even epitome) were pictured as women, in various aspects. In Isa. 54.1, Jer. 3.20, Ezek. 16.8-63 and Hos. 2.19, Yahweh is seen as the husband of the land or the city, for good or ill. In Isa. 49.21, 66.7-11 and Hos. 4.5, Zion and Israel are pictured as a mother, and the picture is completed in Mic. 4.9, Isa. 26.16-18, Jer. 4.31, and 13.21 (and later, Sir. 48.19) where that mother is seen in travail. The imagery is used variously to offer hope to the people of God, or to call them to account. Hence, the pictures can be either positive or negative, from LXX Ps. 86.5, which envisions Zion as a glorious metropolis founded by God, to Jer. 3.6-25, which makes Judah a harlot like her sister Israel.

Because the symbol is so well attested, and has been treated extensively in *Traditionsgeschichte* approaches, it is not necessary to trace its
history here.[30] By the point at which our pieces receive this symbol, it is
no longer important to discern phases in the tradition, nor to determine
such historical questions as whether the tradition arose in the early
monarchical period or later.[31] Any or all of the motifs associated with
the symbol, including the holy City as a refuge, its association with
Yahweh's triumphant creation, Zion as the City of Yahweh the king,
and the City as a mountain peak with flowing river, may have been
intended by the authors of these works, or inferred by those who read
them. It shall indeed be seen that such traditional themes are in some
places explicitly articulated in the texts under discussion. However, the
tradition is so overladen and rich that many of the earlier theologies
accompanying these motifs have been conflated or even left aside. In
tracing the career of the personified woman from the eighth century
through to the poems of Lamentations, Norman Porteous says:

> ...by the time of Jeremiah and Ezekiel...Jerusalem had become the effec-
> tive representative of Israel, people of God, and could be regarded as
> uniting the two streams of tradition, that concerning the Exodus and that
> concerning the monarchy...This results in a certain confusion of metaphors.
> The essential point to bear in mind is that the great hopes associated with
> the chosen people seem now to be linked with the fate of a city, the very
> name of which is in the way of becoming a symbol.[32]

In the poignant poetry of Lamentations, Porteous tells us, the
'personification is more than a poetic device'[33]—indeed, it has become a
well-established tradition by which 'worshippers in Judah were being
taught to react to the shattering experiences they had passed through'.[34]

Our pieces, along with others using the tradition, reflect a positive view
of Zion, so that although suffering and necessary transformation are key

30. For a review of literature and debates associated with Zion, daughter of
Jerusalem in Lamentations and Second Isaiah, and the NT use of the theme, see
G. Fohrer and E. Lohse, 'Σιών, Ἰερουσαλήμ, Ἰεροσόλυμα, Ἰεροσολυμίτης',
TDNT, VII, pp. 292-319, 319-38.
31. E. Rohland, M. Robert versus M. Noth. See B. Ollenburger, *Zion, the City of
the Great King: A Theological Symbol of the Jerusalem Cult* (Sheffield: JSOT Press,
1987), pp. 17-18.
32. N.W. Porteous, 'Jerusalem–Zion: The Growth of a Symbol', in *Living the
Mystery: Collected Essays* (Oxford: Basil Blackwell, 1967), pp. 96-97.
33. 'Jerusalem–Zion: The Growth of a Symbol', p. 96.
34. 'Jerusalem–Zion: The Growth of a Symbol'.

motifs, the notions of perfidy and uncleanness are not part of the profile (versus, e.g., Ezekiel or Lamentations). There are in the New Testament and in various apocryphal works joyful references to the holy City as God's dwelling (Bar. 4.5–5.9, 2 *Apoc. Bar.* 4.1-7, Tob. 13.9-23, *Sib. Or.* 3.787, Heb. 12.22), and also a picture of her as a woman who enjoys God's favour (Gal. 4.26). Baruch and Tobit retain the hope of a promised new Zion, probably earthly, as does the later *Pes. R.* 26.7. In *2 Apocalypse of Baruch*, Hebrews and Galatians, the vision of a present heavenly Jerusalem, hidden in the bosom of God, seems to emerge—this ideal Zion replacing the lost city. Michael Stone traces 'The Heavenly Jerusalem: "the unseen city" '[35] from its origins in Isaiah, Ezekiel and Zechariah, through its articulation in Apocryphal, Pseudepigraphical and New Testament literature, to its exploration in rabbinic and later Jewish apocalyptic writings. He demonstrates from *4 Ezra* and rabbinic literature (especially *Midr. Teh.* on Ps. 90.3) that the unseen city often had bound up with it the idea of pre-existence. Stone is not concerned with the depiction of the holy City as Wife or Bride in his dissertation. However, it is clear that wherever the City is given personality in writings later than the Hebrew Bible, the feminine is adopted, in accord with the earlier prophetic literature.

Whether the hope of an ideal Zion is earthly or heavenly, pre-existent, present or future, the general Old Testament idea is retained that God has as his spouse and habitation those who are faithful, and is preserving them, despite outward appearances. In *Aseneth, 4 Ezra*, the Apocalypse and *Hermas*, this hope is made concrete within the apocalyptic form through the event of transformation or transfiguration experienced by the female figure. The reader does not have to do simply with imagery or metaphor that expresses confidence or hope in God's faithfulness; he or she is presented with the envisioned transformation of a central female character, a transformation which is crucial to the drama of the apocalypse. This figure, because of her innate nobility and protection by the Almighty, is best labelled 'Lady', in the classical (if not etymological or popular) sense of the word: a 'woman who rules', and a 'woman who is the object of chivalrous devotion'.[36]

---

35. M.E. Stone, *Features of the Eschatology of IV Ezra* (PhD dissertation, Harvard, 1965; Atlanta: Scholars Press, 1989), pp. 101ff.

36. *The Oxford English Dictionary* (ed. R.W. Burchfield; Oxford: Clarendon, 1987), VII, p. 582.

Proposed Method

John Collins's invitation in the earliest *Semeia* volume was to add definition to the proposed paradigm through detailed analyses of individual apocalypses. I hope here to take up this challenge, by adopting a twofold method: first, to engage in a close study of the surface structure of each text, disclosing the literary function of the transformation in each; and second, to discover what the element of transformation has to say about the genre apocalypse, specifically, about the Type I genre identified by Collins. So then, Chapters 2 to 5 will demonstrate the appropriateness of considering the work at hand as an example of 'apocalypse', against the backdrop of previous scholarship, and then engage in close observation of the structure of the text. Such techniques as the following will be illuminated so as to reveal a plausible shape for each piece: sequential numbering or signals of a new vision within the work itself; repeated phrases and themes; specific *Leitwörter*; repeated patterns of action; parallelism, chiasmus and contrast; emphasis through 'oracle', hymn, prayer or 'soliloquy'; and departure from a pattern established in earlier sections. Once the structure has been determined, the overall direction of the work will be shown through observing the relationship of the parts, their relative length, the resolution of certain themes and problems, and so on. The episode of transformation will then be placed within the patterns which have been observed, so that its importance to each work can be demonstrated. These observations about narrative shaping do not depend upon an assumption of polarity or an expectation of 'deep' structure which reflects or encodes reality. They do recognize the importance of what has been called 'synchronic' observation, not as hostile to historical concerns, but alongside these. Such pursuits of structure, independent of the ideologies of pure structuralism, have increasingly shown their worth in the past few decades, from the early discussion of 'rhetorical criticism' by James Muilenburg[37]

---

37. 'Form Criticism and Beyond', *JBL* 88 (1969), pp. 1-18. This was an early plea for attention to the style and patterns of the text. His term 'rhetorical criticism' has not been taken up by many, perhaps because of its confusion with the application of classical models in such authors as G.A. Kennedy, *New Testament Interpretation through Rhetorical Criticism* (Chapel Hill: University of North Carolina Press, 1984). The difficulty of finding an appropriate term for a many-sided movement which concerns itself with such matters as structure, narrative and style is complicated by the fact that 'structuralism' proper has adopted 'structural criticism' to describe its method.

(later adapted by such students as Phyllis Trible),[38] to the specific but extremely varied studies of scholars including Robert Polzin,[39] Robert Culley,[40] J.P. Fokkelman,[41] Robert Alter[42] and R. Alan Culpepper.[43]

Often, such discussions have stopped with an analysis of specific texts, although methodological issues have come increasingly to the fore. However, it is clear that a close reading of the text may not only open up the text itself (a worthy enough occupation!), but may also serve to elucidate a text-type, or genre. Since our four texts are spread out over the sub-types of Collins' Type I apocalypse (Ia: *4 Ezra*; Ib: Apocalypse and *Hermas*; Ic: *Aseneth*), we are in a position to note not only the differences and similarities of four apocalypses with a common motif, or event, but also to determine how these shed light on the sub-genre as a whole. Such an endeavour moves beyond a close reading to a comparative study, that is, it engages in genre criticism. Chapter 6 in particular will highlight the question of genre by synthesizing the observations made in the preceding four chapters. Transformation will be seen as providing access to the question of identity,[44] a key focus of apocalypses

38. *God and the Rhetoric of Sexuality: Overtures to Biblical Theology* (Philadelphia: Fortress Press, 1978).

39. 'The Framework of the Book of Job', *Int* 28 (1974), pp. 183-200.

40. *Studies in the Structure of Hebrew Narrative* (Semeia Supplements 3; Philadelphia: Fortress Press, 1976).

41. *Narrative Art in Genesis: Specimens of Stylistic and Structural Analysis* (trans. P. Visser-Hagedoorn; Assen: Van Gorcum, 1975).

42. *The Art of Biblical Narrative* (New York: Basic Books, 1981).

43. *Anatomy of the Fourth Gospel: A Study in Literary Design* (Philadelphia: Fortress Press, 1983).

44. The issue of identity has, of course, a long philosophical history, from Heraclitus, Parmenides and Plato, Aristotle and Epicurus, through Locke and Hume to Gottlob Frege and other moderns. A concise but helpful introduction to such questions is given by A. Stroll in 'Identity', *The Encyclopaedia of Philosophy* (ed. P. Edwards; New York: MacMillan and the Free Press; London: Collier MacMillan, 1967), IV, pp. 121-24. It is a curious feature of the four pieces discussed in this study that transformation is introduced as a kind of *clarification* of the identity issue, rather than as a hard case of the philosophical discussion of 'change'. That is, the difficulty is not in trying to establish that the female figure prior to and after her transformation remains the same person; rather, the transformation itself demonstrates that the figure was *indeed* the beloved of God, despite first appearances. Implicit in these various presentations of transformation are the issues of appearance and reality, as well as the question of novelty as something determined in the past, or arriving in the future. For an

which may be placed alongside the temporal and the spatial axes in Collins' paradigm. It is hoped, then, that the following analyses and study will serve two interests: to continue the discussion of four worthwhile pieces (in particular, *Aseneth*, which has just come to the forefront of scholarly interest through a reconsideration of its dating), and to further the study of the apocalypse genre, by considering the element of transformation in Type I apocalypses.

One further word of explanation may be helpful at this point. Because the approach and purpose of this study are aesthetic and generic, rather than historical, and because the four works are roughly contemporaneous, an extended discussion of *Sitz im Leben* is not necessary. The works will be read as intelligible in their own terms, and largely as they stand, since neither source criticism nor investigation into a precise *Sitz im Leben* has produced a scholarly consensus regarding any of them, and because they have enjoyed considerable popularity beyond their original audience. Although a milieu is certainly helpful in ascertaining the purpose and direction of a work, it is not indispensable, nor is it always invited by the work itself. Of the four works discussed here, perhaps *4 Ezra* and *Hermas* most clearly invite a discussion of *Sitz im Leben*, since the aspect of a ruined city in the former, and the use of actual names and events in the latter, call attention to milieu. Nevertheless, to read behind the lines is not necessarily to read the lines, and often historical study has been mistaken for literary understanding. Where decisions can be made, and seem important, the historical and source arguments will be considered.[45] The focus will remain, however, on the pieces themselves, their artistic arrangement, and the literary function of the transformations within them. This is not to adopt an 'art for art's sake' approach, which may be suitable in treating twentieth-century literature intended as artefacts, but not ancient religious works which obviously served other ends. It is, however, to say that the pieces are of value as literature (both

intriguing discussion of the latter, within a theological perspective, see W. Pannenberg, 'Appearance as the Arrival of the Future', *JAAR* 35 (1967), pp. 107-18.

45. The objections of Paul Ricoeur in 'Biblical Hermeneutics', *Semeia* 4 (1975), p. 29 concerning a naïve commingling of structural and historical concerns are well taken. The juxtaposition of such methods is less inappropriate when structure is examined without the assumptions of structuralism proper, however. N. Frye indeed declares in his 'Theory of Genres', *Anatomy of Criticism* (Princeton: Princeton University Press, 2nd edn, 1971), p. 316 that '[t]here is no need to choose between the two types of criticism'.

in their uniqueness and in their generic configurations) and should be so evaluated, alongside other fruitful endeavours, including historical, socio-logical and theological investigation. To read and appreciate these visions is not only to understand their milieu, nor simply to see their relationship to other religious pieces which continue to hold normative value for at least some of us, but to interpret them as unique expressions of an important, if mysterious, genre.

Figure 1. *J.J. Collins' 'Master-Paradigm' of Apocalypses*[46]

Manner of Revelation

1.	*Medium* by which the revelation is communicated.
1.1	*Visual* revelation may be either in the form of
1.1.1	*Visions*, where the content of the revelation is seen, or
1.1.2	*Epiphanies*, where the apparition of the mediator is described.
1.2	Auditory revelation usually clarifies the visual. Epiphanies are always followed by auditory revelation. They may be either in the form of
1.2.1	*Discourse*, uninterrupted speech by the mediator, or
1.2.2	*Dialogue*, where there is conversation between the mediator and recipient, often in the form of question and answer.
1.3	*Otherwordly Journey*, when the visionary travels through heaven, hell or remote regions beyond the normally accessible world. Revelation in the course of a journey is usually predominantly visual.
1.4	*Writing*, when the revelation is contained in a written document, usually a heavenly book.
2.	An *Otherwordly Mediator* communicates the revelation. Often the media-tion consists of interpreting a vision but it can also take the form of direct speech or simply of guiding the recipient and directing his attention to the revelation. The mediator is most often an angel, or in some Christian texts, Christ.
3.	The *Human Recipient*.
3.1	*Pseudonymity*: The recipient is usually identified as a venerable figure from the past. A few Christian apocalypses are not pseudonymous.
3.2	The *Disposition of the Recipient* notes the circumstances and emotional state in which the revelation is received.
3.3	The *Reaction of the Recipient* usually describes the awe and/or perplexity of the recipient confronted with the revelation.

46. J.J. Collins, 'Introduction: Towards the Morphology of a Genre', *Semeia* 14 (1979), pp. 6-8. Used with permission.

Content: Temporal Axis

4.   *Protology*: Matters which deal with the beginning of history or pre-history.

4.1   *Theogony* (in Gnostic texts, describing the origin of the Pleroma) and/or *Cosmogony* (the origin of the world).

4.2   *Primordial events*, which have paradigmatic significance for the remainder of history (e.g. the sin of Adam).

5.   History may be reviewed either as:

5.1   *Explicit recollection* of the past, or

5.2   *Ex eventu prophecy* where past history is disguised as future and so associated with the eschatological prophecies.

6.   *Present salvation through knowledge* is a major way of salvation in Gnostic texts and distinguishes them significantly from other apocalypses.

7.   *Eschatological crisis*. This may take the form of

7.1   *Persecution* and/or

7.2   *Other eschatological upheavals* which disturb the order of nature or history.

8.   *Eschatological judgment* and/or *destruction*. This is brought about by supernatural intervention. It comes upon

8.1   *Sinners*, usually oppressors, but in Gnostic texts, the *ignorant*.

8.2   The *world*, i.e., the natural elements.

8.3   *Otherworldly beings*, e.g. the forces of Satan or Belial, or other evil powers.

9.   *Eschatological salvation* is the positive counterpart of eschatological judgment. Like the judgment, it is always brought about by supernatural means. It may involve:

9.1   *Cosmic transformation*, where the whole world is renewed;

9.2   *Personal salvation*, which may be part of the cosmic transformation or may be independent of it. This in turn may take the form of

9.2.1   *Resurrection*, in bodily form or

9.2.2   *Other forms of afterlife*, e.g. exaltation to heaven with the angels.

Content: Spatial Axis

10.   *Otherworldly elements* may be either personal or impersonal and either good or bad.

10.1   *Otherworldly regions* are described especially in the otherworldly journeys but also in lists or revealed things in other contexts. Again they may be evaluated in either a positive or a negative way. The Gnostic texts evaluate the lower heavens negatively.

10.2   *Otherworldly beings*, angelic or demonic.

Paraenesis

11.   *Paraenesis* by the mediator to the recipient in the course of the revelation is relatively rare and is prominent only in a few Christian apocalypses.

Concluding Elements

12.   *Instructions to the recipient.* These are distinct from Paraenesis (11) and
       come after the revelation as part of the concluding framework: e.g. they
       tell the recipient to conceal or publish the revelation.
13.   *Narrative conclusion.* This may describe the awakening or return to earth
       of the recipient, the departure of the revealer or the consequent actions of
       the recipients. In some Gnostic texts we find reference to the persecution
       of the recipients because of the revelation.

Chapter 2

CHIASMUS AND TRANSFORMATION IN JOSEPH AND ASENETH

The Story

The romance, *Joseph and Aseneth*, apparently a Jewish work written in Greek between 100 BCE and the early second century CE, has obviously not been in the centre of 'background' or contextual studies. While the Qumran scrolls and Nag Hammadi have become almost household words, this has not been the happy fate of *Aseneth*. The reason for the book's relative obscurity is that it was not edited until the end of the last century and even then it was erroneously described as a fifth-century Christian production. This rendered it of interest to Byzantinists or perhaps early Church historians, but not to biblical scholars nor to the general public.

However, *Aseneth* is no longer quite so 'neglected' as described by S. West in 1974,[1] and is indeed becoming increasingly important to biblical, especially New Testament, studies. Hence, several monographs have focused on the piece in recent years, as well as several articles in the volumes of *NTS* and *JSP*.[2] *Aseneth* nevertheless remains a tantalizing

1. S. West, 'Joseph and Aseneth: A Neglected Greek Romance', *Classical Quarterly* NS 24 (1974), pp. 70-81.

2. E.W. Smith, Jr, '"Joseph and Aseneth" and Early Christian Literature: A Contribution to the Corpus Hellenisticum Novi Testamenti' (PhD dissertation, Claremont Graduate School, 1974); R.D. Chesnutt, *Conversion in Joseph and Aseneth* (JSPSup, 16; Sheffield: Sheffield Academic Press, 1995). In *NTS* 33, see especially C. Burchard, 'The Importance of Joseph and Aseneth for the Study of the New Testament', *NTS* 33 (1987), pp. 102-34. See also sociological studies in *JSP*: R.C. Chesnutt, 'The Social Setting and Purpose of Joseph and Aseneth', *JSP* 2 (1988), pp. 21-48, and R.C. Douglas, 'Liminality and Conversion in Joseph and Aseneth', *JSP* 3 (1988), pp. 31-42. The most recent contribution is by G. Bohak, 'Aseneth's Honeycomb and Onias' Temple: The Key to Joseph and Aseneth?' *Proceedings of the Eleventh World Congress of Jewish Studies, Jerusalem, June 22–29, 1993* (Jerusalem: World Union of Jewish Studies, 1994), pp. 163-70. The *Proceedings* themselves were not available to me during the preparation of this study, but a manuscript copy of the paper, which is preliminary to his Princeton dissertation, was generously provided by the author.

puzzle to scholarship. Despite a limited consensus in certain areas, it has obstinately 'proved difficult to classify'.[3] Not only are there difficulties of genre, but also of proper text, original language, date and provenance, function, and (for want of a better term) 'message'. C. Burchard, who is probably the most competent *Aseneth* critic of recent years, declares, 'If...we ask what Judaism as depicted in Joseph and Aseneth is like, it is easier to say what it is not'.[4] There would, indeed, even be a few who do not consider that the book depicts 'Judaism', but rather Christianity,[5] Gnosticism or mysticism of some sort. With such uncertainty, one is not surprised to find in the work a complexity and richness of allusion which renders it difficult to master.

The story itself is less difficult, indeed rather popular in appearance. Aseneth, the 18-year-old virgin daughter of Pentephres (Potiphar of Gen. 41.45), Priest of Heliopolis, has scorned the advances of many suitors. Breathtaking in beauty, she lives secluded in a tower adjacent to her father's house, worshipping numerous idols, and attended by seven beloved virgins. At harvest time, Joseph, who is gathering grain against the famine to come (cf. Gen. 41.46-49), stops at Pentephres' home for refreshment. The priest intends to offer him Aseneth in marriage, but she refuses arrogantly. She is, however, *bouleversée* when Joseph enters as 'the sun of heaven' and comes to greet him. Joseph refuses to kiss her in greeting, since a Jew who worships the living God and is sustained by gifts of heaven (bread, wine and oil) is forbidden contact with a 'strange' woman. Seeing Aseneth's remorse, he prays for her future blessing, then goes on his way with a promise to return on the eighth day. Aseneth retires to her chamber, where she mourns for a week, destroying her idols and denouncing her pride. The morning star of the eight day heralds an angelophany: God's chief angel visits Aseneth, declares her acceptance, gives her the name 'City of Refuge' for subsequent converts, feeds her with honeycomb (which he says is 'bread of life, cup of immortality and ointment of incorruptibility'), and promises that she will be married to Joseph. Aseneth dresses in bridal

3.   West, 'Joseph and Aseneth', p. 70.

4.   Burchard, 'Joseph and Aseneth—A New Translation and Introduction', in J.H. Charlesworth (ed.), *The Old Testament Pseudepigrapha* (New York: Doubleday, 1985) (hereafter *OTP*), II, p. 194.

5.   This is generally true of older treatments dependent on the view of Batiffol, e.g., the reference by E. Stauffer in 'γαμέω, γάμος', *TDNT*, I, pp. 648-57, which sees the extravagant Joseph imagery as messianic, probably Christian. See especially p. 657.

attire, is transfigured, and greets Joseph, who has been informed of her conversion in a twin (although offstage) vision. They are married by Pharaoh, and Manasseh and Ephraim are conceived. This conversion story comprises chs. 1–21. Chapters 22–29 read as a sequel, perhaps even an afterthought to the conversion story, with the emphasis on action rather than mystery and romance. Aseneth is ambushed by Pharaoh's son. He is aided by Gad and Dan, but opposed by Joseph's other brothers, especially Levi, who has prophetic powers, and Benjamin, who behaves like a young David. At the climax, Aseneth is saved by divine intervention, Pharaoh's son is wounded, and the two treacherous brothers crave forgiveness. This is given, but Pharaoh's son and then Pharaoh himself die, leaving Joseph as king in Egypt.

The Present Consensus

Earlier scholarship tended to see *Aseneth* as a fifth-century Christian work on the basis of M.R. James's 1889 identification of the 'sacramental' passages and alleged indebtedness to a Jewish fourth-century legend.[6] The recent consensus[7] is, however, that the work is Jewish in essence, while a few persist in finding some Christian interpolations.[8] Dates have been given from the second (G. Bohak)[9] or first century BCE (G.D. Kilpatrick)[10] through the first century CE (V. Aptowitzer)[11] to the second century CE (M. Philonenko),[12] by the

6. M.R. James, 'Le Livre de la Prière d'Aséneth', in P. Batiffol (ed.), *Studia Patristica* (Paris: Leroux, 1889), I, p. 37.

7. For two thorough overviews of the summary of scholarship, see Chesnutt, *Conversion*, and C. Burchard, 'The Present State of Research on Joseph and Aseneth', in J. Neusner, P. Borgen, E.S. Frerichs and R. Horsley (eds.), *New Perspectives on Ancient Judaism* (Lanham, MD: University Press of America, 1987), II, pp. 31-52.

8. Especially T. Holz, 'Christliche Interpolationen in Joseph und Aseneth', *NTS* 14 (1968), pp. 482-97.

9. Bohak, 'Aseneth's Honeycomb', prefers a date in the mid-second century BCE, connected with Onias's followers. His argument requires a pre-74 CE dating because of the putative connection of the honeycomb holocaust with the destruction of the Jerusalem temple, and the suggested fastening of hope upon Onias's temple, subsequently destroyed in 74 CE.

10. 'The Last Supper', *ExpTim* 64 (1952), pp. 4-8.

11. 'Asenath, The Wife of Joseph: A Haggadic Literary-Historical Study', *HUCA* 1 (1924), pp. 239-306.

12. *Joseph et Aséneth: Introduction, text critique, traduction et notes* (SPB 13; Leiden: Brill, 1968).

application of various criteria, and none have continued in James's early judgment. Most consider that its latest date must be the early second century CE, with Hadrian's anti-circumcision edict (c. 135) and the revolt under Trajan in Egypt (c. 117, assuming an Egyptian provenance) providing the upper bracket. Other evidence, such as the prominence of Isis symbolism and the lack of audience for a Jewish work after this time in Egypt, would confirm such dating. All but P. Riessler[13] and Aptowitzer have considered the original language to have been Greek, on the basis of weighty phraseological evidence such as ἀθανασία, ἀφθαρσία (8.5) and φαινόμενα ἐκ τῶν ἀφανῶν (12.2).

So then, although much debate continues concerning the purpose, exact audience, and type of Judaism reflected by *Aseneth*, there is now general agreement that the book is a Hellenistic Jewish romance with a religious purpose, most likely written in Egypt from the first century BCE to the early second century CE.[14] Many varieties of Judaism have been suggested for the author, including Essene,[15] Therapeutic,[16] mystic,[17] 'followers of Onias's temple'[18] and non-sectarian.[19] Increasingly it seems to be thought that a pronounced sectarian milieu is not necessary to explain the peculiarities of the work, even though *Aseneth* contains high-flown imagery and quasi-mystical passages, such as that of the honeycomb and bees. How one imagines the author or original readership of this unusual novel will depend on the breadth of social contours traced for Judaism in its formative period. It may well be that

13. 'Joseph und Asenath: Eine altjüdische Erzählung', *TQ* 103 (1922), pp. 1-22, 145-83. We are indebted to Riessler for standard versification, although the situation is now complex because of the debate concerning short and long recension.

14. If the novel reading offered by G. Bohak finds general acceptance, a more precise and half-century earlier *Sitz im Leben* will supplant the general two-century range. No full consideration of his arguments can be given in this study, since his dissertation, '*Joseph and Aseneth* and the Jewish Temple in Heliopolis' (PhD dissertation, Princeton University, 1994) was unavailable to me while preparing this manuscript; the paper offered in *Proceedings*, however, is tantalizing.

15. Kaufmann Kohler, 'Asenath, Life and Confession or Prayer of', in *JewEnc*, II, pp. 172-76.

16. K.G. Kuhn, 'The Lord's Supper and the Communal Meal at Qumran', in *The Scrolls and the New Testament* (ed. K. Stendahl; New York: Harper & Bros., 1957), pp. 75-77.

17. H.C. Kee, 'The Socio-Religious Setting and the Aims of Joseph and Aseneth', *SBLSP 1976* (ed. G. Macrae; Missoula: Scholars Press, 1976).

18. Bohak, 'Aseneth's Honeycomb'.

19. Burchard, in *OTP*, II, esp. 194.

Hellenistic Judaism in Egypt was considerably eclectic, and that mystical leanings and a love of the sapiential were not the exclusive property of sectarian groups. One has only to consider the presence of an Egyptian *temple* in addition to the one in Jerusalem to recognize that our understanding of 'mainline' Judaism (if the term is not anachronistic) must be open to surprising details.

What has emerged from the past half-century of debate over *Aseneth* is an approximate date, very probable location, faith orientation and language, and the inadvisability of allegorical approaches, which are self-demonstrably tenuous by virtue of their very discrepancies and number. Chesnutt's monograph, originally written as a PhD thesis under Charlesworth, reflects this consensus, which will no doubt become the dominant view since Charlesworth's *Pseudepigrapha* has virtually replaced that of Charles. Certainly speculation and probabilities continue to guide our view of the work, but these decisions are not mere guesswork, and are based on careful observation of the text itself. It seems in no way premature to accept the date range and Egyptian milieu, as well as the likelihood of Jewish provenance as a working hypothesis for this discussion, while recognizing that there is still much room for discussion in such areas as purpose and exact *Sitz im Leben*. In terms of text, only Philonenko seems convinced that a short text based on family d of the four families a, b, c and d is adequate.[20] Thus, on the basis of the strong arguments presented by Burchard,[21] this discussion shall use the preliminary eclectic text[22] provided by Burchard which underlies his new translation in the *Pseudepigrapha*.

20. Philonenko, *Joseph et Aséneth*, pp. 21-26, 125-26.

21. 'Zum text von "Joseph und Aseneth"', *JSJ* 1 (1970), pp. 3-34.

22. C. Burchard, 'Ein vorläufiger griechischer Text von Joseph und Aseneth', *DBAT* 14 (1979), pp. 2-53, supplemented by 'Verbesserungen zum vorläufigen Text von Joseph und Aseneth', *DBAT* 16 (1982), pp. 37-39, provides an eclectic text based largely on b, but in consultation with other families, as well as the Armenian, Syriac and two Latin versions. This text is not yet easily available, and has been printed in the bulletin without aspiration or accents: it is due to be published soon in the *Pseudepigrapha Veteris Testamenti Graeci* series. A copy of Burchard's text, provided with accents but unannotated, may also be found in Albert Marie Denis, OP, *Concordance Grecque des Pseudépigraphes d'Ancien Testament* (Louvain-la-Neuve: Université Catholique de Louvain Institut Orientaliste, 1987). Where the English is cited, reference should be made to Burchard's own translation in *OTP*.

2. *Chiasmus and Transformation in Joseph and Aseneth* 35

The Vision Sequence as Apocalypse

Aseneth, although not an apocalypse *per se*, contains within it a vision sequence which, in terms of form, may be associated with the genre apocalypse. An 'apocalypse' within a romance is not totally unexpected: as David Aune points out, 'generally, apocalyptic vision reports are constituent elements of larger texts in Greco-Roman literature'.[23] While a Jewish background for the romance may be seen in the Joseph and Daniel 'novelettes', the Hellenistic influence is also pertinent here. It is therefore not surprising to find within *Aseneth* smaller pieces of various genres, including prayer, hymn and vision. The sequence found in chs. 14–17 may be seen as a vision in apocalyptic form within the host romance; that is, the chapters present a revelation within a narrative framework, a revelation which includes many of the features of the apocalypse noted in the *Semeia* profile. A comparison of the chapters to Collins's chart[24] yields the following characteristics:

23. Aune, 'The Apocalypse of John', p. 78. Aune's discussion of apocalypses within 'host genres' (a term borrowed from H. Dubrow, *Genre* [London: Methuen, 1982], p. 116) is a helpful clarification of the way in which ancient composite texts have been handled by modern critics. Aune points out that 'host' or 'inclusive' genres are 'commonplace' in Graeco-Roman literature, and he distinguishes between 'periodic' macrostructures, which show the influence of formal oratorical theory, and 'paratactic' structures, which are more episodic, and are bound together by such devices as ring composition (pp. 79-80). See also H.W. Attridge ('Greek and Latin Apocalypses', *Semeia* 14 [1979], pp. 159-86) for examples of apocalyptic sequences within a larger structure. Even in the analysis of Jewish apocalypses in *Semeia* 14, several were listed and analyzed which form only one part of a larger text, for example Dan. 7–12 or parts of *1 Enoch*. Most recently, J.J. Collins has discussed the problem of composite texts in the light of A. Fowler's three-phase developmental theory ('The Life and Death of Literary Forms', *NLH* 2 [1971], pp. 199-216). Composites may occur in the naïve phase, before discrete differentiation has occurred, or perhaps in the last phase, where the genre may be 'subordinated to a new context' (*Apocalyptic Imagination*, p. 3). Koch (*Ratlos*) and J.G. Gammie ('The Classification, Stages of Growth and Changing Intentions in the Book of Daniel', *JBL* 95 [1976], pp. 191-204) have considered the apocalypse *itself* to be a composite, *mixtum compositum* or 'major literary genre'.

24. See the chart which is Figure 1, found at the end of Chapter 1.

Manner of revelation

1.1.1	Vision
1.1.2	Epiphany
1.2.1	Discourse
1.2.2	Dialogue
1.4	Writing
2.	Otherworldly mediator
3.1*	Pseudonymous seer
3.2	Disposition of recipient
3.3	Reaction of recipient

Content: Temporal Axis

4.2	Primordial events
6.	Present salvation by knowledge
9.2	Personal afterlife

Content: Spatial Axis

10.1*	Otherworldly regions
10.2	Otherworldly beings

Concluding Elements

12	Instructions to Recipient
13	Narrative Conclusion

* indicates possible, implicit or minor presence.

The omission of element 5 (past events), prominence of 6 (present salvation by knowledge) and 9.2 (*personal* afterlife), and omission of both 7 (upheavals) and 8 (judgment)[25] is consonant with certain Christian and Gnostic apocalypses.[26] These characteristics also distinguish it sharply

25. Note however the presence of judgment at the end of *Aseneth*, chs. 28–29.

26. The element of final judgment is considered by J.J. Collins in *The Apocalyptic Imagination* to be essential to the genre: '[I]n all there are also a final judgment and a destruction of the wicked. The eschatology of the apocalypses differs from that of the earlier prophetic books by clearly envisaging retribution beyond death' (p. 5). Such an absolute statement is surprising in the light of the fact that a few of the later apocalypses are void of any elements in category 8, according to the analyses in *Semeia* 14 (see A. Yarbro Collins, pp. 104-105, which profiles *5 Ezra* 2.42-48, *T. Isaac*, *T. Jacob*, *Resurr. (Bart)*, *Myst. John*, *Apoc. Jas*). It may be that John Collins is here referring primarily to the Jewish Apocalypses in his distinction of them from prophecy. However, in view of the fact that most of these later apocalypses are not discrete, it would be important to read them in context to see if the *idea* of judgment is imported from the book in which they are found. This is certainly the case in Aseneth, where judgment of the enemies of the righteous is declared to be the prerogative of God (chs. 28–29,

from the larger body of Jewish apocalypses—a surprising discovery, considering the normal view of Aseneth's provenance, but understandable
in view of the syncretism of the age. All in all, the section fits best into
the Ic category ('Apocalypses with Only Personal Eschatology [and no
heavenly journey]'). Moreover, the profile demonstrates an affinity with
the apocalypse in content (elements 4–10) as well as form (1–3, 12–13).

The only major problem with actually labelling the passage an apocalypse is its apparent lack of emphasis on eschatology. This would be, of
course, no problem if Rowland's 'disclosure' definition were preferred.
However, even Collins' definition proves friendly to the vision, since
eschatological concerns are not totally absent. Indeed, promises of eternity are given to Aseneth as an integral part of the revealed mysteries.
('Behold, your name was written in the book of the living in heaven...
and it will not be erased forever', 15.5; see also 8.5; 12.15; 15.4-5; 16.14.)
R.T. Beckwith goes so far as to say that in *Aseneth* there is 'a stress on
future life'.[27] Although *Aseneth* seems to correspond most closely to
sub-type Ic, one might even say that the eschatology is not wholly
personal. Aseneth's status as 'City of Refuge' places her in some sort of
relationship to others of the eschatological community, the community
which will 'enter the rest provided for those who have been chosen'
(8.9; 19.8). This is demonstrated visually in the bee episode, where the

esp. 28.8). This concept is demonstrated dramatically by the death of Pharaoh's
villainous son, who is superseded by none other than Joseph. Aseneth's rescue from
the 'abyss' and the 'dark' also implies a dualism of judgment. Within the 'apocalypse'
section itself, the death of the injurious bees (16.17-23) may point to eschatological
judgment. The difficulty, however, is that judgment in all these cases is not *clearly*
future. Pharaoh's son is depicted in an earthly judgment of death, although the
statements about God's retribution are framed in the future tense. We are not sure
whether the death and 'place' of the evil bees is future, or an assurance of God's
ever-present protection for Aseneth. This ambiguity about the time of judgment
parallels the view of salvation, as shall be seen in later discussion. Is Aseneth's status
as City of Refuge present or future? Has she received all her reward from the point of
her vision, or is there also the idea of unimagined bliss in a 'place of rest'? Such
problems point to the difficulty of insisting upon eschatology when dealing with texts
which contain personal present salvation—mostly Gnostic texts, but also here, it
would seem. In what sense is a future judgment or salvation possible when the present has become the arena of eternal light or darkness? See also F.T. Fallon, 'The
Gnostic Apocalypses', in *Semeia* 14 (1979), pp. 123-58 (148), for Gnostic profiles,
where the presence of element 8 is not consistent.

    27. R.T Beckwith, 'The Solar Calendar of *Joseph and Aseneth*: A Suggestion',
JSJ 15 (1984), p. 90.

corporate importance of Aseneth's conversion is highlighted by the building of a honeycomb on her lips, from which all the bees are nourished. It is also demonstrated by the blessing of the seven virgins in solidarity with Aseneth (17.6) who are given a place as pillars in the 'City of Refuge'. The eschatology is not 'cosmic', nor exactly 'political' (Ib); neither is it merely individualistic.[28]

Some might also question the lack of first person narration (Aune), but this is not decisive, and other examples (for one, *Testament of Abraham*) of a third-person apocalypse can be given. Moreover, as A. Yarbro Collins points out, the purpose of the first-person is to establish authority; this has already been done for Aseneth within the host romance, where her status has been carefully established. She is the heroine of a romantic, or at least (to use the terminology of Northrop Frye) a 'high mimetic' piece,[29] one which perhaps even borders on the mythical at times. If the focus of comedy is 'the integration of society, which usually takes the form of incorporating a central character',[30] Aseneth's integration occurs *through* the revelation of the central apocalypse. It is the vision itself which provides the necessary 'twist of the plot'[31] so that integration can occur. Nevertheless, integration becomes a mystery for the benefit of the reader, and not simply a pleasant story to beguile those with leisure on their hands. Aseneth's apocalypse is to be shared with her 'children', the peoples 'under [her] wings' (15.7), and this point is made repeatedly within the entire episode (see 16.16, 20; 17.6; 19.6, 9).

The visionary sequence of chs. 14–17 of *Aseneth*, then, comprises a passage which may be fruitfully considered alongside more 'pure' apocalypses. For the purposes of this discussion, namely the place of transformation within the *structure* of the works being studied, the comparison is particularly apt. In fact, in formal terms, the sequence is best comprehended in terms of 'apocalypse': presence of the *angelus interpres* and other structural details render the more general term 'vision'[32] simply inadequate. Content is more debatable, but this is not

28. See also Stauffer, 'γαμέω, γάμος', *TDNT*, I, p. 657, who says that *Aseneth* 'stops short' of individualism and mysticism.

29. N. Frye, 'Historical Criticism: Theory of Modes', in *Anatomy of Criticism* (Princeton: Princeton University Press, 2nd edn, 1971 [1957]), pp. 33-67.

30. Frye, 'Historical Criticism: Theory of Modes', p. 43.

31. Frye, 'Historical Criticism: Theory of Modes', p. 44.

32. See J.S. Hanson, 'Dreams and Visions in the Greco-Roman World and Early Christianity', *ANRW*, II.23.2, pp. 1395-1427 for a discussion of revelatory literature in general. *Aseneth* as a whole certainly exemplifies such literature, but provides in the

as important to the argument at hand. Without minimizing the particularities of the piece as a whole, and its relationship to other genres (particularly the romance),[33] it is both desirable and essential to recognize the apocalyptic structure and flavour of the section in question. For the sake of brevity, then, I will refer to the vision sequence of chs. 14–17 as the 'apocalypse' from this point.

The apocalypse occurs at the structural centre of the first story (that is, chs. 1–21) which treats the conversion of Aseneth. It will be seen that the structure of the conversion story is carefully framed so as to place the weight on the apocalypse as a whole, and on its central mystery in particular. In fact, a chiastic structure informs the work, with the apocalypse itself providing the central complex of brackets, and sheltering a mystery, to which all the action of *Aseneth* is intimately related.

Chiasmus was, of course, a common tool in the ancient literature of several cultures. It was employed both as a poetic device within a few words or lines (abc*cba* or abc*ba*), and as a general structural technique for a larger section or even an entire book. The presence of such techniques has been extensively demonstrated in the Hebrew Bible,[34] and as chiastic structures also enjoyed popularity in the Hellenistic world,[35] it is not at all surprising that they occur in parabiblical books such as *Aseneth*. Some have preferred to restrict the use of the term 'chiasmus' to a short arrangement of individual words, suggesting other terms such as 'palistrophe' or 'envelope structure' for the structural feature. These

chapters under discussion a close enough parallel to the apocalypse for fruitful comparison.

33. R.I. Pervo, 'Joseph and Asenath and the Greek Novel', in G. Macrae (ed.), *SBLSP 1976* (Missoula, MT: Scholars Press, 1976), pp. 171-82, compares *Aseneth* to various pieces, and contrasts it with the 'historical novel', while arguing for a subgenre of 'sapiential novel', cf. Tobit and Dan. 1–6. Such a study is helpful in furthering our understanding of the book, even if Pervo's adaptations of Merkelbach and Kerenyi (p. 176) concerning the relationship of novel to cult are a little rash.

34. See most recently, and with special applicability to this study, the chiastic reading of B.G. Webb, 'Zion in Transformation: A Literary Approach to Isaiah', in D.J.A. Clines, S.E. Fowl and S.E. Porter (eds.), *The Bible in Three Dimensions: Essays in Celebration of Forty Years of Biblical Studies in the University of Sheffield* (JSOTSup 87; Sheffield: JSOT Press, 1990), pp. 65-84.

35. Aune, 'The Apocalypse of John', discusses the characteristics of popular literature such as the novel, and includes ring composition or chiasmus as one of the structuring devices for paratactic works (pp. 79-80). The genre of apocalypse is, in itself, a prime example of ring composition (in the story frame), although not of the more complex structural chiasmus.

two functions are not entirely independent, however. John W. Welch argues that '[l]ong passages are more defensibly chiastic when the same text also contains a fair amount of short chiasmus and other forms of parallelism as well'.[36] His comment reflects the ongoing debate concerning structural chiasmus and subjectivity in scholarly circles, and the desire to avoid chiasmus-hunts as a mere critical game. Whenever short chiasmus and parallelism can be easily demonstrated in a work, this factor becomes a helpful aid in establishing the likelihood of longer structural patterns in the same mode. Other controls against an eisegetical imposition of chiasmus upon the text are also suggested by Welch, and will be taken into account in the course of the following discussion. Let us consider first the frequency of short chiasmus and parallelism in *Aseneth* as a prelude to an analysis of the larger structure.

Examples of Short Chiasmus in Joseph and Aseneth

Particular parallelism and chiasmus are, in fact, very frequent phenomena in the piece as a whole. Throughout, we hear the parallel repetition or expansion of one idea in 'diptych' or 'triptych' form. A few examples suffice: 'For who among men on earth will generate such beauty,/and what womb of women will give birth to such light?' (6.4); 'Lord God... who gave life to all...and called (them) from the darkness to the light,/ and from the error to the truth,/and from the death to the life...' (8.9); ἀνακαίνισον...ἀνάπλασον...ἀναζωοποίησον...(8.9); 'With you I take refuge...to you I will shout', and so forth (12.3). Inverse parallelism, or chiasmus, also occurs at key points of the action. The best example would be at 12.1, where Aseneth, after two false starts, finally musters the courage to 'open her mouth' to the Almighty. Suspense reaches its apex as she begins her prayer with a striking invocation of the Lord God of ages:

ὁ κτίσας τὰ πάντα καὶ ζωοποιήσας
ὁ δοὺς πνοὴν ζωῆς πάσῃ τῇ κτίσει σου (abccba).

The prayer continues with a briefer chiasmus: ὁ ποιήσας τὰ ὄντα καὶ τὰ φαινόμενα ἐκ τῶν ἀφανῶν καὶ μὴ ὄντων (abba). At an earlier point (11.6) she has described her plight in this fashion:

καὶ πάντες ἄνθρωποι μισοῦσί με
διότι κἀγὼ μεμίσηκα πάντα ἄνδρα (abccba).

36. J.W. Welch (ed.), *Chiasmus in Antiquity* (Hildesheim: Gerstenberg, 1981), p. 13.

These are exemplary of other parallelisms, *chiasmi* and repetitions, found particularly in the poetic and 'blessing' passages. A related feature would be descriptive lists, or suggested actions which are repeated in alternate order at further points of the drama (for example, Aseneth's self-appellation at 6.2; 11.3, 16; 12.5, and 'What should she do?' at 5.1-6; 11.3, 11; 12.6).

We have, in addition, several examples of *short* structural chiasmus, or palistrophe, in the piece, the most striking being 'Aseneth's Psalm' (21.11-21), which sums up the entire first section of *Aseneth* in a manner reminiscent of the Song of Moses (Exod. 15). The structure may be pictured as follows:

ἥμαρτον refrain vs. 11

A   Daughter (θυγάτηρ) of the priest

ἥμαρτον refrain vs. 12

   B   Virgin (παρθένος) in his house

ἥμαρτον refrain vs. 13

      C   I revered (ἐσεβόμην) many gods

ἥμαρτον refrain vs. 14

         D   I lived by idols

ἥμαρτον refrain vs. 15

            E   I trusted not in God (οὐδὲ ἐπεποίθην ἐπὶ τῷ θεῷ)

ἥμαρτον refrain vs. 16

            E′   I trusted in self (ἐπεποίθην ἐπί μου)

ἥμαρτον refrain vs. 17

         D′   (or F)[37] I lived by self

ἥμαρτον refrain vs. 18

      C′   I scorned many men

ἥμαρτον refrain vs. 19

   B′   Virginity (παρθενεία) unassailable

ἥμαρτον refrain vs. 20

A′   Bride (νύμφη) of the firstborn son of the Great King

ἥμαρτον refrain vs. 21

   ἕως…(her conversion and acceptance)

37. Only D and D′ are an imperfect parallel, so that it might be more accurate to label D′ as 'F', a misplaced term. That is, D′ mentions Aseneth's scorn of all males, and in this sense contrasts with C in much the same way as C′. The pride of D′ is more general than that of C′, however, and speaks of Aseneth's scorn for all humankind, and their inability ἐνώπιόν μου (a contrast to the refrain's ἐνώπιόν σου which addresses the Almighty). So then, D′ is distinct in that it pits Aseneth's self-reliance against her reliance on idols (D). Just as D provides an extension of the idea in C, so C′ is an extension of D′: hence, the chiastic shape is generally preserved (ἄρτον… ἄρτον, vss. 13-14; ἐξουθένουν πάντα ἄνδρα…μεμίσηκα πάντας, vss. 17-18).

The chiasmus reaches its climax at E and E′, where οὐδὲ ἐπεποίθην and ἐπεποίθην are contrasted in an obvious way, enveloping the ἥμαρτον refrain:

καὶ οὐκ...
    οὐδὲ ἐπεποίθην ἐπί...
        Refrain
    ἐπεποίθην ἐπί...
καί ἥμην...

This is illustrative of one feature which a recent volume[38] prescribes for good chiasmus—climactic centrality. The chiasmus 'systematically serves to concentrate the reader's interest on the central expression'[39]— here, Aseneth's idolatry and self-absorption. The final effect of the poem is to present a static picture of Aseneth's two sins—idol-reverence (ABCDE) and self-possession (E′D′C′B′A′). The picture is finally shattered at the ἕως clause of v. 21. A slight link is made between the chiastic vv. 11-21 by the foreshadowing hope of v. 20 ('I shall be bride...'). Even here, however, Aseneth's future tense implies her present state. She is now not worthy, but *shall be* the bride of the son of the Great King. Verses 11-20, then, are a confession of misguided reverence and pride, a poetic depiction of her tower existence. The chiastic returns underscore her godless condition, along with the anaphoric ἥμαρτον which intersperses and frames the entire episode. The cycle is broken with the terse phrase, 'until Joseph the powerful one of God came'. With his coming she is brought down, then exalted: the list of καί's in v. 21 lifts the confession to a mode of celebration. This transformation is aided by the change from first to third person, and the placement of the ἀλαζών Aseneth in the passive position (ἐγώ is rendered με). Earthly imprisonment in idolatry and self is, through the agency of Joseph, changed to devotion as a gifted νύμφη for ever and ever. The entire poem appears thus:

38. D.N. Freedman, 'Preface', in Welch (ed.), *Chiasmus in Antiquity*, p. 7.
39. Freedman, 'Preface'.

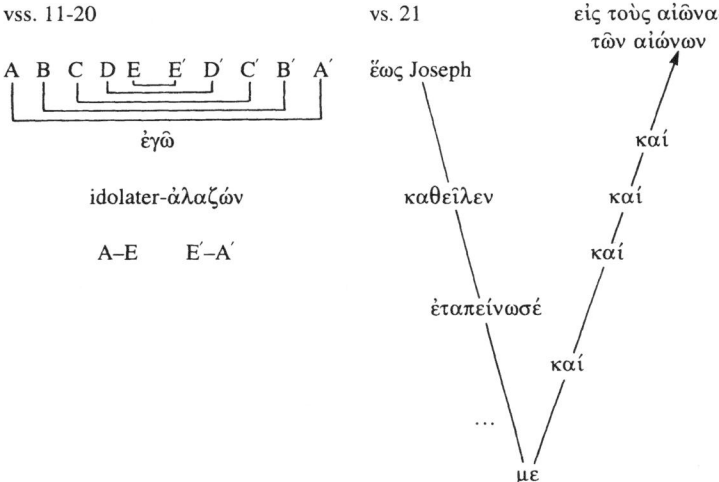

Further intricacies of the poem, such as the polarity of ἐνώπιον σου and ἐνώπιον μου (D′) might be cited. This brief discussion is enough to demonstrate that the author or final shaper[40] of *Aseneth* was appreciative of subtle poetic design, and was prepared to use it.

The Threefold Structure of Joseph and Aseneth

With these examples of chiasmus in mind, we may move on to the structure of *Aseneth* as a whole. Our primary focus will be the conversion story (chs. 1–21), rather than its sequel (22–29), since the transformation of Aseneth occurs in the first story, which is a well-conceived whole. Further, although the two stories are connected by various themes, and follow chronologically, they appear to differ in shape and genre, the first moving more slowly as its story unfolds, the second having a breathless, adventurous quality. Philonenko comments: 'la première partie, bien equilibrée, est toute entière centrée sur la prière d'Aséneth qui marque sa conversion'.[41] Chesnutt also cites Aséneth's

---

40. Philonenko does not include Aseneth's Psalm as authentic, while Burchard feels it represents an early tradition. Even *if* the psalm is a later creation, the redactor correctly saw its form as continuing the poetic devices scattered throughout the piece which had come to his hand.

41. Philonenko, *Joseph et Aséneth*, p. 27.

actions, but sees her repudiation of idols as the 'decisive event'.[42] Such a statement is understandable in the light of Chesnutt's purpose, which is to examine Aseneth's conversion in relation to contemporary paradigms. This emphasis on anthropology might predispose a reader to see Aseneth's own actions as the critical ones, hence her confession as the turning point. It would then follow, as stated by Chesnutt, that the vision is confirmatory, and that the angel's words at 15.4 announce what has already taken place.

However, it seems more likely that the angel's announcement is *performative*, and enacts what God is doing for Aseneth. Aseneth's prior confession, after all, ends with various petitions, not with utter confidence of God's acceptance: her stance is that of the unworthy child of an all-powerful Father,[43] a perspective which emphasizes the divine initiative. Moreover, Chesnutt's argument that 15.4 ('Behold, he has written [ἐγράφη] your name in the book of the living') is aorist, and therefore indicates that the *peripeteia* is past, neglects the thrust of the entire verse: Aseneth's name, the mother of converts, has been and will be 'in the book' eternally, just as God's will is eternal. The aorist indicates finality and security in God's will, not an event which has just now been precipitated by Aseneth's confession. The initiative for change in Aseneth's psalm came through God's agent (ἕως..., 21.21). This divine initiative is mirrored in the structure of the piece as a whole. Certainly, the careful balance of chs. 1–21 is undeniable; it will be seen, however, that the centre of the piece, both in terms of action and in terms of thought, is found a little later than the confessional prayer, that is, at the 'apocalypse' of chs. 14–17.

This structuring can be traced by observing the action of the piece, through the resolution of various themes, and through words which carry illocutionary force. We note first of all the action. The scene is set, marriage is proposed and refused, Joseph arrives to be entertained, and Aseneth mourns and confesses. After the visitation from heaven, she is transfigured, Joseph arrives again, he is entertained with a difference, they

42. Chesnutt, *Conversion*, p. 249.

43. For this emphasis on the fatherhood of God and its attendant themes, by which *Aseneth* parallels other canonical and apocryphal works, see A. Strotmann, *Mein Vater Bist Du! (Sir 51,10): Zur Bedeutung der Vaterschaft Gottes in kanonischen und nichtkanonischen frühjüdischen Schriften* (Frankfurter Theologische Studien 39; Frankfurt am Main: Knecht, 1991).

are married, and the scene is put in a larger context. The atmosphere is that of intrigue and action, broken by reflective prayer and vision. When the action is resumed, Aseneth is transformed, and all is resolved. Suspense builds up until the first announcement of the angel at 18.3, the apocalypse enriches our understanding of what is happening to Aseneth, and chs. 19–21 act as the resolution of the drama.

Various themes underscore this threefold structure of suspenseful action, caesura and resolving action. For example, descriptions of Aseneth's dress serve to punctuate key points of the drama. She dresses to meet her parents, to mourn, to receive the revelation, to prepare as a transformed bride for Joseph, and she is crowned at the wedding. Her dress in the first, middle and concluding parts corresponds to the state of the action—heroine *manquée*, penitent and glorified bride. Related to these stages is the focus on brightness in *Aseneth*. The first part (chs. 1–9) emphasizes the brightness of beauty of Joseph, the apocalypse (14–17) emphasizes the brightness and beauty of heaven and its inhabitants, and the last part (18–21) emphasizes the brightness and beauty of Aseneth.

As is common in religious stories, prayer functions 'as denoting the turn of a predicament'.[44] The plot is set in motion by Aseneth's soliloquy at 6.2, when she first sees Joseph. At 8.10-11, Joseph's proleptic blessing adds to the suspense (and hope) of the reader regarding Aseneth's inclusion in Israel. Two soliloquies come from Aseneth at 11.1 and 11.16, and are 'false starts' to her actual prayer of repentance. Finally, it is Aseneth's prayer of confession which marks her *volitional* turning point, but not the actual reversal of the piece (*contra* Chesnutt). Nor does the section make sense as the centerpiece of Aseneth's own change, if the anthropological studies of Van Gennep and Victor W. Turner are given any weight. Their observations of inititation rites have disclosed three stages of separation, liminality and aggregation, which have been applied with profit to Aseneth's journey by Rees Conrad Douglas.[45] In these terms, Aseneth's prayers correspond to the initial stage of conversion only; in literary terms, the prayers signal the change of plot, but must await their fulfilment in the blessing of the angel (16.16) as confirmed by Joseph (19.8.)

44. *OTP*, II, p. 220 n. 12a.
45. R.C. Douglas, 'Liminality and Conversion in Joseph and Aseneth', *JSP* 3 (1988), pp. 31-42.

An observation of the food theme is also instructive: Joseph is gathering produce while Aseneth admires the yield from the 'family inheritance'; Joseph is feasted in isolation, Aseneth abstains from food and is fed individually by the angel; Joseph is feasted in communion with Aseneth and the family; and a national feast marks their marriage. There is a movement from separation to communion, from denial to fulfilment. The theme of integration which is common to comedy is found, therefore, in the feast situations. If we see the divine feast of honeycomb as the apex, it becomes clear that the other meals organize themselves in brackets around this event. What was denied in the beginning is solved by the middle, and resolved at the end. Isolation (Aseneth's rejection by Joseph) becomes salutary (her confession), then privilege (her vision); as a result, true fellowship with the chosen community becomes possible.

Attention to such words as ἰδού ('behold') confirms this structuring. ἰδου occurs at Joseph's arrival (5.1), Aseneth's repentance (11.1; 13.1), Aseneth's acceptance (15.2-5), Joseph's return (18.1) and their marriage (21.3). It also occurs at other points in the drama, but there it is a matter between the characters (for example, 'Behold, here I am') and not a narratival interjection calculated to attract the attention of the reader (for example, a string of nine 'beholds' in Aseneth's prayer and eight in the angel's acceptance). These themes and devices of dress, brightness, prayer, eating and repeated ἰδου all confirm the basic threefold structure of *Aseneth* 1–22.

The Structural Chiasmus of Joseph and Aseneth

We are left, then, with the outline of a story marked by 'complications', broken into by a salutary vision, and recommenced with the complications removed. When we hear the servant announce, 'Behold, Joseph the powerful one is coming to us today' (18.1), we know that the vision is over, and recognize this as an echo of the beginning (5.1). Our expectation is that the story of Joseph meeting Aseneth will be retold, but in comic rather than tragic form. Our expectations are not disappointed. The structure, however, is not a simple rehearsal of the story in transformation, but a careful *reversal* in chiastic style. It may be pictured thus:

I *Story Initiated*

  A Setting: καὶ ἐγένετο/πᾶσαν τὴν γῆν Αἰγύπτου 1.1;
     τῇ οἰκίᾳ αὐτοῦ (Pentephres') 2.1

  B With father 3.6; She dresses in diadem 3.11;
     'My child'; right hand, kiss, inheritance given 4.1-5

  C Proposed and refused marriage 4.8-9

  D Wonder at Joseph chs. 5–6; his light and beauty throughout

  E Feast: enters, feet washed 7.1-6; Aseneth absent; Joseph on throne,
     separated

  F No embrace, threefold prayer 8.5-9; pushes away στῆθος

  G Aseneth, virgins alone in solitude 10.2; 'door closed'

  H In black, mourning, undressing 10.15, 'feared a great fear' 10.1

  I Inward transformation of the 'miserable' Aseneth 11.1–13.15 (3 speeches)

II *Apocalypse 14–17*

III *Story in Reverse*

  I′ Outward transformation into glory 18.5-11

  H′ In white, rejoicing, dressed, 'feared a great fear' 18.10-11

  G′ Aseneth, Joseph, virgins alone in privilege 19.3; 'gates closed'

  F′ Embrace, threefold kiss 19.10–20.10; falls on στῆθος 19.10

  E′ Feast ch. 20: enters, feet washed by Aseneth; Aseneth hostess,
     with family, on throne

  D′ Wonder at Aseneth 20.6-8; Her beauty and light 18.10, 11; 19.4; 20.6;
     21.4; 22.7

  C′ Proposed and 'refused' marriage 20.8–21.1

  B′ With 'father' Pharaoh 21.2-8; 'child' 21.4; right hand—blessing 21.6;
     husband and crown given 21.5

  A′ Setting—larger context 21.8-9; πάσῃ τῇ γῇ Αἰγύπτου 21.8; καὶ
     ἐγένετο...ἐν τῷ οἴκῳ Ἰωσήφ 21.9

The piece divides, then, into three major parts, chs. 1–13 (A to I),
chs. 14–17 (the apocalypse) and chs. 18–21 (I′ to A′). The poem in ch. 22
sums up the action of the first story and paves the way for the sequel,
which will not be considered here in any detail. With regards to balance,
it will be noted that the first half of the chiasmus is far longer than the
return motifs. This is not surprising, since the rhythm of the story
demands the building of suspense, followed by a quick resolution. We
are not dealing here, after all, with a lyric poem (in which the chiasmus
might be balanced in terms of length of lines) but with a romance. Nor

does the difference in length spoil the dramatic balance of chs. 1–21. As we have noted, resolution of themes and problems creates a sense of the story retold with a difference. What *is* surprising is the length of the vision sequence (that is, the apocalypse) itself. One would expect in a romantic piece that such a passage might be used as a mere *deus ex machina* to provide a solution to the problems. In fact, the apocalypse acts in this way, but goes far beyond this purpose to present revelatory material in such an involved manner as to call attention to itself. We hear (among other things) about the angels of heaven, about the heavenly virgin Μετάνοια, about paradise, about the bees of heaven, about the food of the blessed, and about the mysterious book of the Most High. It would seem, then, that a good deal of weight falls upon the apocalypse by virtue of its complexity. The threefold structure of *Aseneth* 1–21 also calls attention to the middle term, the apocalypse, which we will now examine in more detail.

The Structure of the Vision Sequence

When we turn to the apocalypse itself, we may again be guided by several thematic and verbal pointers. Central to the episode is the question of identity:[46] both the identity of the heavenly visitor and that of Aseneth. This issue is complemented by the action of blessing or concept of blessedness. Throughout the revelatory passage we are compelled to move in two directions—first, to recognize the mysterious blessedness of those who represent heaven; and secondly, to pay heed to the blessing which is afforded Aseneth, as a new inhabitant of that realm.

---

46. The identity of Aseneth is an important issue in the resolution of the dramatic problems: how can Joseph and Aseneth be united? and, how can Aseneth be united with the Almighty? The transformation comes as a clear solution to the difficulty, demonstrating Aseneth's foreordained identity as City of Refuge and Bride of the Son of Heaven. So then, there is no pausing over the philosophical questions of identity and change, but glorious change is an answer to the dilemma of identity. Aseneth's new-found standing with the Almighty is disclosed through a suitable new 'appearance' of glory. (Here, it would seem, the two connotations of δόξα come together!) Moreover, something new appears to have taken place as the result of the ἀποκάλυψις to the heroine; Joseph's preliminary prayer, however, and the angel's revelation that her name 'has been written' in a heavenly book, makes the metamorphosis appear more as an epiphany of what *actually* is, despite her initial pagan 'appearance'. In a naïve and commonsense manner which one would expect of a romance, the various perspectives on identity and change have been offered.

As in the piece as a whole, 'behold' becomes a prime indicator. So too do the references to ὄνωμα, μακάριος/α, εὐλογημένος/η, and God's mysterious βίβλος, where all these things are recorded by his own hand.[47] This is the shape of the apocalypse which emerges:

A   *Theophany* **Who are you?** ch. 14

    a   Prayer, comment
    b   Arrival
    c   On face (does not see)
    d   Call
    e   Description of visitor
    f   Preparation

B   *Behold Declaration* **Who she will be** 15.1-10

    'Your name is written', so

    1.   You will be renewed
    2.   You will be city
    3.   You will be bride

C   *What is your name?* 15.11-12

    Angel's name is blessed, hidden in book

B′   *Signs Verification* 15.13–17.1 'So you will know' **Who she will be**

    1.   Honeycomb found—'happy', wise Aseneth
    2.   Honeycomb shared—who she shall be—city, mother
    3.   Honeycomb and bees—Aseneth at centre

A′   *Conclusion* 17.2-10 **I did not know [a] god**

    f′   Preparation to leave (comb disappears)
    d′   Call them (virgins blessed)
    c′   Face turned (does not see)
    e′   Description of chariot
    b′   Departure
    a′   Prayer, comment

47. Collins labels a 'writing' a 'mode of revelation' (1.4). While this is accurate of some apocalypses, as in the letters to the churches in the Apocalypse, more often the books form an actual part of the revelation itself, filling in some of the 'scenery' of heaven. Hence, they are an item of content as well as form, even though they themselves impart authoritative revelation. Perhaps an additional category could be envisioned under content (whether temporal or spatial is a moot point), with 'writing' being seen as one of the revealed things. This is in fact a common motif in apocalypses, and found in each of the pieces studied here.

As the reader reflects on the mysterious content of the apocalypse, central questions and answers emerge. Section A poses the question 'who are you?' to the divine messenger. Aseneth is put off with a general answer ('commander of the armies...', 14.8), and instead finds out in section B who *she* is, or rather, who she is destined to be from this time on. Great emphasis is placed on this announcement through the list of 'beholds' (ch. 15). Not to be put off, Aseneth again in section C enquires the name of the divine being, and is roundly refused: that is a mystery. Section B' verifies the announcement of 'who Aseneth will be' through a demonstration of her spiritual receptivity, the sharing of divine food, and the mysterious bee episode. Throughout B', Aseneth remains the central figure, pictured in a remarkably goddess-like position encircled by the bees of heaven,[48] whom she sustains. Section A' answers the question of Section A (Who are you?), in a general way,

48. The association of the bee with reason, divinity and virginity is well-attested; cf. W. Telfer, '"Bees" in Clement of Alexandria', *JTS* 28 (1926–27), pp. 167-78. Isis, and in particular, her counterpart Neith, was associated with bees, so that her Temple in Sais was named the 'house of the bee'; see M. Lurker, *The Gods and Symbols of Ancient Egypt* (trans. B. Cummings; London: Thames & Hudson, 1980). H.M. Ransome, in *The Sacred Bee in Ancient Times and Folklore* (London: George Allen & Unwin, 1937), also tells us that swarms were 'supposed to announce the attainment of sovereignty', and points to the association of bees with divinities such as the Ephesian Artemis or the god Ra (his tears). However, to extrapolate from such images to a confident reconstruction of cultic or mystic practice as being reflected in *Aseneth* would be impulsive. The syncretism of Egyptian Judaism is only imperfectly understood at this point, and it is impossible to tell how much of this kind of symbolism had been appropriated by the 'mainstream' Jewish imagination. Such a discussion would have also to take into consideration such discussions as that of E. Saltman, who argues that the first Jewish inhabitants of Asia Minor were not affected by the Deuteronomic reform, and hence were not hostile to goddesses; see R. Kraemer, 'Hellenistic Jewish Women: The Epigraphical Evidence', *SBLSP 1986* (ed. K.H. Richards; Atlanta: Scholars Press, 1986), p. 199. At any rate, cases for a cultic background to *Aseneth* have been cumulative, taking into account both the symbolic possibilities of this passage, and the possible theophoric explanations for Aseneth's name (cf. Philonenko). It is extremely speculative to move beyond the presence of such imagery to any one cult, especially when *Aseneth* itself does not present anything other than conversion to Judaism *per se*. J.J. Collins has suggested that the presence of mystic symbolism and theophanies does not mean that 'such high revelation is...opposed to the Jewish law' (*Between Athens and Jerusalem: Jewish Identity in the Hellenistic Diaspora* [New York: Crossroad, 1983], p. 203), and points out that it finds its expression in other Hellenistic Jewish apocalypses. The association of Isis with wisdom may also account for the symbolism.

when Aseneth comments, 'I did not know a God came...'

Section C, then, is rendered the sheltered mystery. The name of the visitor is never divulged. He is like Joseph, only more glorious: he writes and speaks with the authority of the Most High, just as Joseph is the vice-regent of an earthly king. Synopses of the plot of *Aseneth* often state that the visitor is 'Michael', presumably on the basis of other biblical and extra-biblical materials that label him the chief of hosts. In fact, this name is never given, nor is any other. The messenger more glorious than Joseph works in concert with Μετάνοια, speaks with authority as God's mouthpiece, and has a first-written name in the book which can be neither known nor mastered. Aseneth's response, 'Forgive me: I did not know', is reminiscent of Job, and the only appropriate answer to such an epiphany. She has beheld mysteries connected with the Almighty himself. His name has not been divulged, but rather, her new name has been given. The mystery of the central section is itself a revelation, however. It is through respecting the mysterious and meditating upon it in her time of confession that Aseneth herself has found a name (12.1-2) To know that there is a mystery is a revelation in itself. Οὐκ ᾔδειν ὅτι θεὸς ἦλθε πρός με (17.9) is the conclusion of the matter.

The Transfiguration of Aseneth as Confirmation

Now that we have examined the general structure of *Aseneth* (that is, chs. 1–21) and also that of the 'apocalypse' at its centre, we are in a position to consider the transformation of Aseneth, City of Refuge. Remember that the actual declaration of Aseneth as City of Refuge occurs *within* the apocalypse, at B and again at B'. In the words of the messenger:

> Your name shall no longer be called Aseneth, but your name shall be City of Refuge, because in you many nations will take refuge with the Lord God, the most high, and under your wings many peoples trusting in the Lord God will be sheltered, and behind your walls will be guarded those who attach themselves to the Most High God in the name of repentance (15.7)

> and you shall be like a walled mother-city of all who take refuge with the name of the Lord God, the king of the ages (16.16).

In both places, the renaming of Aseneth takes place within the context of mystery, and amid language of rebirth or transformation. Section B names Aseneth the City as it talks of mysterious books, of Μετανοια in the heavens, and of the renewal, reformation and revitalization (15.5) of the convert. Section B′ restates the concept of the 'mother-city' after it has declared Aseneth μακάρια because of her insight into God's mysteries (16.14), and during the honey 'communion'.[49] At the same time, distinct language of transformation is used:

> From today your flesh will flourish like flowers of life from the ground of the most high, and your bones will grow strong like the cedars of the paradise of delight of God, and untiring powers will embrace you, and your youth will not see old age, and your beauty will not fail for ever. And you shall be like a walled mother-city...(16.16).

This paradisal description is consonant with the one which follows the apocalypse, at the actual point of Aseneth's transfiguration. There (18.9), she sees herself as 'a rose of life', 'a vine in the paradise of God...', an 'all-variegated cypress'. When her beauty is beheld by Joseph, he declares her *name* 'blessed', and speaks of her 'walls' as 'walls of life' around the 'City of Refuge'.[50] It is interesting, as well, to note that Joseph's first response on seeing her is the question, 'who are you?'—a continuation of the apocalypse theme.

It is obvious, then, that the revealed mystery of the apocalypse, Aseneth's identity, is directly linked to her transfiguration. It is a changed Aseneth, one who has been heard by the Almighty, shown the mysteries, fed with honeycomb from the 'breath of [his] mouth', and pronounced an immortal City, who is physically transformed in the next

49. The suggestions of Kilpatrick, Philonenko and D. Sänger ('Bekehrung und Exodos: Zum jüdischen Traditionshintergrund von "Joseph und Aseneth"', *JSJ* 10 [1979], pp. 11-36, and 'Jüdisch-hellenistische Missionsliteratur und die Weisheit', *Kairos* 23 [1981], pp. 231-42), that some actual cultic practice, a 'honeycomb communion', is reflected here, cannot be substantiated by the thrust of the text nor by our knowledge of sectarian Judaism and the mystery religions. The assertion of an underlying cult or sect also founders by virtue of the numerous conflicting suggestions that have been made. The text's own significance for the honeycomb is, after all, given at 16.11—it is the fruit of the word and spirit of God. Aseneth is sustained by it, since she is now in a position to eat the food of the angels. The meal is the beginning of her new life, and honeycomb acts as a pregnant image of the word and wisdom of God, which by the time of *Aseneth* already has a long history (cf. Ps. 18, Sir. 24.23, etc.).

50. U. Fischer, *Eschatologie und Jenseitserwartung im hellenistischen Diasporajudentum* (BZNW 44; Berlin: de Gruyter, 1978), pp. 115-23, notes the similarities of Aseneth as City, her walls, fruitfulness, and so on, to the New Jerusalem in the Apocalypse.

scene. Just as the period of mourning prepares her for the revelation, so the transfiguration indicates that the words spoken by her visitor are true. Aseneth is no longer 'fearing a great fear' (10.2), but herself instils fear in those who behold her (18.11). Suspense ends at the first statement of the angel (15.1), since we now know that God has accepted her, but the effect of the transformation is to fulfil and verify the apocalypse, thus giving dramatic satisfaction. This sense of completion is then continued through the renewed action, as all the obstacles of the first section are overcome, and resolution occurs. Aseneth's transfiguration is therefore the direct outcome of the apocalypse, and in some ways the goal towards which the entire drama has been moving. To what do the three-fold prayer of Joseph for renewal (8.11), the prayer of Aseneth for God's incorruptible inheritance (12.15) and the declarations of the angel (15.5) refer, if not to this point? Joseph's prayer is:

ἀνακαίνισον αὐτὴν τῷ πνεύματί σου
καὶ ἀνάπλασον αὐτὴν τῇ χειρί σου τῇ κρυφαίᾳ
καὶ ἀναζωοποίησον αὐτὴν τῇ ζωῇ σου (8.11).

The angel, who *is* hand of the hidden God, declares: ἀπὸ τῆς σήμερον ἀνακαινισθήσῃ καὶ ἀναπλασθήσῃ καὶ ἀναζωοποιηθήσῃ (15.5). At her transfiguration, Aseneth is clearly pictured as possessing all that she has lacked: a daughter-relationship with the Almighty, brightness and divine beauty, lively strength, solidarity with other penitents as *prima inter pares*, and potential union with the glorious Joseph. In the words of her 'foster-father', '*At last*, the Lord God of heaven has chosen you'.

Aseneth, the Recipient of Mysteries

Aseneth, then, in fleeing to God as daughter, becomes the mother-city of penitents and the bride of Joseph. The inevitability of all these roles is underscored by reference to God's past actions. She has been betrothed to Joseph since eternity (21.3), her name has been written by the finger of God in the beginning (15.4), her bridal attire and crown are from eternity (15.10 and 21.5) and her walls have been founded 'in the highest' (19.9). Fittingly, it is Aseneth herself who answers Joseph's amazed question 'who are you?', for she has become the recipient of divine favour, life and wisdom, and can now speak for herself.[51] She is

51. R.C. Douglas cites B. Lincoln in his description of women's initiation rites as

both happy and blessed because she has perceived divine mysteries (16.14). It is with unveiled face that she has received the ἀποκάλυψις from her divine Father (15.1). These mysteries include the power of the Almighty to move a penitent from darkness to light, and her prominent place as City of Refuge in this action; they also include ineffable secrets to which *Aseneth* alludes but which are not actually revealed to the reader. Such intimations of glory are seen in the uninterpreted mysteries of the bees and the ever-sustaining honeycomb.[52] Mystery also resides in Pharaoh's prayer that the Almighty increase δόξα for those who belong to him (21.6), in the threefold grace-giving kiss of Joseph and his beloved (19.11), and (in the sequel) in Levi's priestly divulging of mysteries and hidden books to the devoted Aseneth (22.13). We have seen that, in terms of the action, there is a central mystery to which the whole book points, and which finds fulfilment in the transfiguration of Aseneth. This was the question of identity: who is Aseneth; and, by association, who are her children?[53] From another viewpoint, however, the book spins off into various speculative directions, its central mystery 'who are you?' (directed to the divine messenger) never answered, and suggestions of esoteric knowledge lurking everywhere. Aseneth becomes daughter, mother and bride; in the sequel, she also 'grasps the hand' of the quasi-mystic Levi (22.13).

rendering the initiate 'more creative, more alive, more ontologically real' and possessing 'a cosmic status' ('Liminality', p. 33). *Aseneth*'s emphasis on identity *via* transformation is supported by Douglas's own analysis of the book, in which he discerns an emphasis 'both on maintaining and overcoming boundaries...suggest[ing] a group which was conscious of its own identity' (p. 39). While I am less comfortable dealing with the community around a text than analyzing the text itself, Douglas' findings are suggestive and provide a sociological complement to a literary investigation.

52. Burchard notes (*OTP*, II, p. 230, n. h2) that this passage has never been 'interpreted satisfactorily'. Perhaps the resistance is inherent in the text, and not simply due to the denseness of critics. That is, it may well be that the passage is for mystification, not for interpretation.

53. For the sociological implications of these questions, see again Douglas, 'Liminality', and also R.D. Chesnutt, 'The Social Setting and Purpose of Joseph and Aseneth', *JSP* 2 (1988), pp. 21-48. Chesnutt here gives priority to the social tensions inscribed in the narrative and sees Jewish identity as the penultimate concern addressed by *Aseneth*, with its ultimate purpose being 'to enhance the status of gentile converts in the Jewish community' (p. 42). He has been countered, however, in a preliminary way by G. Bohak ('Aseneth's Honeycomb'), who sees the authentication of a community around Onias's temple—also a matter of identity!—as the *raison d'être* for the book.

This centrifugal aspect is one of the features which *Aseneth* shares with Type II apocalypses. It is in these esoteric apocalypses, too, that the seer is transfigured as a reward for insight, or as a result of beholding the mysteries (for example, *1 En.* 39.14, 71.11; *2 En.* 22; *2 Apoc. Bar.* 51; *Apoc. Zeph.* 8.3). The 'apocalypse' in *Aseneth*, while technically sub-type Ic—Apocalypses with Only Personal Eschatology (and no other-worldly journey)—provides a conceptual link between these esoteric Type II apocalypses and those other Type I apocalypses under discussion here. Great mysteries are intimated by the vision to which she is privy, yet Aseneth does not actually travel the heavens. As in other Type I apocalypses, the initiative for revelation comes from God. So too does her transformation, which is confirmatory of God's word and not a reward for esoteric exploits. Aseneth, while exemplary, keeps her feet planted firmly on the ground. While there are romantic elements to her story, the serious hope offered by her transfiguration is that converts are acceptable to the Almighty and to the community of God-fearers. To be blessed by the Most High is to be nourished by the divine hand, and incorporated into a holy people. The mysteries implied by such language are suggested but never made explicit. There is never the sense, as is sometimes the case in Type II apocalypses, that divine mysteries can be mastered. They are a gift from God, to be received in hope and humility. The stance of Aseneth is that of penitent and bride, not that of mystic.

The Breadth of the Apocalypse

An analysis of chiastic structure in *Aseneth*, then, highlights its centri-petal aspect, the centering of action around Aseneth's important identity. Such a structuring lends strength to the view of Aune and Hellholm that apocalypses may be actually defined (in part) by structural chiasmus or equivalent structures which call attention to a central message. In both *Semeia* 36 and *The New Testament in its Literary Environment*,[54] Aune refers to the role of structural chiasmus as 'sheltering' a central mystery from the impious, but emphasizing this message to the seeker. The chiasmus (or its equivalent) therefore has a conceal–reveal dynamic analogous to that found in the genre of parable. In demonstrating this function, Aune makes use of Hellholm's text-linguistic analysis of the

---

54. *The New Testament in its Literary Environment* (Philadelphia: Westminster Press, 1987), p. 145.

Apocalypse[55] and the *Shepherd*.[56] Literary function is a key issue here,
since the devices and structures are seen by Hellholm and Aune virtually
to simulate the original visionary experience for the reader/hearer.

While such analysis is helpful, there are weaknesses in Aune's thesis.
One of these is the emphasis on a central revelatory message, a point
which, in the words of A. Yarbro Collins, 'calls to mind A. Juelicher's
procedure in interpreting parables'.[57] Just as a central core became a
straightjacket for the interpretation of parable, so a central message
might prevent the critic from appreciating the richness and characteristi-
cally paratactic form of this ancient literature. While the centripetal
movements in *Aseneth* are stronger, there are also certain indications of
what might be called a centrifugal force. This force, one which points to
numerous secrets and divine knowledge not directly bearing on the
'central revelatory message', is no less a part of what the book is saying.
Such seeming digressions may also be seen, even more full-blown, in
other apocalypses such as the Enoch literature, where much space is
devoted to sheer speculation, in which 'plot' or *dianoia* is not advanced.
We may be critical of such a style, but it is obvious that these sections
were no less important to the authors. It is this feature which has led
some, of course, to link apocalypses with *merkavah* mysticism.[58] Side by
side with certain distinct messages comes speculation and interest in the
esoteric (presumably for its own sake), an interest which is to some
degree or another hidden. So then, any discussion of chiastic structure
and a 'central message' must be balanced by a respect for the encyclopaedic interests of the piece. Such interest seems endemic to the revelatory genres, and insensitivity to this robs the critic of full understanding.
The structuring of *Aseneth* around an *unsolved* mystery underscores the
presence of the unknown. The transfiguration of Aseneth confirms both
God's revelation and its mysterious glory.

55. 'The Problem of Apocalyptic Genre and the Apocalypse of John', *Semeia* 36
(1986), pp. 13-64.

56. *Das Visionenbuch des Hermas als Apokalypse: Formgeschichtliche und
texttheoretische Studien zu einer literarischen Gattung* (ConBNT 13.1; Lund:
Gleerup, 1980).

57. A. Yarbro Collins, 'Introduction: Early Christian Apocalypticism', *Semeia* 36
(1986), p. 4.

58. See I. Gruenwald, *Apocalyptic and Merkavah Mysticism* (Leiden: Brill, 1980),
and H.C. Kee, 'The Socio-Cultural Setting of *Joseph and Aseneth*', *NTS* 29 (1983),
p. 407.

Chapter 3

VERBAL AND VISUAL TRANSFORMATION IN 4 EZRA

Unity as a Presupposition

There is at present a general consensus regarding the structure of *4 Ezra*
(2 Esdras 3–14), although this has not always been the case. Earlier
scholarship from Richard Kabisch[1] on tended to see the book as an
uneasy alliance of five sources: *S*, the 'Salathiel Apocalypse' (most of
visions 1 through 4); *A*, the Eagle Vision; *M*, the Son of Man Vision; *E*,
the concluding Ezra Vision; and an *E2* source for the eschatological
parts of the first four visions. These sources were discerned mainly on
the basis of competing eschatologies and theologies. This dissecting
explanation of the peculiarities of *4 Ezra* was strongly denied by some,
including H. Gunkel[2] and Bruno Violet.[3] It was not until fairly recently,
however, that their contentions of unity won the day, since the source
theory had gained great popularity through its enunciation by G.H. Box[4]
in the standard Pseudepigrapha edited by R.H. Charles. It is fair to say
that the 1918 desire of M.R. James has in recent scholarship been fulfilled:
'the Apocalypse of Salathiel, the centre of all theories of dissection, is a
ghost-book: conjured up by Kabisch in 1899, it has hovered about us
long enough. I never liked the look of it, and I earnestly hope that it may
now be permitted to vanish.'[5]

Leaving aside the question of the Apocalypse of Salathiel, or similar
sources, we are confronted by *4 Ezra* itself, a fascinating and undisputed

1. Kabisch, *Das vierte Buch Esra auf seine Quellen untersucht* (Göttingen:
Vandenhoeck & Ruprecht, 1889).
2. Gunkel's review of Kabisch's theory in *Theologische Literaturzeitung* 16
(1891), pp. 5-11.
3. B. Violet, *Die Esra-Apokalypse (IV Esra). I. Die Überlieferung* (GCS 18;
Leipzig: Hinrichs, 1910).
4. 'General Introduction' to *IV Ezra*, in R.H. Charles (ed.), *The Apocrypha and
Pseudepigrapha of the Old Testament* (Oxford: Clarendon, 1913), II, pp. 542-60.
5. 'Salathiel qui et Esdras', *JTS* 19 (1918), p. 347.

representative of the 'historical' apocalypses 'without heavenly journey'
(Ia). The following discussion of *4 Ezra* will proceed from the hypothesis
that the book may be intelligently read as a unity, even if the source-
critical studies give some insight into the possible genesis of the book.
The warnings of Michael Stone regarding the sometimes facile assumption of unity in modern criticism must certainly be heeded: 'This view
has predominated in recent scholarship without a really satisfactory
explanation being found for the inconsistencies of style and thought
which led the source critics to their conclusions'.[6] Nevertheless, it would
seem that in a work which has such a definite movement, purpose and
structure as *4 Ezra*, the burden of proof must lie with the proponents of
multiple sources, and not with the advocates of unity. As Stone has said
elsewhere, 'The preliminary hypothesis must always be that the author's
thought was coherent...[especially] in as meticulously crafted a work as
4 Ezra'.[7] If a convincing reading of the book can be made without
recourse to sources, it is its own justification. This is especially so when
dealing with a work within the generic framework of apocalypse; the
genre itself is so noted for its compilation of various styles, forms and
traditions that it has often been dubbed a 'macro-genre'. We should not
be surprised to find within *4 Ezra* a variety of smaller literary forms;
'theologies' at variance are more of a problem to unity, but may also be
explicable within the breadth of the genre.[8] With Stone's caveat in mind,
then, the structure and problem of *4 Ezra* will be considered as depicted
by representative scholars. This will be preliminary to a proposed
reading of the work, in which the double aspect of the woman in the
wilderness will be seen as crucial to the structure and direction of
4 Ezra. It will be seen that the problems of theodicy and Israel's (or
even humankind's) fate are superseded in the narrative by the issue of
Zion's identity, as presented in vision 4, and as it finds its resolution in
God's final words to Ezra.

    6.   'Apocalyptic Literature', in M.E. Stone (ed.), *Jewish Writings of the Second
Temple Period* (Philadelphia: Fortress Press, 1984), p. 414.
    7.   'Coherence and Inconsistency in the Apocalypses: The Case of the End in
4 Ezra', *JBL* 102 (1983), p. 242.
    8.   For a helpful discussion and proposed approach to the 'logic' of inconsis-
tency and integrity in apocalypses, see the newly published dissertation by M.S. Stone,
Features of the Eschatology of IV Ezra (Atlanta: Scholars Press, 1989), pp. 21-33.

The Role of Vision Four

Common to virtually all the recent treatments of *4 Ezra* is the observation that the fourth 'vision' or sequence provides the solution, key, or turning point of the book. That such a key is necessary is aptly argued by A.P. Hayman:

> The transition from Ezra's sceptical questioning in visions I–III to the radiant optimism expressed by him in visions V–VII…is harsh. What can have been the author's purpose in permitting his chief character to undergo such a metamorphosis?[9]

It may be that 'radiant optimism' is a little overstated with regards to Ezra's stance in the final chapters; A.L. Thompson, with perhaps more accuracy, calls it 'guarded optimism'.[10] Nevertheless, Ezra is certainly transformed, changing not only his attitude but also his role. The pivot occurs in the central section of the book, *4 Ezra* 9.26–10.59. Up until this point, Ezra has been in violent dialogue with the angel Uriel concerning matters of theodicy, both with regards to Israel and the plight of humankind in general. Three sequences, properly called 'visions' because of the appearance of a heavenly being, impress upon the reader the seriousness of Ezra's difficulties. The fourth sequence, however, is signalled as different from the outset—Uriel's instructions at 9.25 differ from the previous ones—and proves to be so. The expected dialogue with Uriel following Ezra's lament is pre-empted by his dialogue with a lamenting woman, whom he sternly 'comforts' by reference to the ravished Jerusalem. After a lyrical and striking description of Zion's fate, Ezra repeats his plea for a proper perspective on her part. His words are rewarded by a shocking transfiguration of the woman and her transformation into 'an upbuilt city'[11] or at least, 'ciuitas aedificabatur',[12] 'a

9. 'The Problem of Pseudonymity in the Ezra Apocalypse', *JSJ* 6 (1975), p. 48.

10. *Responsibility for Evil in the Theodicy of IV Ezra* (SBLDS 29; Missoula, MT: Scholars Press, 1977), p. 148.

11. This is the translation of the Syriac, Ethiopic and Arabic readings; see B.M. Metzger, 'The Fourth Book of Ezra: A New Translation and Introduction', in *OTP*, I, p. 547, note f.

12. The Latin edition used throughout will be R.L. Bensly, *The Fourth Book of Ezra: The Latin Version Edited from the MSS* (Texts and Studies III.2; Cambridge: Cambridge University Press, 1895). Where the English is quoted, it will be taken from the translation of B.M. Metzger, 'The Fourth Book of Ezra', in *OTP*, I, pp. 516-59. Metzger's translation is based on the edition of Bensly.

city [which] was *being built*'. He cries out in bewilderment to Uriel, who as *angelus interpres* explains the events, and then he is invited to explore the glorious building and remain in the field for further revelations.

Two of the further visions (5 and 6) are eschatological in character—gone are the questioning dialogues, and there is no return of the skeptical Ezra of the first three visions. Rather, he takes on the role of comforter for his lamenting and nearly hopeless people. Uriel also drops from view, and Ezra is addressed by the Most High himself. This dialogue with the Almighty is implicit in visions 5 and 6 ('dixit ad me', 12.10; 13.21, 52) and becomes explicit in the seventh vision. There, Ezra is revealed as a second Moses, who speaks to God on behalf of his community, and to the community on behalf of God, passing on not only a copy of the destroyed Law, but also the seventy books for 'the wise'.

Author as Bold Skeptic: Harrelson

It is easy to see that the fourth vision is the turning point of the book. What is not easy to explain is just how that *peripeteia* works. Walter Harrelson avoids the problem by considering Ezra's advice to the woman as 'ironic', and removing the final three sections in Procrustean fashion. In this way, Ezra is given the last word of the structural unity chs. 3–10, and Uriel's platitudes are 'given the lie' by the appearance of a vast city, 'a Zion the limits of which are beyond human capacity to conceive'.[13] Unfortunately, in *4 Ezra*, the city is never said to include those who might have fallen under God's judgment. W. Harrelson is thus driven to find parallels in Isaiah 2, Micah 4, and above all Apocalypse 21–22: 'Zion has become the sign of the triumph of glory over despair, of love over mere flat justice'.[14] As for the angel's 'prosaic and allegorical interpretation', it 'may well not belong to the original vision'.[15] Such a suggestion makes one wonder whether Harrelson is indeed viewing the first four visions as unified, or whether his reading is rather a revival of the Salathiel Apocalypse, for reasons very similar to those of Kabisch *et al.* Harrelson has thus provided a reading which is emotionally satisfying to the modern reader, through the tentative excision of passages,

13. 'Ezra among the Wicked in 2 Esdras 3–10', in J.L. Crenshaw and S. Sandmel (eds.), *The Divine Helmsman: Studies on God's Control of Human Events* (New York: KTAV, 1980), p. 36.

14. Harrelson, 'Ezra among the Wicked', p. 37.

15. Harrelson, 'Ezra among the Wicked', p. 38.

and through (ambitiously?) inferring universalistic dogma from the vision. He does recognize, however, the crucial position of the sequence when he labels the appearance of the city as the climax of *4 Ezra*.

The Consolation of a Community: E. Breech

Harrelson is one of the few today who resorts to sources as a means of securing a satisfactory interpretation of *4 Ezra*. If Harrelson sees Ezra as the voice of the author, E. Breech strives to show how the work provides a pattern for *Ezra*'s consolation (not the author's). The pattern moves Ezra, spokesman of the community, from lament to consolation, in the central section of the book, so that there is a 'rationale for the Most High's response to the community's dilemma'.[16] The Zion vision is the 'real beginning of Ezra's consolation',[17] and marks the *peripeteia* between the triptych dialogues and the two eschatological visions and conclusion. No intellectual answer is given to Ezra's concerns, but we can nevertheless observe an act of invocation, referral and waiting, followed by consolation. In Breech's view, it is sight of the great upbuilt city, plus the two night visions which provide the emotional strength necessary to effect a change. As with Harrelson, the appearance of the lamenting woman is not a part of the solution. Rather, it serves to make 'concrete' the lament of the community. The strengths of Breech's position are in his inclusion of the entire piece, his insistence on observing the action of *4 Ezra*, rather than the elusive interior life of the author, and his serious consideration of the lament theme. However, it is difficult to see what is gained by transferring an interest in the psychology of the author to a concern for the catharsis of a community—both are psychological approaches which probe the backdrop of the work, rather than the work itself.

Uriel as Author's Voice:
Harnisch, Brandenburger, Collins, Longenecker

Harrelson and Breech have, in different ways, cast Ezra in the role of spokesman, but there is a group of others who contend that Uriel speaks

---

16. 'These Fragments I Have Shored against my Ruins: The Form and Function of 4 Ezra', *JBL* 92 (1973), p. 272.
17. Breech, 'These Fragments'.

for the author. E. Brandenburger,[18] Wolfgang Harnisch,[19] J.J. Collins[20] and Bruce W. Longenecker[21] argue that Ezra undergoes a 'conversion' to Uriel's position, from skepticism to faithfulness. For Brandenburger, this conversion is 'das mysterium der Verwandlung'[22]—inexplicable and immediate in the fourth vision—while for Harnisch and Collins, the transformation begins gradually during the first three visions, but reaches its climax at the Zion vision. The earlier pieces of Harnisch and Brandenburger tended not to deal with literary devices, but with the theological problems of *4 Ezra*. Breech then complained that Harnisch's equation of Uriel with the author in *Verhängnis* was 'unsupported by literary analysis'.[23] This cannot be said of the later writings of either Harnisch or Brandenburger, which are far more sophisticated in their literary appeal to irony and structure.[24] The reading of *4 Ezra*, however, remains essentially the same: Ezra is converted, and takes the angel's part, whether this be shown by a change in theology or by literary method.

Longenecker, who appears unconvinced by such explanation for Ezra's change, asserts that it takes place 'outside the context of argumentative debate', so that Ezra 'simply appears in Episode IV a transformed character'.[25] However, in the literary discussions of Harnisch, Brandenburger and Collins, it is the dialogue with the woman which is essential to Ezra's change. Harnisch points out the irony of Ezra's consoling role, showing how he is 'tricked by the truth into the truth'.

18. *Adam und Christus: Exegetische-religionsgeschichtliche Untersuchung zu Röm. 5.12-21* (WMANT 7; Neukirchen: Neukirchener Verlag,1962) esp. 27-36, and *Die Verborgenheit Gottes im Weltgeschehen: Das literarische und theologische Problem des 4 Esrabuches* (ATANT 68; Zürich: Theologischer Verlag, 1981).

19. *Verhängnis und Verheissung der Geschichte: Untersuchungen zum Zeit- und Geschichtsverständnis im 4. Buch Esra und in der syr. Baruch-apokalypse* (FRLANT 97; Göttingen: Vandenhoeck & Ruprecht, 1969); 'Die Ironie der Offenbarung: Exegetische Erwägungen zur Zionvision im 4 Buch Esra', *ZAW* 95 (1983), pp. 74-95; and 'Der Prophet als Widerpart und Zeuge der Offenbarung: Erwägungen zur Interdependenz vom Form und Sache im 4 Buch Esra', in D. Hellholm (ed.), *Apocalypticism*, pp. 461-93.

20. *The Apocalyptic Imagination* (New York: Crossroad, 1987), pp. 159ff.

21. *Eschatology and the Covenant: A Comparison of 4 Ezra and Romans 1–11* (JSOTSup 57; Sheffield: JSOT Press, 1991).

22. *Verborgenheit*, p. 87.

23. 'These Fragments', p. 269.

24. These two also see evidence of sources lying behind the text, while moving beyond source criticism to a reading of the text as a whole.

25. *Eschatology*, p. 279.

Brandenburger shows by a structural study how the *Zionepisode* (9.38–10.24, excluding the vision of Zion), is unique ('ganz eigener Abschnitt'),[26] as compared to the dialogues or the following visions; hence, he reasons that it must be the key. Similarly, Collins compares the technique of this episode to the David–Nathan confrontation, showing how the king condemns himself by his own behaviour, and so is compelled to shift his ground. All four consider that Ezra has taken on Uriel's perspective, either gradually or suddenly, so that vision 4 either makes explicit his change, or effects it.

To speak (with Longenecker) of a sudden and inexplicable change in Ezra is to reassert the problem of the narrative, rather than to explore its dimensions.[27] The other three readers engage in such an exploration by reference to the arguments between Ezra and Uriel that precede this critical episode. What are we to make of their suggestion that Ezra is 'worn down' by Uriel in the triptych? Harnisch is clearest on this point, arguing that Ezra's protestations grow less pointed, and that vision 4 signals that a change has already occurred in Ezra.[28] Collins describes the action of the angel as 'the psychological process of calming fear' so that 'the fears are gradually eroded'.[29] Even Brandenburger, who argues for a sudden transformation, tells us that Ezra has come to the point in the fourth vision that he still laments, but can no longer ask an explicit question of the Almighty.[30] However, neither a gradual conversion nor a reduction to undisputing lamentation bears the weight of observation. Ezra does not forbear questioning: rather, he is interrupted by the spectre of a lamenting woman. If we consider the pattern of the laments up to this point, it is clear that the question asked of the Almighty follows a meditation upon various themes: vision 1 commences by meditating upon salvation history (3.4-27), and ends with a question concerning theodicy (3.28-36); vision 2 commences by musing upon God's election of the vine Israel (5.23-28) and issues in a similar question (5.28-30); vision 3 starts by considering the days of creation (6.38-54), and

26. *Verborgenheit*, p. 73.

27. Of course, Longenecker's study is theological rather than literary in orientation. He himself has called again for 'a literary reading' (*Eschatology*, p. 157) of *4 Ezra*. Attention to characterization and plot, as well as to the sequence of imagery from woman to city in the central transformative episode, may well shed light on the mystery of Ezra's own transformation.

28. 'Ironie', p. 75.

29. *Apocalyptic Imagination*, p. 162.

30. *Verborgenheit*, p. 68.

poses its question (6.55-59). In the same way, vision 4 begins with meditation, this time upon the Law and its vessel, Israel (9.29-37). With the appearance of the woman, Ezra dismisses his meditation (9.39), and asks another seemingly unrelated, but in fact most significant question, 'Why are you weeping (9.40)?' The question has been altered by the situation, but *not* because Ezra has been gradually brought to this point. The tyranny of the immediate situation (an unrecognized revelation of mourning Zion!) has begun the transformation of Ezra.

Secondly, it seems far too simple to say that Ezra is 'converted' to Uriel's position in the sense that he foreswears one view and takes on another. There is, after all, no repentance or humiliation on Ezra's part, as in the Job theophany. Ezra's reaction of fear in 10.28-36 does not focus upon any previous impiety in questioning God. Job could say, 'I have uttered what I did not understand...I despise myself, and repent in dust and ashes' (Job 42.3-6). Ezra cries out in words which echo Job, 'I have seen what I did not know, and I have heard what I do not understand' (10.35), but only after reproaching Uriel for putting him in such a situation (10.28).[31] The allusion to the words of Job thus underscores the awe of the seer, but not the admission of unrighteousness. Ezra is at no time blamed or considered irreverent for his questioning mode. It is hardly the case that 'der eine radikale Wende im Verhalten Esras zu erkennen gibt, mit einer Offenbarung der eschatologischen Gottestadt honoriert wird'.[32] Rather, it is *on account of* his true distress for Zion, and not because of a change from skepticism, that Ezra has been rewarded by the view of Zion in glory: 'Et nunc uidens altissimus quoniam ex animo contristatus es, et quoniam ex toto corde pateris pro ea, ostendit tibi claritatem gloriae eius et pulchritudinem decoris eius' (10.50). This is underscored by the fact that his distress is mirrored in the woman herself—9.38 parallels 10.50. Ezra *fears* that his prayer has become a 'reproach', but is assured that this is not the case. Brandenburger tells us that both Ezra and his people must change so as to be receptive to God's apocalyptic wisdom.[33] In fact, it is on account of their heart-felt lament, with all its skepticism and questioning of God, that an answer will be given!

31. On other, especially structural differences between the Job and *4 Ezra* laments, see C. Westermann, 'Struktur und Geschichte der Klage im Alten Testament', *ZAW* 66 (1954), pp. 44-80, esp. 78ff.
   32. 'Ironie', p. 93.
   33. *Verborgenheit*, p. 70.

Ezra in Tension: Thompson and Desjardins

A tertium quid between these various positions is to be found in
A.L. Thompson and M. Desjardins, both of whom depict Ezra in
unresolved tension. Thompson demonstrates through literary argument
how (but not *why*) in vision 4 the seer moves from a position of doubt to
confidence. Ezra's comfort of the woman redirects her attention from
the many to the few at 10.7-9: thus does Ezra regain his own confidence.
The 'confidence', however, remains the 'guarded optimism'[34] of a
'sensitive'[35] person: still there is no real answer for 'the many' who,
seemingly, must perish. Ezra's consolation may direct the mind away
from the 'many' and the present time, so as to focus upon the remnant
and the future glory, but this is not done casually. A certain reserve
rescues the apocalypticist from exclusive 'triumphalism'.

Desjardins accords less unity to the book: *4 Ezra* 'leaves a host of
questions unresolved'.[36] While there is a 'transition' in the fourth vision,
this is not a smooth one, and it may be beside the point to ask how and
in what way the seer has been changed. Despite a lack of thematic or
tonal unity in the piece, he does not argue for a source explanation.
Rather, the disjunction serves to document the author's extreme *Angst*
in a post-holocaust situation: 'It is not only the angel's replies which
serve to express the religious problematic facing the community, but
Ezra's questioning as well...We are in the presence of a man who is
driven to express viewpoints which at times are irreconcilable.'[37] So
then, we meet in *4 Ezra* an author 'in tension', a tension which is left
unresolved, despite the movement from pessimism to optimism on the
seer's part. What Desjardins is describing is the same tension noted by
Thompson. Desjardins, however, grants the tension far more autonomy,
since the transition, in his own experience, 'does not console an alert
audience'.[38] Unconvinced by the undeniable shift in the fourth vision,
Desjardins assumes that this lack of resolution also troubled the author.
The difficulty is, of course, a perennial one: can we always be sure that
what is not convincing to us may be explained by authorial ambivalence?
In fact, what can be documented in *4 Ezra* is indeed a transition, even a

34. Brandenburger, *Verborgenheit*, p. 231.
35. Brandenburger, *Verborgenheit*, p. 357.
36. 'Law in 2 Baruch and 4 Ezra', *SR* 14 (1985), p. 31.
37. Desjardins, 'Law', p. 32.
38. Desjardins, 'Law'.

transformation, difficult though it is to explain. If the author had intended to express *Angst* or lack of resolution as his final word, we might have expected the irreconcilable statements to continue side-by-side throughout the piece, rather than to be found at dead centre, with a movement away from doubt to faith. All this, is, of course, guesswork: what *can* be known about *4 Ezra* is that the figure Ezra moves from one stance to another, and this is the proper object of observation prior to any psychologizing.

'Experience' as the Key: Hayman and Stone

A final approach to *4 Ezra* accentuates one aspect of several other treatments. Two recent critics, A.P. Hayman and Michael Stone, point to the power of 'experience' in explaining the dynamics of the apocalypse. In the proposal of Hayman, Ezra is consoled through an 'experience' unrelated to his questions, but sufficiently strong to take him beyond his doubts—an acute expression of Breech's position. In the fourth vision, Ezra 'is lifted out of his doubts'[39] through the sight of the woman's metamorphosis into Zion. Over against Desjardins, Hayman finds the transition satisfying, since 'it seems to be a clear fact of religious psychology that overwhelming religious experience can dissolve any kind of doubt'.[40] On the other hand, there is no facile or 'easy capitulation' on the part of Ezra,[41] and the author refuses to 'gloss over an insoluble problem'.[42] Hayman argues that visions 1 through 3 present the general problem of the individual and human sin, and that the debate between Uriel and Ezra runs into the ground at 9.37 'without reaching a definite conclusion'.[43] Doubt concerning the fate of humankind is *dissolved* but never fully answered by the experience of vision 4.[44] A second problem, that of Gentile domination over Israel (the subject of visions 5 and 6) *is* adequately explained by the eschatological visions given there.

A second, and more nuanced, formulation of the 'experience' hypothesis is found in the recent commentary by Stone, who traces the

39. 'Pseudonymity in the Ezra Apocalypse', *JSJ* 6 (1975), p. 53.
40. Hayman, 'Pseudonymity', p. 56.
41. Hayman, 'Pseudonymity', p. 53.
42. Hayman, 'Pseudonymity', p. 55.
43. Hayman, 'Pseudonymity', p. 55.
44. Hayman, 'Pseudonymity', p. 54, in argument with P. Volz, *Eschatologie der jüdischen Gemeinde* (Tübingen: Mohr, 1934).

'Odyssey of Ezra's soul'[45]—a gradual development in the triptych,[46] followed by a 'profound religious experience'[47] in the vision of glorified Zion. Stone weds a psychological approach to literary insights: the angel, the lamenting Ezra and the weeping woman are all expressions of Ezra's own experience; Ezra's conversion is complete as, faced with the externalized lament of the woman, the externalized arguments of the angel become internalized. In contrast to Hayman, Stone sees a real unity between the dialogues and the transformation of Ezra, so that although Uriel's answers may not address the 'intractable'[48] theological issues seen by a modern audience, they are religiously satisfying to the author. Uriel's position is accepted in a complex dynamic of advancement and regression; final doubts are laid to rest by the experience of the fourth vision. An important implication of Stone's argument is that Ezra's encounter of and reaction to the heavenly Zion are 'not mere 'stage dressing',[49] but a reflection of the author's actual religious experience.[50]

Both of these expositions of *4 Ezra* illuminate important aspects of the text. Hayman's treatment is helpful, in that it takes seriously the tensions, transformation and final reserve of Ezra. Like Breech's discussion, it suffers, however, from a lack of concentration upon the *whole* of vision 4, and puts too much weight upon the vision of glorified Zion. Collins, Brandenburger and Harnisch have argued well that Ezra's conversation with the woman is at least as important to Ezra's change

45. *Fourth Ezra: A Commentary on the Book of Fourth Ezra* (Hermeneia; Minneapolis: Fortress Press, 1990), p. 32. See also his article, 'On Reading an Apocalypse', in J.J. Collins and J.H. Charlesworth (eds.), *Mysteries and Revelations: Apocalyptic Studies since the Uppsala Colloquium* (JSPSup 9; Sheffield: JSOT Press, 1991), pp. 65-78. This article, while dated after the commentary, actually antedates it (see Stone's references to his *forthcoming* volume). Here, he highlights his own text-immanentist, psychological approach to *4 Ezra* by contrasting it with Brandenburger's theological-literary perspective. He then goes on to make suggestions regarding a possible social setting for the book.
46. Stone, *Fourth Ezra*, pp. 24-28.
47. Stone, *Fourth Ezra*, p. 33.
48. Stone, *Fourth Ezra*, p. 36.
49. Stone, *Fourth Ezra*, p. 33.
50. In 'On Reading', Stone suggests that the tripartite community of seer–inner circle–faithful inscribed in *4 Ezra* may well correspond to social reality. Such a statement might harmonize his seemingly contradictory statements concerning the book's visionary impulse and its reserved attitude to esotericism—the mystical is for the wise, the inner circle; the Law (also given directly by God in the last vision) is for the community at large.

as his view of the city. Further, it is not so easy to divide up the concerns of *4 Ezra* between the 'human condition' and the plight of Israel.
Visions 1 to 3 concern both of these. An analysis of the questions posed
at the end of each lament (3.28; 5.28; 6.59) shows that these are concerned with the Israel question; however, they are attached to the preceding and following laments, which explore the more general questions.

Stone's discussion does not divide up the two issues of theodicy, nor
does he ignore the important contributions of the literary approaches. His
insistence on the visionary backdrop to the apocalypse, and his subtle
use of the literary and experiential insights of *4 Ezra*, are unprecedented.
A main difficulty with this reading is its extreme intricacy. Stone claims
to have discovered a progression of thought (admittedly erratic) so that
at 9.14, '[t]he seer has moved from questioning to acceptance, albeit
grudgingly'.[51] A major question that needs to be posed, however, is
whether Ezra's statement at 9.14-16 is an admission of Uriel's position
or the most pointed formulation of his own complaint. Ezra certainly
does not frame his statement as a concession. It is rather a decisive
declaration of his continued resistance: 'Olim locutus sum et nunc dico
et postea dicam...' Hence, the seeming development of thought seen by
Stone in the triptych might as well explained by the give-and-take of
argument. Formal or temporary concessions are given by Ezra so that
Uriel's position can be heard in full: these do not reduce the tension.

Another difficulty in both of these treatments is the transfer from seer
to author—in Hayman, a seemingly easy and perhaps naïve transition,
and in Stone a deliberate and sophisticated one. This difficulty is met
head on in the recent article of P.F. Esler, who rejects the attempt to tie
explanations 'to an authorial personality...utterly unknown'.[52] It may be
that Esler has overstated the case, under heavy influence of (now not-
so) 'new criticism'. The transfer of anguish from Ezra to the author is a
pitfall which is difficult to avoid in any attempt to make sense of the
book's 'meaning' or 'intent'. However, to read the piece in these terms
is to reduce its resonance for audiences other than what is deduced to be
its original one, and to be overconfident concerning the relationship of
the actual and implied author, or author and protagonist. The popularity

51. Stone, *Fourth Ezra*, p. 293.
52. 'The Social Function of *4 Ezra*', *JSNT* 53 (1994), pp. 99-123. Esler's
understanding of the dynamics of the literary Ezra's transformation through attention
to social scientific concepts such as 'cognitive dissonance' and 'introversionist
religious response' is fascinating, but outside the scope of this study.

of *4 Ezra* is in itself a testimony to its continued power to speak. Let us then leave aside the question of the author's own distress, and trace the movement of the seer throughout the book, especially his change in the universally acknowledged turning point of vision 4.

The Complexity of Ezra's Lament

A quick review of the entire book will show that the major question in view is the plight and fate of Israel. It has been seen that each of the laments issue in a specific question regarding the problem of Israel. Moreover, at both the beginning of the triptych and towards the end of it, Ezra establishes clearly that his interest is for Israel alone:

Non enim uolui interrogare de superioribus uiis, sed de his quae pertranseunt per nos cotidie: propter quod Israel datus est in obprobrium gentibus, quem dilexisti populum datus est tribubus impiis...(4.23);

...de omni homine tu magis scis, de populo autem tuo quod mihi dolet, Et de hereditate tua propter quam lugeo, et de Israel propter quem tristis sum, et de semine Iacob propter quod conturbor (8.15-16).

However, the scope of the introductory laments and further discussion indicate that this question of Israel is not easily extricable from the questions which Ezra intends to leave with the Almighty. Connected to the very specific concerns of the lamenting prophet are those concerns which he realizes are not his proper province at all. His intention all along has been to represent Israel to God: 'sed ueni hunc locum ut deprecarer pro desolatione Sion, et ut quererem misericordiam pro humilitate sanctificationis uestrae' (12.48). At every turn, however, this role opens up into one which questions the lot of humankind in general.

Consider the consistent movement from lament, to particular question, to general discussion in the structure of the first three visions:

Vision 1

3.1-2	Setting
3.3-27	Introductory lament
3.28-36	Question
4.1-11	Wisdom reply
4.12-25	Further discussion
4.26–5.12	Eschatology
5.13-20	Conclusion

Vision 2

5.21	Setting
5.22-27	Lament
5.28-30	Question
5.31-55	Wisdom rely
5.56–6.10	Further discussion
5.11-28	Eschatology
5.29-34	Conclusion

Vision 3

5.35	Setting
5.36-54	Lament
5.55-59	Question
7.1-25	Wisdom reply
7.26-44	Eschatology
7.45–9.23	Extended discussion
9.24-25	Conclusion

Although the *questions* detail Israel's fate, the larger discussion of all three sequences points to the persistent problems of humankind's situation and the justice of God. This is especially the case in each of the introductory laments, but comes increasingly to the fore in the sections entitled 'further discussion'. By the third vision, this concern is given a clear and extended voice (7.45–9.22), but comes to a dead end. Ezra continues to lament, 'Olim locutus sum et nunc dico et postea dicam, quoniam plures sunt qui pereunt quam qui saluabuntur, Sicut multiplicat fluctus super guttam' (9.14-15); Uriel continues to insist that this is the will of God (9.17-23). The discussion regarding these insoluble questions is even more lengthy in the third vision if one includes the so-called 'lost' passage of 7.[36]-[105] which deals with the plight of 'earth', the punishment and joy of the dead, and further laments over Adam and his progeny.[53] The increasing treatment of problems which are declared outside of Ezra's domain, and which seem to have no solution forthcoming make it clear that although the point of Ezra's questions concerns Israel, further problems are involved. Ezra's questions touch on a whole complex of concerns that require a complex response from the Almighty. This response we see in vision 4.

---

53. R.L. Bensly, *The Missing Fragment of the Fourth Book of Ezra* (Cambridge: Cambridge University Press, 1875), and B.M. Metzger, 'The "Lost" Section of II Esdras (= 4 Ezra)', *JBL* 76 (1957), pp. 153-57, provide an introduction to this problem passage, explaining possible doctrinal reasons for its omission in Codex Sangermanensis, etc.

The Complexity of Vision Four

It is customary to speak of vision 4 as containing an introduction, dialogue, vision, interpretation and conclusion. In fact, the dialogue is also a vision, into which the seer mysteriously enters, participating with one whom he understands at first as part of his own plane of existence, but whom he sees in retrospect as the 'similitudo' of Zion (10.49).[54] Vision 4, then, contains a two-part revelation, the first of which is only recognized as visionary in retrospect. The second part of the vision is equally mysterious, since Ezra beholds the transfigured Zion, and is then invited to enter and see her 'splendorum et magnitudinem' (10.55) as far as he can, a view which we do not as readers have described for us. The mystery of the first part of vision 4 lies in its unrecognizability as such; the mystery of the second in its ineffable quality. During the course of this twofold vision, Ezra receives his 'answer' in communicating with a visionary figure unawares, and in beholding a vision that is in essence incommunicable.[55]

The dual vision acts as a unifying device for the whole of *4 Ezra*, in that the dialogue with the 'similitudo' of Zion shows similiarities to the first three dialogues, whereas the sight of glorified Zion is more consonant with the transcendent visions of the latter half. Ezra's 'solution' may be characterized in the first place as dialogical, sapiential and verbal; in the second it is experiential, 'apocalyptic' (that is, revelatory) and visual. That is, Ezra's conversation with the mourning woman has a parabolic cast, and his advice to her fits well within the framework of wisdom discourses, whereas the following vision is more typical of the stupefying visions found in apocalypses. The latter vision is characterized by amazing phenomena ('fulgebat...subito emisit sonum uocis magnum

54. J. Myers makes an apt reference to Exod. 25.9, showing that the Latin word often has the technical meaning of 'figure' or 'heavenly pattern' (*I and II Esdras* [AB 42; Garden City, NY: Doubleday, 1974], p. 276).

55. The integration of human endeavour-response with divine initiative in the pivotal chapter may suggest the need for a refinement to Longenecker's characterization of *4 Ezra* (in contrast to Romans). It seems an overstatement to say that '[d]ivine grace is excluded from the scene' (*Eschatology*, p. 281)—it is certainly in abundance amidst this dual revelation! The contrast of a 'works' (*4 Ezra*) versus 'grace' (Romans) transcendence of the human condition is too stark: in *4 Ezra*, visions, intepretations, esoteric mystery and law are all given by God. Nonetheless, the participatory theme is also very strong, and worked out in a different manner than in the Pauline solution.

timore plenum...', 10.25-26), which have a stupefying effect[56] on the seer ('eram positus ut mortuus', 10.30), who requires an interpretation. Neither mode of divine response—sapiential or apocalyptic—is noted for its directness.[57] Wisdom works by parable, repartee, or induced self-questioning to suggest a sort of answer to problems; apocalyptic is elusive, and often remains resistant to an exact decoding of the message into straightforward language, despite the angelic interpretation.[58]

It should be noted that not all of the elements of the woman's story and transformation are interpreted by Uriel. The interpretation itself is not so univocal as to prevent commentators from disagreeing over the exact meaning of the 'son' and the 'mother'. Moreover, at the end of the vision, Ezra's eyes and ears alone perceive the edifice, for he is 'beatus...prae multis' (10.57). This exclusive status seems to preclude the presentation of his experience of the glorious Zion within the actual text of *4 Ezra*: the readers are tantalized by the suggestion that they will behold mysteries, but this takes place offstage. In this Ia apocalypse, we are not rewarded with a description of exactly what Ezra has seen and heard, as we might expect by comparison with such writings as *1 Enoch*. May it be presumed that 'the wise' will find ways and means to fill in the picture? Alternately, we might conclude with Robert Kirschner that

56. Esler's understanding of this phenomenon in terms of a 'process of defamiliarization' ('The Social Function', p. 113) is helpful. His reading is marred, however, by an inability to see *both* the prospect of the lamenting woman and Ezra's dialogue with her as revelatory—this, despite his observation that change has already begun before the consolation. Key to this problem might be his assumption that the glorious Zion is only a *future* destiny while the lamenting woman is a present state.

57. See again Esler, who point out that the reduction of cognitive dissonance 'seems to outsiders to involve an unconvincing rationalization' ('Social Function', p. 110).

58. N. Perrin has assumed, in *Jesus and the Language of the Kingdom* (Philadelphia: Fortress Press, 1976), pp. 21ff., that the symbolism of apocalyptic vision is 'steno' rather than 'tensive', and therefore inferior. This has been challenged, in my view rightly, by E. Schüssler Fiorenza in *The Book of Revelation: Justice and Judgment* (Philadelphia: Fortress Press, 1985), pp. 183ff., who demonstrates the 'open' quality of the book of Revelation. Even in apocalyptic literature, the vision is far broader than its interpretation, and the interpretation sometimes serves to add to the mystery, rather than to dispel it. An exception to the tensive use of symbolism in apocalypses would be the lengthy sheep allegory in *1 Enoch* 85–90, which is patently decodable. Many have followed Perrin in seeing this type of one-to-one allegory as typical of other apocalyptic writings, and have interpreted passages along these lines, without any feeling for the flexibility of the language and referents.

4 Ezra 4.8 'explicitly denies that Ezra ascended into heaven',[59] or with Stone that the author of *4 Ezra* 'consistently ignores, or indeed pole-mically opposes all the aspects of speculative knowledge'.[60] Kirschner's reading of Uriel's comment is not the only possible one, however, since the angel's words are placed within a conditional clause, and formulate a traditional argument concerning the ignorance of God's ways on the part of humankind. It is too extreme to suggest that there is an absolute eschewal of the mystical experience. Such judgments fall just short of explaining why we are induced by the text to ask, 'But what did he see?' both here, and also at 8.19b ('priusquam adsumeretur'). The author is not denying the traditions of Ezra as a special intimate of God and his mysteries. Indeed, he calls attention to these where he simply might have omitted them. The reserve with which the matter is treated is in fact due to a reverence for esoteric knowledge; it is too holy for common dispensation (14.48) and so is not given within the confines of the narrative itself. At any rate, Ezra's dual vision contains much in it to demonstrate its oblique and mysterious character. The entire episode serves to lift Ezra above his paralysis of doubt, and yet does not cast that lamentation in a poor light.

The Mourning and Glorious Zion

If both parts of Ezra's vision are of equal weight, then this explains why Ezra is not reproached for his laments, nor pulled up short by the divine revelation. An analogy may be made to the rhythm of receiving a vision, in which the seer is not actually rebuked for being fearful, but is told to stand up to receive the vision. There is a time for the awed human response to divine majesty; there is also a time for the confident reception of wisdom, so that God's word may be given out. Failure to respond in humility to the glory would not only be unthinkable, it would be liable to censure. Just as falling prostrate before the splendour is the appropriate attitude for a pious visionary, so Ezra's litanies of grief over Zion are the appropriate attitude for one who stands between his people and God. It is the city of the Almighty, the 'seal of Zion' which has been desecrated.

---

59. 'Apocalyptic and Rabbinic Responses to the Destruction of 70', *HTR* 78 (1985), p. 32 n. 21.

60. *Jewish Writings*, p. 413. But see also his seemingly contradictory comments regarding 'inner circle' mysticism in 'On Reading'.

Who could not lament? The fact that Lady Zion herself is in mourning
underscores the aptness of Ezra's stance: Jacob M. Myers says 'Ezra
was not alone in lamenting her fate';[61] Harnisch reminds us, 'Nicht erst
die sich verwandelnde, sondern schon die trauernde Frau, die mit Esra
redete, entsprach Zion'.[62] Part of Ezra's answer, then, is to recognize
that heaven also mourns the fate of Zion, and that to lament is not in
itself to be in opposition to the Almighty. Moreover, lamenting unto
death does not preclude a resurrection: the weeping Zion is the glorious
Zion incognito.

It is interesting to note that Ezra is given two different pictures of the
'glory' of Zion as an answer to his cry that the 'seal of her glory' has
been lost. His first vision is the sight of the woman's transfigured face,
which shines like the sun and flashes like lightning (10.25); his second
vision is the metamorphosis of this woman into the great city of Zion.
The seer's reaction to the first picture is one of reserve, terror and
wonder. The reserve and terror are explicable by reference to the narrative itself. It is Ezra's statement that he wondered over the meaning of
the transfiguration which gives pause. Within the text of *4 Ezra* there
are two other references to the shining face: 9.97, where the faces of the
righteous are to shine like the sun, and 9.125, where they are to shine
more than the stars. There seems to have been a well-established tradition concerning the eschatological glorification of the face of the
righteous, a concept found also in *2 Apoc. Bar.* 51.3 and *1 En.* 51.4.
Michael Stone points out that in some of the material which uses this
motif, there seems to be an association or even identification of the
righteous in their eschatological state with angels.[63] This seems to be the
case, for example, in *1 En.* 43.1-4 and 46.7. However, he questions the
wisdom of assuming such an eschatological position in *4 Ezra*, since
there are at least two traditions at issue, that is, the tradition of bright
faces (used both for angels and righteous) and the tradition of the
righteous as similar to angels or stars. Moreover, the dominant image in
4 Ezra is brightness like the sun, rather than that of the stars. Ezra, in
seeing the brightness of the woman, 'wonders what this might mean',
and does not assume an angelic identity for Zion (as opposed to the
intimations of astral immortality in *1 En.* 43).

61. *I and II Esdras*, p. 280.
62. 'Die Ironie', p. 90.
63. Stone, 'Apocalyptic Writings', in *idem, Features*, pp. 206-11.

Such reticence in filling out the eschatological picture is consonant with the attitude of the writer to the esoteric in general. Is it necessarily the case that there is an actual 'rejection of those areas of special knowledge which have no bearing on [the book's] problems' or that the book 'shows...very little interest in the future state as such?'[64] Silence can have, after all, more than one motive, and the attention called to the mysteries of the city, albeit undescribed, does not suggest either rejection or lack of interest. There is, however, a reserve in such matters, whether eschatological, supernatural or cosmological. Hence, in the transformation of the woman into Zion, the 'how' or 'when' or encompassing 'whom' of the glorified state are not given (despite the hopeful reading of Harrelson). Such questions are not answered even in the following eschatological visions 5 and 6. There we hear about the destruction of the Eagle and the victory of the Son of Man, but are given no insight into the glory of Zion. We are only told that 'refrigeret omnis terra' (11.46) and 'non poterit quisquam super terram uidere filium meum uel eos qui cum eo...' (13.52). The building of the Almighty is one made without hands and the deliverance of the faithful comes, as it were, from the sea (13.3). The city's ineffable quality makes it difficult to determine whether we are to conceive of Zion as possessing a present, although hidden glory, or whether this state is solely in the future. Ezra's remarks about the possibility of the future 'rest' for the woman (10.24) and her son's restoration 'in tempore' (10.17), as well as the future setting of visions 5 and 6, suggest an eschatological Zion. However, there is a sense in which Zion may be said to be 'prepared and built' already.[65]

This concept of a hidden glorified Zion may be seen in such phrases as 'antequam aestimaretur scabellum Sion' (6.5, where the foundation of eternal Zion is set amidst various other primordial events), 'Vobis... aedificata est ciuitas' (8.52), and 'Sion...ueniet et ostendetur omnibus parata et aedificata' (13.36). Such references throughout the work make the Latin reading at 10.27 ('aedificabatur') rather surprising, unless Zion is thought of here as in the process of preparation, but elsewhere as already built ('aedificatam', 10.44). Most editors, for example,

---

64. Stone, *Features*, p. 226.
65. Contrast the passage in *Pes. R.* 26, where Lady Zion is comforted by the word of God that she *will* be built by God's hand in the future (L. Ginzberg, *The Legends of the Jews* [Philadelphia: Jewish Publication Society, 1928], VI, p. 403).

B.M. Metzger in Charlesworth's *Pseudepigrapha*, have preferred the alternate reading (translated 'upbuilt') offered in the Syriac and other supporting texts. At any rate, when Ezra is invited to enter the city, it is the vast proportions which are emphasized, and not the process of preparation. This is in contrast to the visions of building in *The Shepherd of Hermas*, where the process itself is highlighted. Before Ezra's eyes, the mourning Zion is shown to be the glorified Zion. The Zion who mourns is in fact the Zion who is glorious. The identification of these two figures is explicit in the on-stage transfiguration, and implicit in the interpretation (10.38-54), which treats the figures as one, explaining the woman's story, and ending with a reference to her 'pulchritudine' (10.50). The one over whom Ezra has been distressed is in fact full of glory and beauty.

The transformations of the city and of the seer Ezra are sudden and mysterious. No explicit reasons are given for their change, nor is the manner of transformation discussed. It is the story itself which must give us a clue to the transformations. Is it going too far to suggest that the Lady's mourning, like that of Ezra, effects her change, or at least prepares for it? It is with a great cry, a cry which moves the whole earth, that her transformation is accomplished: 'Et ecce subito emisit sonum uocis magnum timore plenum, ut commoueretur terra a sono. Et uidi...civitas' (10.26-7). Similarly, it is Ezra's most poignant lament (10.19-23) which heralds the transformation of the lamenting Zion. It is as though the seer, spokesman for his lamenting community, merges with the twofold vision of Zion, both in sorrow, and ultimately in joy. A charting of the action, showing the double linking role of vision 4, would appear as in the following diagram, which shows the artful movement from visions 1 through 3, the change signalled at the end of 3 and beginning of 4, the dual focus of vision 4 and its preparation for visions 5, 6, 7, and the increased interest of the community in the latter half. Vision 7 does not follow the exact pattern of visions 5 and 6, since it does not require an interpretation, but is similar enough to match, and different enough to serve as an adequate conclusion for, the entire book. *4 Ezra* begins with Ezra taking the initiative and concludes with the Almighty himself taking over this role. How the piece moves from one to the other through the complexities of dialogue and vision has been described above in general, but a further dynamic, that is, the inside–outside movements of the characters, will be explored in the next section in order to demonstrate this more clearly.

Vision 1		Vision 2		Vision 3	
3.1-2	Setting	5.21	Setting	6.35	Setting
3.27	Lament	5.22-27	Lament	6.36-54	Lament
3.28-36	Question	5.28-30	Question	6.55-59	Question
4.1-11	Wisdom Reply	5.31-55	Wisdom Reply	7.1-25	Wisdom Reply
4.12-25	Discussion	5.56-6.10	Discussion	7.26-44	Eschatology
4.26–5.12	Eschatology	6.29-34	Eschatology	7.45–9.23	Extended Discussion
5.13-20	Concl./Prep.	6.29-34	Concl./Prep.	9.24-25	Concl./Prep.
[5.16-19	Phaltiel's interruption]				

Vision 4

↑	9.26-28	Changed Setting (Ardat)
	9.29-37	Lament
└─	9.38–10.4, 5-25	*Revelation 1* Dialogue and Response
┌─	10.25-27, 28-31	*Revelation 2* Vision and Response
	10.32-54	Interpretation
	10.55-58	Intimated glory
↓	10.59a	Conclusion and Preparation

Vision 5		Vision 6		Vision 7	
10.59b	Setting	13.1	Setting	14.1	Setting
11.1–12.3	Dream	13.2-13	Vision	14.1b-18	Rev. 1 Call
12.4-9	Response	13.14-20	Response	14.19-22	Response
12.10-27	Interpret.	13.21-50	Interpret.	14.23-26	Instruction
12.38	Concl./Prep.	13.51	Question	14.27-36	Preparation of people
12.40-45	People's Question	13.52a-56a	Response	14.37-44	Rev. 2 Writing
12.46-49	Ezra's Response	13.56b-58	Concl./Prep.	14.45-47	Instruction
12.50-51	Preparation			14.48	Response

The Blessing of Ezra

An important clue to the way in which vision 4 acts as a transition for Ezra appears when we chart the parallel movements of the weeping woman and the lamenting prophet. Both Ezra and the woman come outside of the city to lament: 'Et profectus sum...in campum' (9.26); 'ueni...in hoc campo' (10.3). Both the woman and Ezra are enjoined to come out of the field, and enter the city: 'Ingredere ergo in ciuitatem' (19.17); 'Ingredere' (10.55). The woman herself declines to return, but becomes the city into which Ezra enters. Note that Ezra has been *instructed* to seek out the desolate place, since no work of man could endure 'ubi incipiebat altissimi ciuitas ostendi' (10.54). It is both in the 'going out' and the 'entering' that Ezra is blessed: his isolation is the necessary prerequisite to his enlightenment, and his going in is the reward for an appropriate sorrow.

Why 'going out' and 'entering' should be so important as movements for Ezra and the woman is explicable in terms of Exodus–Canaan and Exile–Return symbolism. The desert has acquired throughout the pages of the Hebrew Bible a double aspect: it is the place of desolation, punishment and evil spirits; it is also the place of communion with God, testing and preparation.[66] The later prophets viewed the exile in harmony with the wilderness wanderings of the early Hebrews, and looked for a return parallel to the entry of the Promised Land. So then, they framed their hope not only in terms of a new creation, but in terms of a new Exodus (cf. Isa. 44.16; Jer. 31.2; Ezek. 36.33, 37.21; Hos. 2.14-15). Movements such as the Rechabites, and practices such as the annual sojourning in tabernacles, attest to the understood rhythm of desert/ Canaan and desolation/rejoicing. Within the symbolic network of *4 Ezra*, desolation and desert are complemented by the images of barrenness and bereavement. Although the woman does not dwell on God's wrath as responsible for her plight, the images of desolation and bereavement function in a similar way to the motifs of divorce, barrenness or widow-hood in the prophetic writings. The extreme nature of the woman's state-ments at *4 Ezra* 10.4 are consonant with the polarities of the prophets, who swing from sheer judgment to jubilant hope. The expectation set up by the woman's determination to mourn unto death is not her continuing desolation, but a divine reversal of the situation.

The comforting of the woman is riddled with logical and textual difficulties, particularly in the unexplained connection of Mother Zion and Mother Earth (10.6-17). A.L. Thompson's reading of the passage is ingenious, but fraught with difficulty because of the need to reconstruct[67] in order to show clearly the movement from 'many' to 'one'. It seems too tidy to suggest, as does Thompson, that Ezra's consolation lies in the

66. For a useful summary of the biblical material, see O. Böcher, 'Wilderness', in C. Brown (ed.), *DNTT* (Grand Rapids: Zondervan, 1978), III, pp. 1004-1008.
67. *Responsibility*, p. 228.

redirection of his attention towards Israel alone and away from the human condition. Here, in the fourth vision, as in the first three, we see an explicit consideration of the Israel problem, but also an extension of this to the connected problem of Mother Earth and her children. Ezra begins by appealing to Zion's loss (10.5-9), moves laterally in the discussion to speak of Mother Earth's loss (10.6-15), and then moves back to a lyrical expression of Zion's destruction (10.19-25). The recognition of both weeping and glorified Zion puts his own experience in context and perspective, but never touches the broader questions which continually have been broached.

It is possible that the extent of the city, and the later references to the whole earth's refreshment and a peaceable multitude 'aliqui adducentes ex eis qui offerebantur' (13.13), touch on the question of fallen humanity, but if so, only indirectly. Ezra's task throughout has been that of a prophet/priest to his own community, as may be seen especially in the first (5.16-18) and last (14.13, 27) visions. Though his lament may lead into general questions about humankind, the revelation does not explicitly address these. By entering into the woman's grief, and entering into the city, Ezra comes to a place where he can be not only the spokesman of his people, but also the spokesman of God; how his consolation is gained remains as much a mystery as the logic of his response to the woman, or the undescribed glory of Zion. Perhaps the comfort is to be found in the knowledge that Zion's lament, as well as her transformation, is divinely approved, and even divinely ordained. Finally, however, Ezra accepts that he is 'beatus' and not one of those 'qui spreuerunt'. He is, in the second half of *4 Ezra*, a 'lucerna in loco obscuro' (12.43), not because of his easy removal from the sinful crowd nor because of a facile acceptance of orthodox answers, but because he has voiced Israel's grief and yet has seen her glory: 'Confide Israel,... non est oblitus uestri in contentione. Ego enim non dereliqui uos neque excessi a uobis' (12.48).

'Apocalypse' and 'Revelation'

Israel, then, has not been forgotten in her distress, and is herself, unawares, a figure of great glory. In the hour of lament, it could be asked, 'Quid enim nobis prodest...Et quoniam ostendetur paradisus... uero non ingrediemur?' (7.119-123). In the hour of revelation, it is commanded 'ingredere et uide' (10.55) to the one who insists on numbering himself with those who are still outside. Ezra enters, and in so doing leaves behind his former despair, but not so as to abandon those with whom he is identified. His enlightenment, and likewise that of his people, is to know that Zion has not been abandoned. Her time of mourning has meaning (a great enough assurance!), but this is not even the whole story. There is far more to know, but this can only be understood by 'the wise', and remains a closed book due to its very nature. The problems of theodicy and the humiliation of Zion are therefore put into perspective by a greater issue—the identity of God's own people, who even in sorrow are bound for, indeed, connected with, unspeakable glory. The dual vision of Zion, lamenting and yet mysteriously glorious, is a sign that there remains both a 'semita' (i.e. the Law, 14.22) for the humble and a 'uena intellectus, et sapientiae fons et scientiae flumen' (14.48) for those with keener eyes and ears. If the way involves mourning, then Israel can be assured that there is far more glory waiting to be entered, even though this must not be humanly articulated. Ezra's 'answer' lies in what is not spoken, as much as in what has been clearly expressed. The medium of 'apocalypse', hiding while it reveals, comes firmly to the fore in what has often been considered the least speculative of the apocalyptic writings, *4 Ezra*.

This description of the structure and movement of *4 Ezra* has been anchored to the actual text, in which 'Ezra' and his 'people' actually play concrete roles. One wants continually to shift the ground and ask about the author and the community to which he addressed himself, or the context out of which he wrote. This transition is perhaps more supportable in the case of *4 Ezra* than in other narratives, since the appearance of a community is encoded within the text itself, inviting such an action. It may add depth to the narrative to suggest that the author experienced his visions while daily meditating at the site of ruined Jerusalem, or to refer to a 'post-Holocaust' mentality, or a cathartic 'pattern of consolation' for a sociological group. When all is said and done, however, what the reader possesses is the text—undated save for clues in the introduction and Eagle vision,[68] not situated except through speculation on the content, and at any rate resonant to other groups than its original readers. *4 Ezra*, with all its richness, ambiguity, tension and complexity, reads well as a unity. A classic example of Type Ia apocalypses (those with historical review but no heavenly journey), it

---

68. The almost unanimous dating accepted by scholars is 100–120 CE. This date is decided by a literal application of the thirty-year time frame given at 3.1 to the Destruction of 70, and the judgment that the piece could not easily have passed from synagogue to church after the revolt of Bar Kochba.

takes its point of departure from the historical situation, but then searches out the connected question of Lady Zion's identity.

Some have sought to formulate the issue of *4 Ezra* in terms of *destiny*—where is Israel headed?—rather than the more foundational question of identity. However, the crucial episode is vision 4, not the eschatological visions that ensue: in the central episode, Ezra comes to see that the lamenting and heavenly Zion are one. To settle the question of identity is to prepare the way for hope. While the historical review and eschatological vision of episodes 5 and 6 provide part of the hope for which Ezra is seeking, these are only possible because of the new perspective offered by the central episode. All the debate and revelation centre around the issue of identity: the status of Zion, and her relationship to the Almighty. In contrast to *Aseneth*, where the individual salvation of the proselyte seems to be most clearly in view, and where a 'City of Refuge' is named, but never described, *4 Ezra* pictures Zion as a corporate entity—a family with a divinely-given personality and a divinely-offered hope. The city's grandeur is emphasized and Ezra is seen standing alongside his people within the text.[69] The apocalypse *4 Ezra* is the story of a representative's sorrow and new-found understanding, a sorrow which is transformed and not belittled, and an understanding which is passed on (though not in entirety, 14.47) as an authoritative message. To say this is not to reduce the story to one core 'meaning', nor to detract from the multifarious forms and expressions found within. The visions, parables, allegories, interpretations, laments, dialogues, lyrical passages and mysterious silences all form a part of that story, the framework of the apocalypse; no detour can adequately travel through the book in its entirety.

69. *Pace* Longenecker, who sees in *4 Ezra* the closest thing to 'individualistic legalism' (*Eschatology*, p. 277) and considers the community aspects of the book mere 'posturing' (p. 276). The vacuum sensed by Longenecker is more precisely identified by C. Rowland, who comments that in *4 Ezra* (over against the Apocalypse) 'the eschatological spirit is not active in the community of the elect' ('The Parting of the Ways: The Evidence of Jewish and Christian Apocalyptic and Mystical Material', in J.D.G. Dunn [ed.], *Jews and Christians: The Parting of the Ways AD 70–135* [WUNT, 66; Tübingen: Mohr, 1992], p. 218). It is evident that in *4 Ezra*, identity and community will be configured differently than in a Christian piece: however, the practice of the Law and the (implied) pursuits of the wise take place in context, not in individualistic isolation. Moreover, the 'blessed place' of those who heed Ezra is envisioned as a glorious *city* with huge proportions—presumably more than a few will find a habitiation there.

Figure 2. *Eight Representative Outlines of the Apocalypse*

CHARLES	LUND	BOWMAN	FARRER
Prologue 1.1-3 I *John's Letter to the* *7 Churches* 1.4-20	A Prologue 1.1-20	Title 1.1-3 Letter vss. 4–6 Prologue, vss. 7–8	I *7 Messages* chs. 1–3
II *Problem of the* *Book* 7 Letters 2.1– 3.22	B *7 Epistles* 2.1–3.22	*Act 1* 1.9–3.22	
III *Vision of God and* *the Sealed Book* 4.1–5.14	C *7 Seals* 4.1–8.5	*Act 2* 4.1–8.1 (7 scenes)	II *7 Seals* chs. 4–7
IV *Judgements* 6.1– 20.3 3 series listed in sequence			
	D *7 Trumpets* 8.2, 6- 12; 8.13; 9.1-21; 11.14-19	*Act 3* 8.2–11.18 (7 scenes)	III *7 Trumpets* 8.11– 11.14
	E *Church's Testimony* *in Empire*, 10.1-11		
	F *Church's Testimony* *in Judaism* 11.1-13 F′ *Persecuted by* *Judaism* 12.1-17 E′ *By Empire* 13.1-18	*Act 4* 11.19–14.20; 15.2- 4 (7 scenes)	IV *7 Unnumbered* *Series* 11.15–14.20
	D′ *7 Bowls*, 15.1, 5-8; 16.1-21 C′ *7 Angels* 14.1-20; 15.2-4 B′ *7 Angels* 17.1–22.5	*Act 5* 15.1, 5–16.21 (7 scenes) *Act 6* 17.1–20.3, 7-10	V *7 Bowls* chapters 15–18 *Babylon Appendix* 17.1–19.10 VI *7 Unnumbered* *Series* 19.11–21.8
V *Millennial* *Kingdom* 21.9–22.2, 14-15, 17; 20.4-6, 7-10 VI *Great White* *Throne* 20.11-15		*Act 7* 20.4-6, 11–22.6	
VII *Everlasting* *Kingdom* 21.5a, 4d, 5b, 1-4abc, 22.3-5			*Jerusalem Appendix* 21.9–22.5
Epilogue 21.5c and other displaced verses.	A′ Epilogue 22.6-21	Epilogue 22.6-20 letter form 22.21	Epilogue 22.6-21
Revelation, I, pp. xxv- xxviii	adapted from *Chiasmus*, pp. 327-28	adapted from 'The Revelation to John', p. 436	*A Rebirth of Images*, pp. 55-56

FIORENZA	AUNE	ROUSSEAU	BEAGLEY
A *Epistolary Framework* 1.1-8	A Epistolary Prescript and Title 1.1-2	*7 Cycles* I *Letters* 1.1–5.14	Title 1.1-3 Salutation 1.4-6 Drama 1.7-8
B *Promise* (Letters) 1.9–3.22 C *Sealed Scroll* (Trumpets) 4.1–9.21; 11.15-19	B *4 Series of 7* 1. *7 Letters* 2.1–3.22 2. *7 Seals* 4.1–8.1	 II *Seals* 6.1–8.1	*Act I* Church on Earth (militant): 1.9–3.22; Setting: 7 Letters *Act II* Preservation of Church: 4.1–8.6; Setting: 7 Seal-visions [Interlude: 7.1-17]
	3. *7 Trumpets* 8.2–9.21; 11.15-18 [10.1–11.14 Intercalated]	III *Trumpets* 8.2–11.18	*Act III* Judgment upon earth; Setting: 7 Trumpet-visions, 8.3–11.19 [Interlude: 10.1–11.14]
D *Prophetic Scroll* 10.1–15.4 (excluding 11.15-19)	(*3 Digressions*) 11.18–14.20	IV *Protagonists* 11.19–14.5	*Act IV* Salvation of Saints; Setting: 7 Salvation-visions (*Central*): 12.1–14.13
		V *Transition to Future* 14.6–15.4	
C′ *Sealed Scroll* (Bowls) 15.5–19.10	4. *7 Bowls* 15.1–16.21	VI *Bowls* 15.5–19.10	*Act V* Judgment upon Earth: 15.1–16.17; Setting: 7 Bowl-visions
B′ *Fulfillment* 19.11–22.9	C *2 Visions* 1. 17.1–19.10 [*Intercalation* 19.11–21.8] *CENTRAL CORE	VII *Nations* 19.11–22.21	*Act VI* Judgment of Harlot: 17.3–20.10; Setting: 7 Visions of Judgment
			Act VII The Church Triumphant: 20.4–22.5; Setting: 7 visions of Consummation
A′ *Epistolary Framework* 22.10–22.21	2. 21.9–22.9		Epilogue 22.6-15 Imprimaturs 22.16-20 Benediction 22.21
'Composition and Structure', pp. 174-75	*Literary Environment*, pp. 240-43 (chart deduced from text)	*L'Apocalypse et le Milieu Prophétique*, p. 28	*The Sitz im Leben*, p. 181 (chiastic chart adapted)

Chapter 4

TRANSFORMATION AND CONTINUITY IN THE APOCALYPSE

Assigning a place to the transfigured woman within the Apocalypse of John is a difficult task since there is little agreement among scholars concerning the surface structure of the book as a whole. This is in marked contrast to the consensus concerning the shape of such an apocalypse as *4 Ezra*. John Wick Bowman in 1955 charted eight representative outlines of the Apocalypse,[1] to which might be added at least six others which have been conceived since that time.[2] The very number of suggestions witnesses to the frustration of scholars in adequately comprehending the piece. This frustration is also, it seems, expressed in two opposite attitudes: over-confidence regarding a new scheme as 'the key' to understanding, or a failure of nerve in some commentators seen in the conspicuous lack of any outline at all. In the words of David Aune, 'the Apocalypse...has yet to be satisfactorily analyzed'.[3] Whether this is due to the 'structural...complex[ity]'[4] of the piece, as Aune insists, or to a lack of organizational interest or skill on the part of the writer/redactor(s), is a question which must be carefully weighed, not simply assumed one way or the other. The following pages will provide a brief consideration and analysis of the various approaches to structure which have been adopted in the past. No detailed alternate outline will

1. 'The Revelation to John: Its Dramatic Structure and Message', *Int* 9 (1955), pp. 436-53.

2. See Figure 2 at the head of this chapter, which selects four representatives from Bowman's chart, and adds four more recent schemes. It will be noted that corrections have been made to Bowman's understanding of Charles's scheme, based on Charles's own outline in his commentary. Moreover, some adaptations have been made in the cases of Charles, Bowman, Lund and Rousseau for the purposes of simplifying the chart.

3. *New Testament in its Literary Environment* (Philadelphia: Westminster Press, 1987), p. 241.

4. Aune, *Literary Environment*.

be offered (a ludicrous attempt, considering the past failure rate!), but common features of the most careful outlines will be highlighted. *En route* we will note the importance of design and symmetry within the book, as seen through various internal indications. Of real interest in this discussion is the place afforded the persecuted mother (ch. 12) and New Jerusalem bride (ch. 21) within the various schemes. It will be seen that not a few critics have cited these chapters as crucial to an understanding of the book for various reasons. Finally, the relationship between the two chapters will be explored and their functions outlined.

Traditional Source Theory: Spitta, Völter, Charles

Older criticism tended to explain the structural problems of the Apocalypse by recourse to source theories, clumsy revision or redaction and displacement. In such authors as Friedrich Spitta[5] and Daniel Völter,[6] a frank *Quellentheorie* was employed to account for breaks, digressions, doublets, theology in tension and surprising sequences. Their methods have been continued more recently by such scholars as M.E. Boismard[7] and J. Massyngberde Ford.[8] Less extreme in his use of the traditional method was R.H. Charles,[9] who remains a luminary in the study of the book, as in all things apocalyptic. Charles thought that the author intended to describe a progressive series of events, which was at times disrupted through proleptic visions (for example, ch. 14) or flashbacks (ch. 12). However, he also found it necessary to posit a meddling redactor, whose activity is seen mostly at the end, but also throughout the book. Other inconsistencies are resolved through appeal to the resistance of traditional material. Such explanations rise and fall on the intricate hypothesis of Charles that the Semitic author was heavily influenced by sources, and that his work was botched by a subsequent

---

5.   *Die Offenbarung des Johannes untersucht* (Halle, 1889), cited in the discussion of source theory by A. Yarbro Collins, *The Combat Myth in the Book of Revelation* (HDR 9; Missoula, MT: Scholars Press, 1976), pp. 6-9.

6.   Various works from 1882 onwards cited in Yarbro Collins, *Combat Myth*.

7.   ' "L'Apocalypse", ou "les apocalypses" de S. Jean', *RB* (1949), pp. 507-27. Structural disjunctions are accounted for by a revision theory, in which the same author edits two earlier versions of the text, both by his own hand.

8.   *The Revelation of John* (AB 38; New York: Doubleday, 1975).

9.   *Studies in the Apocalypse* (Edinburgh: T. & T. Clark, 1913) and *A Critical and Exegetical Commentary on the Revelation of St John* (2 vols.; ICC; New York: Scribner's, 1920).

editor. Moreover, in dealing with a writer who supposedly displayed real problems with grammatical coherence, it was not natural to expect structural coherence. Charles departed from earlier source critics in expecting a certain amount of design on the part of the author, but enough of that school's legacy remains in his comments to prevent a real examination of the text as it stands. In his own day, however, and also in more recent years, Charles's arguments for *bona fide* Semiticisms,[10] sources and redaction have been queried. Few today would appeal to sources and redaction in explaining (away) the structure of the book. However, even where authors continue to cite linguistic and structural irregularities as important keys to understanding the growth of the corpus, the final shape is usually recognized as of some importance. A. Yarbro Collins[11] is a good example of one who appeals to sources, yet also incorporates the more recent text-immanentist methods. The trick with such eclecticism is, however, to use all the methods fairly; there is a strong temptation to resort too quickly to sources when an *impasse* in understanding is reached. It is always a delicate matter to determine whether an *aporia* is in the eye of the beholder, or in the text.

No Attempt to Structure: Rissi, Kraft

Another group of scholars may be treated together—those who do not attempt to subdivide the main central section of the Apocalypse, but simply list the elements sequentially. Most of these use 1.19 as a structural principle, ἃ εἶδες referring to the inaugural vision of 1.9-17, ἃ εἰσίν to the state of the seven churches (chs. 2–3) and ἃ μέλλει to all the remaining episodes of the book, save for the finale (chs. 19 or 20–22.5 and closing messages).[12] The content of the visions from chs. 4 through 19 or 20 is not structurally shaped, so that the divisions appear more like a table of contents than like a scheme. Good examples of this

10.   E. Lohmeyer, *Die Offenbarung des Johannes* (HNT 16; Tübingen: Mohr/Siebeck, 2nd edn, 1953 [1927]), p. 193, and H. Kraft, *Das Offenbarung des Johannes* (HNT 16a; Tübingen: Mohr, 1974), p. 17, argue for a deliberate Semitic style, coherent with the 'prophetic' flavour of the Apocalypse.

11.   *The Apocalypse* (NTM 22; Wilmington: Glazier, 1979), pp. xii-xiv.

12.   References to the Greek text of the Apocalypse are to *Novum Testamentum Graece* (ed. Nestle–Aland; Stuttgart: Deutsche Bibelstiftung, 26th edn, 1979).

procedure would be M. Rissi (I = chs. 1–3; II = ch. 4–19.10; III = 19.11–22.21)[13] or Heinrich Kraft,[14] who also describes 4.1–19.10 as the main section. The main advantage of such formats is that the interpreter is preserved from forcing patterns onto the work, or entering into what seems to be a never-ending controversy. However, to tell us that chs. 4–19.10 are the 'main section' is hardly informative,[15] and does little to explain why the author has put the visions the way that they appear. Little is lost, but little is also gained. Surely more can be said about the shape of the Apocalypse than this.

Intricate Structuring: Lund, Bowman, Lohmeyer, Rousseau, Gager

At the extreme opposite pole are those who envision a very clear and detailed structure of the book, notably N.W. Lund,[16] who has produced an intricate example of ring composition for his study on chiasmus. His scheme is complicated by a theory of 'deliberate projections'[17] of blocks of material which do not fit the scheme. Of real difficulty is, unfortunately, his central chiasmus, a chiasmus which by all literary rules should be marked and self-evident.[18] Yet it is not at all clear how F (11.1-13) and F' (12.1-17) correspond, nor how they are to be easily identified with 'the Church's testimony in Judaism' and 'the Church persecuted officially by Judaism'.[19] Moreover, Lund does little with his central chiasmus in terms of establishing a main message, hidden mystery, or the like. In the final analysis, he tells us that 'the purpose of

13.   *Zeit und Geschichte in der Offenbarung des Johannes* (Zürich: Zwingli Verlag, 1952).

14.   *Offenbarung*, pp. 5-6. Kraft's interest in design is overshadowed by a theory of deliberate 'prophecy' and successively revised *Grundschrift*. Interest in these other matters has perhaps prevented a thorough examination of structure.

15.   Only a little less general, and probably less well-considered is the attempt to see 5.1–22.61 as a single section; see R.W. Wall, *Revelation* (New International Bible Commentary 18; Peabody, MA: Hendrikson, 1991).

16.   *Chiasmus in The New Testament* (Chapel Hill: University of North Carolina Press, 1942), pp. 327-28.

17.   Lund, *Chiasmus*, p. 327.

18.   D.N. Freedman, 'Preface', in J.W. Welch (ed.), *Chiasmus in Antiquity*, p. 7.

19.   The same is to be said for the next ring out, E (10.1-11) and E' (13.1-18), which Lund details as 'the Church's testimony in the Roman Empire' and 'the Church persecuted officially by the Roman Empire'.

the book is practical. The author sees the impending clash of the Church with Rome. To stiffen the morale of the Christians is his great task.'[20] If it could be proved that chs. 11 and 12 refer to the past testimony and persecution within Judaism, would such a central section actually function to 'stiffen the morale' for Christians in the hands of a world power such as Rome? We are thus left with the impression that the chiasmus is only formal; hence, it is difficult not to dismiss Lund's hard work as yet another attempt to buttress his thesis that the NT abounds in extended chiasmi. Another very different scheme, but one presented with similar confidence, is that of Bowman, who declares that form and content are 'inextricably combined' and that 'only through grasping the nature of [the] dramatic structure of the book can its message be properly apprehended'.[21] No doubt form and content are combined in such a manner: if the Apocalypse were indeed intended as a seven-act, seven-scene drama, it would be of the utmost importance to recognize it as such. Unfortunately, Bowman does not explain why some of the scenes remain unnumbered, while the others are numbered by the author. Rather, he tells us it is 'reasonable to look for all to be so divided' into seven, since the numeral is so pervasive throughout the Apocalypse. It should, of course, be pointed out that at no time were there actual seven-act, seven-scene plays in antiquity (the norm was five acts),[22] so any such special format should be self-evident and undeniable. This is not the case: others attempting to employ a similar key[23] are in

20.   Lund, *Chiasmus*, p. 409.

21.   'The Revelation to John', p. 440.

22.   R.R. Brewer, 'The Influence of Greek Drama on the Apocalypse of John', *ATR* 18 (1936), pp. 74-92.

23.   See F. Palmer, *The Drama of the Apocalypse* (New York, 1903), and more recently M. Wilcock, *I Saw Heaven Opened: The Message of Revelation* (London: Inter-Varsity, 1975). Bowman's own structure has been adapted and modified by R.J. Loenertz, *The Apocalypse of St John* (London: Sheed & Ward, 1947), and by L.C. Spinks, 'A Critical Examination of J.W. Bowman's Proposed Structure of the Revelation', *EvQ* 50 (1978), pp. 211-22. Spinks's own structure has again been modified by A.J. Beagley, *The 'Sitz im Leben' of the Apocalypse with Particular Reference to the Role of the Church's Enemies* (Berlin: de Gruyter, 1987), especially p. 181, in an attempt to enhance a chiastic arrangement. Although the particulars of these chiasms seem a little forced (e.g. Act II has as much to do with judgment as with 'The Preservation of the Church'), the discovery of chs. 12–14 as central is consonant with many other schemes, and with the recent discussion. The most recent attempt at dramatic structuring is to be seen in J. Isaac, *L'Apocalypse de Jésus Christ: Les épreuves de l'alliance et le sens de l'histoire* (Paris: Cerf, 1991). Isaac also posits

disagreement regarding the delineation of scenes within acts, particularly in the latter half of the book. One final weakness is to be seen in his categorical denial of apocalypse as a genre which explains the Apocalypse, and his description of it as a '*sui generis*' letter-plus-drama.[24] This denial and characterization are surely extreme. Critics have by no means been 'tricked by a word (that is, *apocalypsis*)'[25] in their decision regarding genre, but have had concrete reasons to regard the apocalypse as one, or, more often, as the chief informing work of the genre. Bowman's antipathy to the apocalyptic genre of the Apocalypse seems directed more by apologetic constraints, that is, fear of association with extra-canonical literature,[26] than by reason.

Parallel to Bowman's conception are earlier studies which divide the Apocalypse into seven parts, such as E. Lohmeyer,[27] and R.G. Moulton,[28] whose outline is quite similar. More recently, François Rousseau[29] and John G. Gager[30] have put forward two very different but equally intriguing outlines of seven cycles. Rousseau utilizes recurring phrases, inaugural visions and the presence of doxologies/hymns to mark out each section, thus integrating the whole of the Apocalypse, and recognizing the key inaugural passages of 19.11 and 1.9-20. However, the system of cycles has the effect of obscuring certain notable passages, such as the Babylon episode. Gager's study is less thoroughgoing and more tentative, but worth considering. He tells us that two patterns of sevens and twos 'meet to create a "machine" for transcending time'.[31]

seven acts, the first four roughly the same as Bowman, the last three (as anticipated) with different demarcations—chs. 12–14 remain central.

24. Bowman, 'The Revelation to John', pp. 437ff.

25. 'The Revelation to John', p. 438.

26. Bowman states, 'It is high time that we cease to be tricked…into imagining that the major associations of John's work are to be found with the extra-canonical apocalyptic literature' ('The Revelation to John', p. 438).

27. *Offenbarung*.

28. *The Modern Reader's Bible* (New York: MacMillan, 1907), in Bowman's chart.

29. *L'Apocalypse et le Milieu Prophétique du Nouveau Testament: Structure et Prehistoire du Texte* (Tournai: Desclee & Cie; Montreal: Bellarmin, 1971), p. 28.

30. 'The Attainment of Millennial Bliss through Myth and the Book of Revelation', in P.D. Hanson (ed.), *Visionaries and their Apocalypses* (Philadelphia: Fortress Press, 1983), pp. 146-55.

31. *Attainment*, p. 149.

His method is to travel sequentially through the book, noting seven alternating sequences of victory–hope and oppression–despair, plus a concluding section of victory and hope (21.1–22.5). Such an alternation may in fact have a certain psychological effect upon the reader. However, the alternations are not entirely clear: see his central section of oppression–despair, which inconveniently includes a hymn of praise and rejoicing (12.10-12). Again, the four clearly marked series of sevens that we do have in the book itself have been cut across by his scheme, so that structural clarity has been obscured by a psychological theory. Given such difficulties, can we be persuaded that the Apocalypse functions so as to 'transcend time'?

Scrolls as a Structuring Device: Bornkamm, Yarbro Collins,
Schüssler Fiorenza

A final group of critics pays great attention to the scrolls of the Apocalypse as a structuring device. Gunther Bornkamm[32] was the first to point to the *Siebensiegelbuch* as a key. Following a variant reading of 5.1, he writes that the scroll is to be conceived of as a *Doppelurkunde*,[33] with the table of contents ἔξωθεν and the details sealed within. Only after the seals have been broken can the contents be discerned: this 'Inhalt der Urkunde'[34] begins with the trumpets at 8.2, and is recapitulated at 15.1 with the bowls sequence. So then, two cycles of visions, 8.2–14.20 and 15.1–19.21, are discovered, preceded by the letters and opening of the scroll, and followed by concluding judgment and salvation. Bornkamm demonstrates parallelism between chs. 12–13 and 17–18, and other key passages to strengthen his argument. Chapters 10 and 11 are seen as the contents of the little book, and dubbed a *Fremdkörper*;[35] that is, they displace the seventh trumpet, and point to the mysterious completed history of Israel.

Bornkamm has been followed in different ways by Adela Yarbro

---

32.   'Die Komposition der apokalyptischen Visionen in der Offenbarung Johannis', *Studien zu Antike und Urchristentum: Gesammelte Aufsätze Band II* (BEvt 28; Munich: Chr. Kaiser, 1959), pp. 204-22.

33.   Bornkamm, 'Komposition', p. 205.

34.   Bornkamm, 'Komposition', p. 221.

35.   Bornkamm, 'Komposition', p. 217.

Collins[36] and Elisabeth Schüssler Fiorenza.[37] Both of these accentuate the importance of the scroll of 5.1 as a structural device, but also highlight the open βιβλαρίδιον (10.2), which the prophet eats (10.10). Like Bornkamm, Yarbro Collins construes two cycles of visions. However, she traces different contours, so that the first half of the Apocalypse is associated with the sealed scroll (1.9–11.19) and the second half is related to the little scroll (12.1–22.5). Yarbro Collins sees a distinct break between 11.19 and 12.1 because 'only the vision sequence of the 7 trumpets is integrated compositionally with the opening of the seals',[38] and a new beginning seems to occur here. It might be pointed out that she is not alone in seeing 12.1 as the central point, since H.B. Swete also cited the same two halves, labelling the first 'the work of the ascended Christ' and the second 'the destinies of the Christian church'.[39] Yarbro Collins works out the structure more carefully than Swete. The sealed scroll consists of three sevenfold visions which are intensified by the three sevenfold visions of the open scroll. Here, Yarbro Collins basically follows Austin Farrer's first structure[40] in discerning the unnumbered series.[41] Her purposes, however, in delineating structure are related directly to the combat myth presented in ch. 12.

Schüssler Fiorenza has a different view of the contents of the little book, and sees an *inclusio* within an 'architectonic pattern',[42] rather than a two-part recapitulation, as the appropriate outline. The little scroll (D) is the central section, surrounded by the sealed scroll (C and C'), a

36.   Yarbro Collins, *Combat Myth*.

37.   'The Composition and Structure of the Book of Revelation', in *The Book of Revelation: Justice and Judgment* (Philadelphia: Fortress Press, 1985), pp. 159-80 (= *CBQ* 39 [1977], pp. 344-66). She employs the same structure, differentiating the sealed scroll from the 'bitter-sweet' scroll, in her recent rhetorical/compositional commentary, *Revelation: Vision of a Just World* (Proclamation Commentaries; Minneapolis: Fortress Press, 1991).

38.   *Combat Myth*, p. 26.

39.   *The Apocalypse of John* (London: Macmillan, 1922), p. xlii.

40.   *A Rebirth of Images* (Westminster: Dacre, 1949; repr. Boston: Beacon, 1964), pp. 36-58. See p. 8 of *Combat Myth* for her indebtedness.

41.   Her organizing principle is not Farrer's liturgical hypothesis, however, which she deems 'arbitrary', but the two scrolls format.

42.   'Composition', p. 175. Schüssler Fiorenza's most recent presentation of structure, in *Revelation: Vision of a Just World*, gives rhetorically appropriate titles to the same sections, but also stresses the compositional tension between the concentric structure and the dynamic, forward spiralling movement of the Apocalypse (see esp. *Revelation*, pp. 35ff.)

promise and fulfilment section (B and B'), and a prologue and epilogue (A and A'):

A	Prologue 1.1-8	
B	Promise 1.9–3.22	
C	The sealed scroll 4.1–9.21; 11.15-19	
D	The little scroll 10.1–15.4	
C'	The sealed scroll, continued 15.1, 5–19.10	
B'	Fulfilment 19.11–22.9	
A'	Epilogue 22.10-21.	

Actantial analysis is especially invoked to demonstrate the difference of the little scroll (D) from the rest of the book. A change in actants, coinciding with the introduction of a new scroll, signals the crucial centrality of this section. Since the little prophetic book holds central place, 'the structure of the book underscores that the main function of Rev is the prophetic interpretation of the situation of the community'.[43] Schüssler Fiorenza supports her chiastic construction by explaining it as an extension of the epistolary *inclusio* (prescript and closing). The Apocalypse is less an 'apocalypse' in genre than a 'unique form-content configuration',[44] a 'Christian prophecy' expressed by an 'epistolary framework' and using various 'dramatic, liturgical, mythopoeic, prophetic, and Christian...patterns'.[45]

Both Yarbro Collins and Schüssler Fiorenza point to ch. 12 as the central one, although they work out different schemes. The main difficulty in arbitrating between them is that the author of the Apocalypse does not himself trouble to tell us where the contents of the little scroll begin or end. Schüssler Fiorenza is indeed correct when she argues, 'the author does not divide the text into separate sections or parts, but joins units together...It is therefore more crucial to discern the joints of the structure which interlace the different parts than to discover the "dividing marks".'[46] That is, in pieces such as *Aseneth* and *4 Ezra*, traditional markers such as time, locale and an orderly progression of events make the division of the whole text into parts (for the sake of analysis) a fairly simple and fruitful procedure. With the Apocalypse, however, the numbering of the visions and the flow of action are disturbed again and again: sections are linked together by a process

43. Schüssler Fiorenza, 'Composition', p. 175.
44. Schüssler Fiorenza, 'Composition', p. 177.
45. Schüssler Fiorenza, 'Composition', p. 170.
46. Schüssler Fiorenza, 'Composition', p. 173.

of displacement, where the beginning of a new section commences before the first section has completely ended. The effect is one of phantasmagoria, and, as Schüssler Fiorenza notes, the technique used to achieve it must be recognized for an adequate appreciation of the book.

However, the arguments of both Schüssler Fiorenza and Yarbro Collins depend upon a division of parts as well as a perception of their connections. That is, both scholars base their posited structures upon a *division* of the two scrolls, a difficult task in a work which is so determined to conceal its seams. As we consider both schemes, several questions arise. Of Yarbro Collins we must ask, is it fair to include the first four chapters of the Apocalypse as part of the sealed scroll, which scroll is not even introduced until ch. 5? Again, why not include ch. 11 as part of the contents of the little scroll, since this chapter follows its introduction in ch. 10? Of Schüssler Fiorenza, it must be asked, what evidence is there that 15.1, 5 resumes the content of the sealed scroll? It would seem that Yarbro Collins's format requires a far more complex defence than that of Schüssler Fiorenza, since it claims far more—series of sevens, including unnumbered ones, intricate recapitulation, and so on. Moreover, the scheme suffers from the use of the term 'appendix' for the Babylon and Jerusalem sections.[47] Babylon's downfall may be more fairly dubbed an appendix, since it is formally connected to the bowl sequence; to consider 21.9–22.5 a mere appendix, however, is to subordinate the climax of the action. It seems unlikely that anyone would have called this section an 'appendix' had the total of seven visions for a posited unnumbered series not already been reached. We have already seen that the discovery of unnumbered sevens is a risky venture. The comments of Martin Kiddle are sobering:

> [I]t is pressing this fact too hard to insist that the whole literary structure of REVELATION is based on the number 7, and that all the material not included in one of the seven-fold series is an 'interlude', or, alternatively, an interpolation. Frequently the so-called interludes are intended to be of the utmost importance (e.g. vii., xi., xii.); and can it be reasonably argued that chaps. xvii.–xxii. (following the completion of the vision of the seven bowls) are nothing more than an editorial appendix?[48]

47.   This is apparently a legacy from Austin Farrer (*Rebirth*, p. 56).

48.   *The Revelation of St John* (assisted by M.K. Ross; MNTC; London: Hodder & Stoughton, 1940), p. xxxii. Kiddle would likely have been even more nonplussed at the curious innovation of some newer critics who label these awkward passages 'digressions' or 'appendices' and yet plead for their centrality. Aune, for example, argues that the digressive passages are sheltered mysteries, of primary

Schüssler Fiorenza's concept of the book is less risky, but has its problems as well. The greatest difficulty is her insistence, in the company of Bowman, that the Apocalypse is a *sui generis* composition. This view opens up the vexed question of mixed genres: a reading of Fiorenza gives the impression of one hedging her bets, most comfortable with the idea of the book as a prophetic letter, but unable to give up the idea of its 'apocalyptic' quality.[49] In fact, the main structural purpose of the epistolary frame for Fiorenza, that is, as a clue to the 'onion' structure of the Apocalypse, would be demonstrated equally by reference to the definition for apocalypse adopted in *Semeia*. That is, the *narrative framework* of the apocalypse genre will do as well as the epistolary framework to set up an *inclusio*. That the framework has an epistolary cast[50] would then be simply one of the particulars of a specific example of the genre, comparable to various peculiar forms found in other apocalypses (dialogue and debate in *4 Ezra*, parable in *1 Enoch*, and

importance in determining the theme or meaning of the book, yet concealed by the structure. The hearer/reader has to work at understanding the book, hence re-experiences the mysterious revelation of the original seer. For Aune, these passages include 11.18–14.20 and 12.11–21.8. He cites the linguistic work of D. Hellholm, 'The Problem of Apocalyptic Genre and the Apocalypse of John', in K.H. Richards (ed.), *SBLSP 1982* (Chico, CA: Scholars Press, 1982), pp. 157-98, to support such claims. While something is to be said for the sheltered mystery hypothesis, Aune's structure seems a curious mixture of the general and the particular. The result is an indigestible scheme which sheds some light on the problems of the text.

    49.   Fiorenza's compositional study was written in 1977, prior to a major colloquium on apocalypticism held in Uppsala in 1979 (proceedings are reflected in Hellholm [ed.], *Apocalypticism in the Mediterranean World and the Near East*) and prior to the discussion of the SBL group in *Semeia* volumes (1979 and 1986). In the latter two studies, it is both argued and assumed that the Johannine Apocalypse should be categorized as Type Ib—one of the 'Apocalypses with Cosmic and/or Political Eschatology (which have neither historical review nor otherworldly journey)'. Fiorenza does not appear to have been particularly influenced by these discussions, however, and continues to speak in her latest (1985) essay, 'Visionary Rhetoric and Social-Political Situation', in *The Book of Revelation*, of the book as having 'prophetic-apocalyptic setting', and in her Proclamation commentary (1991) of it as an 'open prophetic letter' which utilizes apocalyptic vision.

    50.   To consider the prologue and conclusion an actual epistolary framework, as does Fiorenza ('Composition', p. 176), is to ignore the fact that the epistolary aspects of 1.4-5 and 22.8 are both obscured and modified by the prophetic and visionary character of these sections. Who, after all, is the sender—John, Jesus or God Almighty (1.1, 4, 8; 22.8, 12, 16)? Moreover, who is the recipient—the seven churches in Asia (1.4) or the 'blessed' in general (22.7)?

paraenesis in the later Christian apocalypses). To miss the dominating influence of the genre apocalypse is to rob the critic of the most helpful points of comparison available within ancient literature.

The other basic problem is one which Schüssler Fiorenza shares with Yarbro Collins, that is, the lack of explicit delineation of the scrolls which are argued to provide the structure. We are never told within the Apocalypse itself that certain sections provide the contents of either scroll. However, the opening of seals followed by visions (ch. 6) and the eating of a scroll, followed by a commission to prophecy (ch. 10), would probably imply that the contents of the heavenly books are being disclosed, at least to some degree. Schüssler Fiorenza, unfortunately, does not give strong arguments for the resumption of the seven-sealed scroll in ch. 15. Given the movement back to God's visitation of wrath at this point, however, and the inner connection of chs. 10–14,[51] it would seem worthwhile to look for clear indications that ch. 15 continues the movement which was interrupted at ch. 10.

Genre and Symmetry:
Reflection and Analysis of the Proposed Structures

We have seen that in the formats which emphasize the final shape of the Apocalypse rather than its possible sources or revisions, various symmetries have been stressed. The foundational symmetrical structure of the text seems to be that shared with other works of the same type: that is, the narrative framework which sets off the visions of an apocalypse. Given that some have demurred from such a classification, it is perhaps helpful to reflect upon the larger issue of genre and the use to which generic categories may be put. In debating the merits of assigning a particular piece to one genre or another, critics have perhaps sometimes been guilty of assuming, or at least of giving the impression, that genre is an absolute category. A more fruitful approach would be to see the pursuit of genre as heuristic, so that any one piece (including the Apocalypse!) might be approached from various angles, including different types of intertextuality. We name a work, after all, to befriend it, and not to master it. In any one selection of writings, it is obvious that some will have more consistent and unequivocal intertextual echoes, whereas others will hover on the borders of recognized generic

---

51. Even Yarbro Collins admits the connection of ch. 10 with chs. 12–14; see *Combat Myth*, pp. 27-28.

categories. The reasons for a more or less 'hybrid' writing may be naïveté or sophistication on the part of the composer, the development of a particular genre at the point when that form was expressed in the piece at hand,[52] or even a difference in conventions and expectations between the ancient world and our own.

In dealing with the Apocalypse, a question that has been raised concerns the awareness of a first-century audience of the genre 'apocalypse'. Are we imposing a modern category infelicitously upon an unsuspecting body of literature? A second question concerns the advisability of considering the Apocalypse as an apocalypse when it is clear that the piece can be fruitfully understood by reference to other types of literature. These two questions are particularly pertinent when genre is conceived as a quasi-Platonic ideal, something that is 'there' outside of its particular manifestations. However, when genre is approached in terms of a fruitful reading strategy, the problems of anachronism and exclusivity fade. What is at issue is not whether the Apocalypse is written self-consciously as an apocalypse, so as to exclude other connections. Rather, we ask, what if we see the Apocalypse as a particular example of the genre, comparable to other similar pieces, but with its own peculiar flavour? Then, the epistolary introduction can be seen as standing in the place of pseudonymity—a point made even by Schüssler Fiorenza!—authenticating the visions within their Christian setting. Again, the easy connection of the letter form with a common apocalyptic theme, heavenly writings, renders the form not so very surprising. Further, the 'anti'-apocalyptic quality of the Apocalypse (that is, its lack of pseudonymity and its 'open' rather than sealed quality) associates the piece strongly with the genre: does the book demonstrate here an ability to play with traditional expectations of visionary works? I am convinced, then, that the genre apocalypse is the best pair of specatacles from which to view John's revelation, although other viewpoints may yield complementary results. Part of seeing the work as an apocalypse is to take seriously its character as a macro-genre, complete with a grand-narrative, and search for categories which open this narrative to us.[53]

52.   See A. Fowler, 'The Life and Death of Literary Forms', *NLH* 2 (1971), pp. 199-216, for an exploration of genre formation, development and anti-types.

53.   A plea to analyze the Apocalypse as a narrative (i.e. attention to plot, characterization, etc.) is made cogently by W.S. Vorster, '"Genre" and the Revelation of John: A Study in Text, Context and Intertext', *Neot* 22 (1988), pp. 103-23. His word

The symmetrical quality of this unusual and complex narrative has often provided a starting point for the structures traced by various critics. Certain structural designs dominate: all authors have recognized the importance of the four series of sevens, although some have unfortunately removed the letters to the churches from the 'main body' of the work. Many have pointed to the similarities between the plagues, particularly the parallelism of the trumpets and bowls. Others have pointed to the similarity of inauguration scenes, to the fulfilment of the epistolary promises in the final chapters, to the two measurings of the temple, and to the contrast between whore and bride. In every analysis, the attempt to depict the structure of the Apocalypse has led to two observations— signs of design, such as numbered sequences and symmetry, and surprising interruptions or displacements of this. It would be easy to follow the course of the nineteenth-century critics and argue for a confusion of parts by compiler or editor. However, even where episodes interrupt the action or seem misplaced, there are strong internal indications that they are intended to stand as they are. For example, ch. 10 imposes upon the flow of the 12 trumpets, yet includes within it references to this delay, and to the time when the trumpet is 'about to be sounded' (ὅταν μέλλῃ σαλπίζειν, 10.7). Similar to this delay of the trumpet is the deliberate hiatus between the sixth and seventh seals in ch. 7.

Reinforcement of the Two-Scroll Structure

Although it seems wisest not to subdivide the larger sections, as many who note these designs have tried to do, it is clear that symmetry and repeated phrases do provide clues to the shape of the Apocalypse. The use of the scroll revelations seems to be one of the better internal indicators of the flow of the action, and Schüssler Fiorenza's broad divisions seem plausible. However, it has been noted that Schüssler Fiorenza does not give strong reasons for the resumption of the large scroll at 15.1. Of help in establishing this return to the large scroll might be the numbering of three woes which passes through the central section, the sections labelled by her as C and C'. In 8.13, the last three trumpet angels (trumpets five, six and seven) are introduced in this manner:

needs to be heard again, however one assesses his radical and deconstructionist challenge to generic distinctions.

οὐαὶ οὐαὶ οὐαὶ τοὺς κατοικοῦντας ἐπὶ τῆς γῆς ἐκ
τῶν λοιπῶν φωνῶν τῆς σάλπιγγος τῶν τριῶν ἀγγέλων
τῶν μελλόντων σαλπίζειν.

The first woe is numbered at the end of the fifth trumpet (9.12), the second woe is numbered prior to the sounding of the seventh trumpet (11.14), but the third woe is not numbered as expected at the end of the seventh trumpet. Two problems present themselves: why is the numbering of the sixth trumpet/second woe delayed until 11.14, when we should naturally expect it following 10.21; and why are we told that the third woe is 'coming soon', but never explicitly satisfied in this expectation?

The first problem is not so acute, since the numbering of the second woe is delayed along with the sounding of the seventh trumpet. That is, if the last three trumpets followed sequentially and without interruption, the natural order would appear as follows:

> Contents of the fifth trumpet
> > Link 1—First woe over, two to come
> Contents of the sixth trumpet
> > Link 2—Second woe over, one to come
> Contents of the seventh trumpet
> > Conclusion—All woes complete.

However, there is a break between the sixth and seventh trumpet, so that link 2 is also delayed. The problem is really why the seventh trumpet is delayed, and this has been adequately explained by the technique which has been called variously 'interlocking' (A.Y. Collins), 'intercalation' (Fiorenza) and 'loi de l'emboîtement' (E.-B. Allo).[54] To introduce link 2 at 11.4, and to say that the second woe is past, and the third will soon come, is a way of resuming the trumpet series. It is a signal that we will now move on to the seventh trumpet after a delay of a chapter and a half. The seventh trumpet, then, is tucked into the 'alien material' of the little scroll, interlocking the two scrolls.

Why the third woe itself is not numbered after the contents of the seventh trumpet is a more perplexing question. Why is there no 'conclusion' corresponding to links 1 and 2, which tells us that the woes

---

54.   *Saint Jean: L'Apocalypse* (EBib; Paris: Gabalda, 4th rev. edn, 1933), pp. lxxxii-lxxxv, cited by Collins, *Combat Myth*, p. 49 n. 64. As Yarbro Collins points out, her description of interlocking is more particular than the general observations of Allo. Schüssler Fiorenza's intercalation is also precisely defined and differs slightly. All three conceptions, however, point to the deliberate foreshadowing of the next section's theme for the purpose of linking parts.

are complete? By analogy to the fifth and sixth trumpet, Bowman, Lohmeyer and Charles assume that the seventh trumpet *is* the third woe,[55] even though we are not told this directly. However, no plague or judgment is described during the seventh trumpet sequence (11.15-19); rather, the seventh trumpet episode depicts worship in heaven, declares the arrival of God and Christ's reign, and proclaims the time 'for judging the dead' (11.18). The seventh trumpet is therefore an announcement of victory, and not a description of plagues, as were the other trumpets. Moreover, God's active visitation of plagues is arrested for three more chapters as the drama of the 'little scroll' is enacted (D, 10.1–15.4).

It is not until ch. 15, then, that the process of God's judgment recommences in detail (although we are given a preview of it, from the perspective of heaven, in chs. 10–14, when the angel is sent to reap). The seals and trumpets are followed by the third series of plagues, that is, the bowls. During the seventh trumpet, the worshippers in heaven were aware of ἀστραπαί, φωναί, βρονταί, σεισμός and χάλαζα μεγάλη (11.19)—a great hailstorm poured out upon humankind—although we are not told the effect of these. During the bowl, or vial sequence, we see the effect of God's wrath poured out. The renewal of the plagues is signalled by a renewed reference to God's temple (11.19 // 15.5). Moreover, with the completion of the series, with the seventh bowl, we are again told of ἀστραπαί, φωναί, βρονταί, σεισμός (16.18) and χάλαζα μεγάλη (16.21). It would seem, then, that just as the seventh seal merges into the trumpet visions (8.1-2), so too the seventh trumpet merges into the bowls, and finds its completion in the 'fulfilment' of God's wrath. The bowls are the complete pouring out of judgment, and this process ends in the 'remembrance' (16.19) of Babylon, when χάλαζα μεγάλη...καταβαίνει ἐκ τοῦ οὐρανοῦ ἐπὶ τοὺς ἀνθρώπους (16.21). So then, the seventh trumpet, so to speak, 'contains' the seven bowls, just as the seventh seal 'contained' the seven trumpets. The pause in the momentum of judgment takes us to the perspective of heaven for a brief interval in the seventh trumpet, and for a longer retrospect and prospect in the contents of the little scroll (chs. 10-14, excluding the trumpet). The final woe is therefore not numbered, since it is not described until Babylon is finally judged: it is the end. This reading is confirmed in the Babylon 'appendix', where God's judgment of the city is detailed, and where we are told three times 'woe, woe, O great city' (18.10, 16, 19b). The third woe, the

55.   See the chart which is Figure 2, at the head of this chapter.

greatest, is thus accomplished when the great city falls. In the words of the great voice out of the temple of heaven, γέγονεν (16.17)—it is done.

The Centrality of Chapters 10–14

So, then, the final trumpet does herald the third and final woe, but we do not actually see this until the bowl plagues begin at 15.5. Inserted into this action are chs. 10–14—a picture of the whole of salvation history, and a look behind it into the heavenly events which explain God's conquest. The sounding of the seventh trumpet heralds both God's judgment and his conquest: the kingdom has become God's and Christ's. How has this change occurred? Chapters 10–14 explain that this is a mystery: the seven thunders shout, but cannot be revealed. Instead, the prophet is given a little scroll to eat, a reed to measure the temple of God, and a commission to prophesy again. His prophecy, the little scroll, includes the vision of the two witnesses,[56] the Woman and the Dragon, the two beasts, the Lamb with the 144,000 and the final judgment. Some symmetry is to be seen in these events. The two witnesses are foiled, for example, by the two beasts. This is underscored by the time-period used in both chapters (1260 days = 42 months at 11.2, 3 and 13.5), and by the early reference to the beast at 11.7. It is also highlighted by references to the miracles performed by each couple, by the resurrection of the witnesses and the false resurrection of the beast, and by the contrasting reactions to these wonders: ἔδωκαν δόξαν τῷ θεῷ τοῦ οὐρανοῦ (11.13) over against καὶ προσεκύνησαν τῷ δράκοντι (13.4). Again, just as all peoples, tribes, languages and nations refuse the witnesses burial (11.9), so all peoples, tribes, languages and nations follow the beast (13.7).

Chapter 12 is the central chapter within this scheme. We have seen its importance in other outlines of the book besides that of Schüssler Fiorenza, notably in the works of Yarbro Collins and Swete, who see it as a new beginning, and Lund and Gager, who place it in the centre of their series. The chapter may be outlined as follows:

---

56.   *Contra* Yarbro Collins, but with Bornkamm, Charles and Schüssler Fiorenza.

Intro	Two portents	vss. 1-3
A	Woman persecuted and flight	vss. 4-6
B	War in heaven	vss. 7-9
C	Declaration	vss. 10-12
A′	Woman persecuted and flight	vss. 14-16
B′	War on earth	vs. 17

The declaration itself (C, vss. 10-12) comes in the middle of the narrative,[57] and has a threefold structure: Statement, Explanation, and Response enjoined. The statement (vs. 10) is in fact an enlargement of the seventh trumpet hymn (11.15)—God's reign has come, since the accuser has been conquered. *How* has this happened?—through the blood of the Lamb and the word of testimony (vs. 11). So then? Rejoice, or be woeful, depending on one's situation 'in heaven' or 'on earth' (vs. 12). The μυστήριον of God pre-announced at 10.7 is that the accuser has been overcome through the Lamb and the witness of the faithful. Verse 11 of ch. 12, then, provides the very heart of the Apocalypse. Even the woes are under the authority of the God of heaven, who himself has cast down the accuser, limited the time of his power, and has himself 'given' this destructive ability to the Dragon. Those who have given the word of testimony are in solidarity with the Lamb who has also suffered, and is elsewhere spoken of as the chief witness (1.5; 3.14b; 22.16, 20), or *Kronzeuge*.[58]

Schüssler Fiorenza has provided two actantial models for the entire Apocalypse, by which she sets the complex of chs. 10–14 apart from the rest of the book. The book as a whole is represented by a scheme which makes Christ the Subject, conferring judgment or salvation upon the community/cosmos, and opposed by anti-divine powers. The little scroll, however, follows a different model, in which the Dragon makes war upon the community/ humankind, helped by the evil potentates, and opposed by Christ, Michael and Christians. A diagram of the two models makes this contrast apparent.[59]

---

57.   See Yarbro Collins for interesting discussion of possible sources, *Combat Myth*, pp. 233ff.

58.   Bornkamm, 'Komposition', p. 220.

59.   'Composition', p. 174.

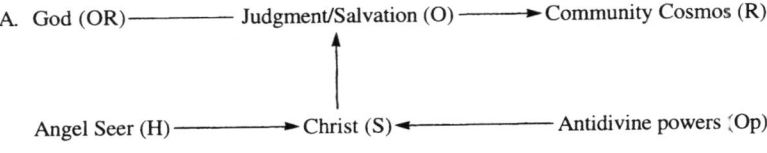

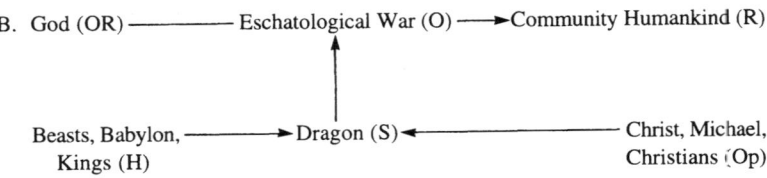

The difficulty with using actantial models for pieces other than folk tales is a source of much debate and discussion for those engaged in tracing surface structure. As far as they go, however, Schüssler Fiorenza's different pictures are largely helpful and faithful to the action of the Apocalypse. We do find, however, a shift from one picture to the other within the scrolls from time to time (for example, model A in the judgment scene of 14.14, or model B at the battle of 20.7). Schüssler Fiorenza's contrasting models therefore represent general tendencies of the two sections. Moreover, to be completely accurate, a fulfilment of action should be noted, both at the central point of the little scroll, and at the finale of the Apocalypse itself. The Declaration of 12.10-12 presents a *static* pattern without opposition, where helper and subject merge. Satan has vanished as Opposer, and has simply become the recipient of God's judgment. Christ and the saints are both instrumental in accomplishing this judgment. The seer envisions a situation in which the cosmic battle actually ceases and the need for actants disappears. This is also true of chs. 21–22, where a static picture in the mode of salvation rather than of judgment emerges. God ordains marriage for the saints, the Subject is Christ, and all opposition is again gone.

These fulfilment sequences serve to show that the two scrolls are complementary and unified, rather than completely distinct in character. It might be said that they portray the same drama, but from a different perspective. The sealed scroll shows God's control over the cosmos and community, victorious even through the opposition of Satan and his cohorts. The little scroll describes the rebellion of the opposers, but also explains how the victory of God over these powers is accomplished, both through the 'blood of the Lamb' and through the suffering of the faithful. Both sequences end with the victory of the Ordainer, either through the establishment of the subject in Schüssler Fiorenza's first picture, or the overturning of the pretender in her second. The little scroll portrays this in the starkest way, by having the peace of heaven embedded within the ongoing war. Yarbro Collins has interpreted the 'open-ended quality'[60] of ch. 12 as emphasizing the partial defeat of the dragon and the continuation of the war on earth after the Declaration at 12.10-12. However, the embedding of a victory-song within a rehearsal of conflict has, from another perspective, the opposite effect. That is, the Declaration provides an understanding of the victory not simply as future but as already accomplished in heaven—a powerful statement for those who see themselves as embroiled within the battle. Even the battle, even the machinations of the dragon are under the control of God. The martyrs and the 'seed of the woman' are in reality citizens of heaven (cf. 18.20). David L. Barr characterizes ch. 12 as 'explaining how, historically, the change of kingdoms has occurred'.[61]

The Woman of Chapters 12 and 21:
A Re-Examination of Collins's Distinction

Now that the general structure and thrust of the Apocalypse has been discussed, we are in a better position to consider the two heavenly women figures who, in the words of Barr, 'dominate the last half of the book'.[62] Barr tells us that these figures played no role in the first part of the Apocalypse, but this is perhaps an overstatement. Implicit reference to them is made at 2.4, 2.14, 3.12, 11.2 and 11.8, where 'first love', 'immorality', 'New Jerusalem', 'holy city', and 'great city' are mentioned. However, it is certainly the case that these full-blown figures are striking in the latter part of the Apocalypse, and serve as vehicles (along with their negative counterpart, Babylon) for understanding the fulfilment of God's purposes. Virtually all the structural pictures suggested for the Apocalypse have indicated that the place of the heavenly women is of prime importance. By its very nature, the vision of the New Jerusalem is given a climactic place in each scheme, although some

60.   *Combat Myth*, p. 145.
61.   'The Apocalypse as a Symbolic Transformation of the World: A Literary Analysis', *Int* 38 (1984), p. 45.
62.   'Symbolic Transformation', p. 44.

critics spend more time questioning the doublet (21.1-5; 21.9-10) than actually discussing the text. Chapter 12 is also highlighted by many: Bowman, who includes it in his important central fourth act, Moulton, who entitles the surrounding section 'Salvation', Swete and Yarbro Collins, who see it as initiating the second half of the book, Lund and Beagley, who place it centrally through chiasmus, and Schüssler Fiorenza, who sees it as part of the little scroll.[63] Even Aune, who considers the ch. 12 narrative one of three 'digressions', considers this digression to be a literary technique which shelters the important centre of the book.[64]

Yarbro Collins's argument is particularly interesting, since she focusses on the narrative of the Woman and the Dragon as central to the entire book, not simply to the last half, to which it belongs: 'Ch. 12 has a pivotal position in the book' and is 'the paradigm of the Book of Revelation'.[65] Its paradigmatic status is due to the explicit depiction of the combat myth, which Collins feels is the 'conceptual framework' governing the entire work. It will be clear by now that this paper is arguing for victory, both proleptic and final, as the dominant thrust of the Apocalypse. Chapter 12 not only 'interprets' the difficult position of the faithful by recourse to the combat myth, but also puts this in perspective by reference to the 'joy' of heaven and the 'limited time' of the oppressor. This is not, in fact, an outright argument with Yarbro Collins,[66] but a shifting of her focus.

It is clear, then, that the two women figures, the Queen of ch. 12 and the Bride of ch. 21, are important to the meaning and action of the book. How are they related, however? The intuitive response of many commentators is that the women figures are to be seen synoptically.[67] This perspective can be traced back to J. Weiss, who identified the woman of ch. 12 with 'the heavenly Jerusalem', citing Gal. 4.26 as

63.	See the chart which is Figure 2, at the head of this chapter, and also Bowman's chart for a visual picture of the centrality of chapter 12 in most schemes.

64.	*Literary Environment*, p. 242.

65.	*Combat Myth*, p. 231.

66.	See *Combat Myth*, pp. 233-34, for her own discussion of how the apocalypse functions in the community.

67.	A notable exception would be the provocative reading of Tina Pippin, in which the woman is left exiled in the wilderness because she is 'no longer useful': see *Death and Desire: The Rhetoric of Gender in the Apocalypse of John* (Louisville: Westminster/John Knox, 1992), p. 76. Pippin's method of reading the female symbolism, however, may have prevented the connection from being made.

evidence for a long-standing tradition, and contrasting the two appearances of the figure with that of Babylon.[68] Austin Farrer tells us that the woman of ch. 12 is to be related both directly to the New Jerusalem of ch. 21 and inversely to Babylon of ch. 17, so that both chs. 12 and 21 present 'the congregation of God', although in different aspects.[69] Martin Kiddle, too, sees the figures as representing the same reality, the 'true messianic people', a woman who is in the 'desert' in ch. 12 but 'decks the bridal garments of joy' in ch. 21.[70] So, too, does J.P.M. Sweet, who speaks of the New Jerusalem and the heavenly woman as 'closely related'.[71] Most recently, J.A. du Rand has understood the text by appealing to a 'myth pattern...which includes the final battle and the mother transformed into the bride after her release from captivity...'[72]

Despite the many who agree on the identity or at least a close relationship of the two figures, there are those who are not convinced of this, notably Yarbro Collins. Her expertise in the areas of apocalypse and Apocalypse of John studies is manifest: while I have not adopted her structure, her arguments for recapitulation and apocalyptic form, and her analysis of ch. 12 in particular have been extremely helpful in this discussion. It is therefore necessary to take seriously her division of the 'Queen of Heaven' in ch. 12 and the 'Bride-City-Temple building' of ch. 21 when she tells us that 'there is no indication that the description of the heavenly Jerusalem in ch. 21 is a continuation of ch. 12'.[73] In Yarbro Collins's view, ch. 12 in its redacted form refers to the 'heavenly Israel',[74] whereas ch. 21 refers to the 'heavenly Jerusalem'.[75] They are in the same category of heavenly counterparts to earthly realities, but distinct in their meaning.

Yarbro Collins adduces four reasons for not associating the two figures. The first reason, no internal indications for a descriptive continuation, has been mentioned in the preceding paragraph. To this should be added: no indication of association of the ch. 12 figure with a city; the inappropriateness of the desert as a setting for the holy city; and

68.   Cited by R.H. Charles, *Revelation*, II, p. 316.
69.   *Revelation*, p. 215.
70.   Kiddle, *Revelation*, pp. 417-18.
71.   J.P.M. Sweet, *Revelation* (Philadelphia: Westminster Press, 1979), p. 302.
72.   J.A. du Rand, 'The Imagery of the Heavenly Jerusalem (Revelation 21.9–22.5)', *Neot* 22 (1988), p. 76.
73.   *Combat Myth*, p. 132.
74.   Yarbro Collins, *Combat Myth*, p. 134.
75.   Yarbro Collins, *Combat Myth*, p. 135.

the improbability of the holy city being first mother, then bride of the Messiah.[76] The first argument seems the most weighty, and will be handled last. Several responses may be made to the assertion that the desert woman is never associated with a city. The first is that a continuity between the two figures does not necessitate such a precise association. The New Jerusalem itself is a complex symbolic female figure, with connotations of temple, bride and new community: it is *called* a city, but refers to far more. If *other* indicators point to the association of the ch. 12 figure with God's faithful people, the exact label 'city' is unnecessary. Secondly, if one does not posit a radical structural break between chs. 11 and 12, as has Yarbro Collins, the reference to 'holy city' in 11.1-2 may in fact shed some light on the plight of the woman in ch. 12. In ch. 11, the holy city is trampled for 42 months, while the witnesses prophesy for the same 1260 days (42 months) in the city where their Lord was crucified; in ch. 12, the woman is protected in the wilderness for the same length of time, and the Dragon is cast down to earth by the 'witness' of the faithful and the blood of the Lamb, for a circumscribed time (by reference to 13.5, the same 1260 days = 42 months). The picture of the witnesses, the persecution and the 'holy city' is, it would seem, parallel to that of the Woman's battle with the Dragon, as complemented by heaven's conquest of him. Sweet has extended this set of temporal parallels, reminding us that the number of days and months are also references to 'three and a half' and so 'bind [chs.] 11–13 together'.[77] In all, the references to three and a half (years) = 42 months = 1260 days occur at 11.2, 9, 11; 12.6, 12 (implied), 14; and 13.5. As the witnesses are clothed in sackcloth, so the woman is in the desert; their power is undeniable, however, as is hers. That power is seen even in persecution, since she is 'clothed with sun', but it will be viewed in full splendour in the events of ch. 21.

It seems likely that a complete hearing or reading of the Apocalypse at one sitting would call great attention to the reappearance of a positive female figure in ch. 21. Since both figures have obvious corporate associations, it seems unlikely that the hearer/reader could be expected to make a fine distinction between two heavenly entities with earthly counterparts. Moreover, Yarbro Collins herself characterizes the symbolism of the whole of the Apocalypse, and specifically of ch. 12, as

76.   Yarbro Collins, *Combat Myth*, p. 132.
77.   *Revelation*, p. 46.

tensive, or, in her own words, 'flexible in application';[78] its recasting by a Christian redactor (Yarbro Collins's theory) makes this flexibility even more prominent. It must be asked how such flexibility, or such symbolism far removed from historical allegory, can support two *specific* interpretations of the female corporate figure.

Yarbro Collins has also suggested that the desert imagery is inappropriate to a glorified city. However, it should be pointed out that the desert is not the first locale of the woman in the story as it stands, but the place to which she flees. It would seem that the time of her persecution is also the time of her nourishment. (Notice that the pursuit continues in 12.15 even after the woman has been given eagle wings and has escaped ἀπὸ προσώπου τοῦ ὄφεως.) Moreover, in connection with the New Jerusalem of ch. 21, it may be said that towards the end of the Apocalypse the tables have been turned. Babylon is now seen in the desert (17.3),[79] appropriately placed within a habitation of demons, unclean spirits and birds (18.3). Jerusalem, on the other hand, has been 'prepared' (ἐτοίμασεν ἑαυτήν, 19.7; ἡτοιμασμένην, 21.2) in her ἡτοιμασμένον place (12.6), and is now alternately on a great mountain (21.10), or coming out of heaven (21.2). The contrast between the whore and bride is well-established by many. If Babylon has taken over the desert *topos*, it is to be expected that the New Jerusalem will no longer be there.

The 'inappropriateness' of desert imagery for the 'heavenly woman' of ch. 12 is therefore intrinsic, and underscores the drama of her unanticipated situation. Such shocking juxtaposition is consonant with the entire method of the author. Paul S. Minear explains, 'One reason why the apocalyptic descriptions seem so grotesque and lurid is this: the bizarre antitheses underscore the deceptive co-existence of two orders of being which are originally and ultimately incompatible'.[80] It is unnecessary to defend the use of Minear's ontological categories to admit that his perception of duality seems incontrovertible. In ch. 12, the woman is both heavenly and in the desert, the Dragon once was heavenly and now is only earthly, and victors overcome by martyrdom (12.11). The two contrasting cities briefly mentioned in ch. 11 (11.2, 8) are kept under surveillance throughout the little scroll (14.1 and 14.8) and throughout the remainder of the Apocalypse, until the reversal,

78.   *Combat Myth*, p. 126.
79.   *Contra* Kiddle, *Revelation*, p. 238.
80.   'Ontology and Ecclesiology in the Apocalypse', *NTS* 12 (1965), p. 102.

destruction and restoration of *topoi* is complete.

Yarbro Collins also argues that it is unlikely that the holy city should be both mother and bride of Messiah. However, an analysis of her foil, Babylon, sheds some light on this. Babylon is, of course, the promiscuous consort of the beast and the kings of this world (17.2); she is also ἡ μήτηρ τῶν πορνῶν [m. or f.] καὶ τῶν βδελυγμάτων τῆς γῆς (17.5). In other words, she is both consort to the kings, and queen-mother, reigning over them (17.18). The fate of whore and beast are the same (17.7-8): they shall be overcome by the King of kings, and supplanted by *his* γυνή (19.7). The voice νυμφίου καὶ νύμφης will not be heard again in the great city (18.23); rather, the holy City, the true Bride, and the all-powerful Bridegroom have come. Farrer's explanation of the relationship between the two figures is instructive: 'For though the mother of Messiah is not, as such, the bride of Christ, both figures are allegories of the same reality, the 'daughter of Zion', the congregation of God'.[81]

It seems therefore, that the 'problems' of no reference to a city in ch. 12, desert imagery, and the conflation of mother with bride are not insurmountable, but indeed reveal the complexity of the woman's identity. But are there any internal indications linking the drama of the pursued woman with the description of the New Jerusalem? In fact, there are, from broad structure down to descriptive detail. Yarbro Collins herself makes use of the structural sweep of the action in defending her chs. 12–22 unit. She speaks of the open nature of 12.17, and of its unfulfilled character. Neither the victory of the Messiah nor the salvation of the woman are completed in ch. 12. So then, 12.5, and 19.11-21, 20.4-6 are seen as a 'literary bracket'[82] surrounding the action. We must wait until the end of the book for the Messiah's office to be fulfilled. Similarly,

> It is not said later in a further narrative section that the woman is brought forth from the desert. But the expectation evoked by this element is later satisfied. The New Exodus of ch. 12 is followed by the New Conquest of 19.11-21. The limited rescue or salvation of ch. 12 is followed by the ultimate rescue or salvation of 21.1–22.5. The function of the open-endedness of the rescue of the woman, then, is to create a tension of expectation in the reader which is finally resolved in chs. 21–22.[83]

81.   *Revelation*, p. 215.
82.   *Combat Myth*, p. 28.
83.   Yarbro Collins, *Combat Myth*, p. 29.

So then, Yarbro Collins herself senses the continuity of action, despite the nice distinction she has made between the two figures. It is difficult to see how evoked expectation of conquest and salvation can be satisfied if there is no relationship between the two women. Perhaps the distinct nature of sources which Yarbro Collins perceives behind the two women has led her to differentiate too strongly in even the final shape of the story. It seems that we are driven back to a general idea of both figures as God's faithful people (18.4), despite the various problems which she has well detailed. It may be, however, that the 'incoherence' of a figure which is both mother of the Messiah and of 'other offspring' was no problem for the writer (in Yarbro Collins's view, redactor) of ch. 12. We need not be required to decide if she is a collective figure or the mother of a group (12.17a), the Old or New Covenant people, Mary or the Church. Such analysis belongs to the interpretation of an allegory, which this manifestly is not. Such tensions *may* bespeak partially adapted sources; they may also be inherent in the nature of a text which uses allusive language, piling on images and making bold strokes. Reference to 'the rest of her seed' thus becomes a *highlighting* of the woman's collective role, rather than a point against it. The author has not shifted his emphasis to the individual from the corporate as Yarbro Collins contends.[84] Rather, both individuals and the whole community are concerned at every point of ch. 12. This double focus on individual and corporate blessedness returns in ch. 21. Kiddle reminds us that the Bride of ch. 21 speaks of 'individual blessedness', but the city speaks of corporate blessing: these are joined in a bold 'figurative inconsistency'.[85]

Hidden and Revealed Glory

Besides the broad structure, other details indicate a close connection between the two ladies. Both the narrative of ch. 12 and the description of ch. 21 are connected with a measuring of the Temple. In ch. 11, John is told to measure the inner court of the Temple (the outer is under siege) with a κάλαμος ὅμοιος ῥάβδῳ, but no dimensions are given; in ch. 21 the angel measures by means of a golden κάλαμος an immense city of almost unimaginable proportions. The pattern followed in chs. 11–12 is measuring–testing, but in chs. 21–22, it is presentation–measuring. Bornkamm suggests this parallelism: 'Man wird endlich auch

84.   Yarbro Collins, *Combat Myth*, p. 233.
85.   *Revelation*, p. 415.

fragen dürfen, ob nicht die Ausmessung und Bewahrung des Tempels,
womit der Inhalt des kleinen Büchleins beginnt (11,1), ein verheissungs-
volles Vorzeichen ist für die Ausmessung des neuen Jerusalem (21,
15ff)'.[86] If this line is followed, then the glory of ch. 12 is hidden; the
glory of ch. 21 is revealed. In 12.11, the witnesses conquer by their
death; in 21.4, there is no more death for those who have conquered.
The settings are related by contrast as well. To the desert–mountain
contrast may be added the 'sea' by which the Dragon (not John) stands
at 12.18, versus the οὐκ ἔστιν ἔτι of 21.1. Where the narrative left off,
the description of transformed reality begins. Again, the demonic river
of the Dragon has been replaced by the river of life in 22.1. Moreover,
the desert imagery has given way to garden symbolism, as the
description of 22.2 makes clear. The hymn of 12.12 blesses οὐρανοὶ
καὶ οἱ ἐν αὐτοῖς σκηνοῦντες while 21.3 tells us that the relationship
between heaven and redeemed earth has changed, so that ἡ σκηνὴ τοῦ
θεοῦ μετὰ τῶν ἀνθρώπων καὶ σκηνώσει μετ' αὐτῶν.

Concerning the description of the heavenly woman and the city-bride
in particular, several observations are to be made. The ch. 12 woman
stands on the moon, is clothed with the sun, and wears a crown of 12
stars; the holy city has no need of sun or moon, since her δόξα and
φωστήρ (21.11) are from God (or are God), and she has 12 gates super-
vised by 12 angels. Farrer comments that the crown of the heavenly
lady has become the 'battlemented crown' of the city, a commonplace in
ancient iconography.[87] The first woman labours under childbirth, the
penalty of Genesis 3, giving a loud cry, while with the second woman
every κατάθεμα is gone, and there are no more tears or crying.
Occasional help is given to the first woman *in extremis* by heaven and
earth;[88] the second woman is pictured in an intimate and permanent
connection with God and the rejuvenated earth.

What we are left with is a close relationship of the two figures, but not
an exact identity. The hidden glory of the persecuted woman (she is only

---

86.   'Komposition', p. 217.
87.   *Revelation*, p. 215.
88.   See P.S. Minear, 'Far as the Curse is Found: The Point of Rev. 12.15-16',
NovT 33 (1991), pp. 71-77, who makes an interesting case for a certain undoing of
the curse in Rev. 12 itself. The mouth of a friendly earth swallows the serpent's flood
in Rev. 12, in contrast to the mouth of a hostile earth which swallows the blood of
Abel in Gen. 4. The re-alliance of the earth with the woman in ch. 12 may be seen as a
portent of harmony to come: we wait until ch. 21 for full peace and integratioan.

a portent)[89] in ch. 12 becomes the evident glory of the blissful bride in ch. 21. The New Jerusalem is the answer to the ongoing war between the Woman and her seed and the Dragon. There is some ambiguity regarding the mode of the heavenly city—is it future, or pre-existent in the mind of God? Both seem to be the case: the separation of God's λαός out of Babylon and the removal of the Dragon and his kingdom seem to be necessary prerequisites for the eschatological declaration, ἰδοὺ καινὰ ποιῶ πάντα (21.5); yet the heavenly city comes down from God, as though she were always there, much as in *4 Ezra* 13.36, where 'Sion...parata et aedificata' is made manifest. Moreover, the persecution is not simply an obstacle to be overcome. Rather, the witness of the saints, even in the negative sense of martyrdom, equals the divine preparation of the city. The time of preparation and the time of persecution are the same. The suffering of the woman, like the blood of the Lamb, becomes a weapon, not a sign of weakness. Just as John is surprised to find that the Lion *qua* Lamb is the answer to his own distress (5.4-6), so the reader discovers that the Queen, *qua* Martyr and Mother, is the portent of the New Jerusalem. In the words of Barr,

> The hearers are decisively changed. They now live in another world.
> Persecution does not shock them back to reality. They live in a new reality
> in which lambs conquer and suffering rules. The victims have become the
> victors.[90]

Epics of Wrath and Return

Northrop Frye, in discussing the features of various forms of epics, has pointed out that it is not unusual for works of an encyclopaedic genre such as the epic to actually contain within them an epic in miniature:

> Often too...a miniature epic actually forms part of a bigger one. The
> prophecy of Michael in Paradise Lost presents the whole Bible as a
> miniature contrast-epic, with one pole at the apocalypse and the other at the

---

89.   C. Keller takes it upon herself to give a name to this 'namenlose Frau', 'Die Frau in der Wüste: Ein feministlisch-theologischer Midrasch zu Offb 12', *EvT* 50 (1990), pp. 414-32. It aseems, however, that the 'Zeit' for her naturalization has come long before Keller's own midrash, that is in ch. 21 of John's own vision—John, looking into the face of the fleeing woman, does not see Hochma or Sophia, but the portent of the New Jerusalem.

90.   'Apocalypse', pp. 49-50.

flood. The Bible itself contains the Book of Job, which is a kind of
microcosm of its total theme, and is cited by Milton as the model for the
'brief' epic.[91]

Certainly the apocalypse is a genre which would qualify as
'encyclopaedic' and indeed has been so characterized by many. Its
inclusion of hymns, oracles, letters, visions, and the like should therefore
make the inclusion of a tiny epic not so very surprising. An understanding of the scope of macro-genres places the discovery of a scroll
within a scroll in a larger context. The central 'little scroll' becomes,
then, not simply a peculiarity of the Apocalypse of John, nor even a clue
to the feature of 'embedded mysteries' within apocalypses in general,
but an example of a feature found in genres of epic proportions. The
focus of the little scroll, as Schüssler Fiorenza has pointed out, is the war
of the Dragon, who is, unawares, the tool of the Ordainer. It is as though
we have a miniature 'epic of wrath' (ending in judgment at 14.19-20)
within the larger Apocalypse, which is, by and large, an 'epic of
return'.[92] At ch. 21, the harried Church of the letters 'returns' to her
ordained home and position, just as the 'Lamb' is now seen in his
proper aspect of glory. Chapters 12 to 14 explain the same events from
an inverse perspective, disclosing the war of the Enemy as part of God's
own purpose, the Lady's suffering as God's own preparation, the 'woe'
as the other side of the 'rejoice'. Within the logic of each epic, the Lady
appears as persecuted, or glorified: such states, although outwardly in
contrast, are really an indication of identity. The identity is underscored
in each 'epic' by the hidden mystery of triumph in the little scroll
(12.10) and the necessary exploration of judgment throughout the main
narrative.

The envelopment of the little scroll within the sealed scroll is a phenomenon analogous to an 'embedded' text. In considering embedded
texts, literary critics have pointed to the various relationships that the
secondary fabula may have to the primary text: the embedded text may
explain the story or it may *resemble* it. In the latter case, the embedded
text may function as a kind of 'mirror' to the primary story.[93] With the
little scroll, we are not dealing technically with an embedded text, since
embedded texts are signalled by direct or indirect speech, and occur

91.   'Theory of Genres', *Anatomy of Criticism*, p. 324.
92.   'Theory of Genres', p. 317.
93.   M. Bal, *Narratology: Introduction to the Theory of Narrative*, pp. 142ff.

when a particular character of the primary fabula relates a story, or even sequence of stories of his or her own (as in the stories of the endangered queen in the *Arabian Nights*). An actual example of embedded text within the Apocalypse would thus be the seven letters of Jesus to the churches, in which we forget, for a while, the visionary setting of the apocalypse. However, we may also see the function of the little scroll as analogous to the function of embedded text, since the events of chs. 11–14 transpire after John has eaten the scroll, and as a result of the commission to prophesy (10.8-11). The little scroll events thus do not represent the voice of the seer alone, but the direct and authoritatively written word of God. It is not the case of an *actor* in the primary narrative plunging into a second narrative, but that of an *actant* in the primary story (the scroll, a symbol of God's own word) telling its story through the mouthpiece of the seer. Just as the seventh seal contains the trumpets, and the seventh trumpet contains the bowls, the sealed scroll gives rise to the little scroll.

What is helpful about the analogy to embedded text is the idea that a secondary fabula may resemble the first text, and act as a 'sign'[94] for it, giving signals as to its interpretation or outcome. Mieke Bal notes that the placement of the mirror-text in the primary story 'determines its function'.[95] Placed near the beginning, the subtext may give veiled hints concerning the outcome of the story. This is certainly the case in the complex of the seven letters, which function as promise ('tree of life', 'second death', 'new name', etc.) and give clues to the grand finale of the Apocalypse, that is, the visions of judgment and salvation (19.11–22.9). The veiled quality of the subtext's resemblance to the primary story maintains the suspense of the action. When a mirror-text is presented towards the end of the primary text, the function is usually not to provide suspenseful clues, but to 'enhance' the significance of the story.

It would seem that the little scroll, coming dead-centre in the Apocalypse, fulfils both functions. In that the story interrupts the sounding of the trumpet, and the series of woes, and in that it provides an uncompleted story of the refugee woman and her seed, the little scroll maintains suspense. It also foreshadows both the conquering of Satan and the downfall of Babylon without telling the end of the story—that is, it refrains from giving a picture of the wedding of the Lamb and the New Jerusalem. In ch. 14, we are given a glimpse of the 144,000,

94.   Bal, *Narratology*, p. 146.
95.   Bal, *Narratology*.

and told about the voice from heaven ὡς φωνὴν ὑδάτων πολλῶν καὶ ὡς φωνὴν βροντῆς μεγάλης (14.2), which sings the new song; it is not until 19.6 that we learn that this voice ὡς φωνὴν ὑδάτων πολλῶν καὶ ὡς φωνὴν βροντῶν is the song of a great multitude, and that the new song is the song of the reign of God and the marriage of the Lamb and his wife. One function of the little scroll, then, is to prefigure the outcome of the conquest. However, its function within the Apocalypse is also to explain and add significance to the overall narrative pattern. The understanding of events of persecution through the perspective of a cosmic battle—a battle which has already been won!—adds depth to the conquest in the larger epic of return.

The little scroll is curious because its finality of judgment is juxtaposed with open-endedness. Within the narrative, the reader is presented with both a *fait accompli* and an ongoing war. Michael and his angels have been successful in dislodging the pretender; the accuser of people of God has been cast down through the blood of the Lamb and through τὸν λόγον τῆς μαρτυρίας (12.11); and the salvation and power and reign of God and the Christ have come. However, the casting down of the dragon means also 'woe' and 'wrath' to the earth, and war for the seed of the woman. So, then, the little scroll acts as a 'sign' for the understanding of the events of the entire Apocalypse, providing the σημεῖον μέγα (12.1) of the woman who is to be prepared and redeemed (12.6) and ἄλλο σημεῖον (12.3) of the dragon who is her enemy and over whom victory is sure. The perspective of the little scroll sees the ongoing war as consonant with the peace of heaven. Interposed within the rehearsal of conflict is the victory song of 12.10-12, which provides an understanding of the victory not simply as future but as already accomplished in heaven—a powerful statement for those who see themselves embroiled within the battle. Even the battle, even the machinations of the dragon are under the control of God. What seems to be abandonment for the people of God is really a time of preparation, a portent of glory.

The People of God

The relationship between the women of chs. 12 and 21, then, is one of continuity and transformation. The author, who has continuously echoed Second Isaiah, presents his New Jerusalem as a combined picture of Isaiah 35.1-10, 52.1-12, 54.1-17 and 60.1-22—a panorama of glorious transformation. Schüssler Fiorenza has told us that 'the great harlot is in contrast to the woman in ch. 12 as well as to the bride of the Lamb, the New Jerusalem'.[96] This is true, even though the prophet suggests that there may be something of the character of Babylon[97] in the unpurified people of God (ἐξέλθατε ὁ λαός μου ἐξ αὐτῆς, 18.4). At the same time as the people must be called out, lest they receive the plagues, they can also be radically separated from the unholy city: the voice goes on at 18.6 to distinguish sharply between what 'she' has done and what 'you' will do (third-person singular versus second-person plural). The contrast between the desert woman and Babylon is thus in a different mode than that of the Whore and the Bride. The first contrast is between holy weakness and evil dominion; the second is between deceptive power and God-given triumph. The first positive woman must become the second, through a painful testimony (12.11); their foil Babylon will cease altogether, through the outcome of the same events. The θλῖψις and βασιλεία, despite outward appearances, are inter-related.

The identity of the people of God is a complex one indeed in the Apocalypse. The symbolic language used within two distinct but inter-related narratives calls up a picture of the holy Lady which has far more depth and imaginative power than could ever have been suggested by such propositional language as 'God's people must suffer', 'God's people must be distinct from his enemies', 'God's people will triumph'. Within the drama of the narrative, an imperative such as 'Come out from her' implies several thoughts, including logically opposite ones. On the one hand, the holy people must be distinct, otherwise they could not be separated. On the other, the command is issued as a warning, and so a certain 'taint' may be rightly inferred. Within the logic of the narrative, there is no problem. John does not have to decide whether the New Jerusalem already exists or whether it must be prepared. For him, the symbol has its own power, both to encourage and to warn. He is not presenting a static reality in pictures, but evoking a dynamic symbolic

96.   'Composition', p. 171.
97.   The function of Babylon as a foil to the righteous city makes it quite beside the point to enter into a debate regarding the intended historical identity of the city as Rome (the usual view) or Jerusalem (see Beagley). Her description as a μυστήριον (17.5), in which image is piled upon image, is reminiscent of Babel, Babylon, Rome and apostate Jerusalem—she is the archetypal city set up as an alternative to the protection of God. That is, Babylon is a true symbol, and not merely a cipher. As such she is a foil to the New Jerusalem, but also can be depicted as a temptation to the people of God.

world which interprets—indeed, impinges on—our own. In the words of
Leonard L. Thompson, the 'symbolic universe' is not 'apart from the
world of actual, social relations'.[98] Rather, '[t]he seer's view [is that of]
an unbroken world',[99] a world of dynamic change, in which
'boundaries...locate the place where transformations occur'.[100] The
recognition that human identity, even corporate human identity, is in
process, is a sophisticated one, yet one which emerges naturally from the
narrative.

The recognition of a complex and dynamic symbolic world in the
Apocalypse should serve as both an invitation and a warning to readers.
Critics have been quick to see both the infelicitous cashing out of
symbols and the imaginative intertextual connections made by popula-
rizers and even cult figures.[101] However, the creative methods congenial
to our own postmodern situation may carry their own dangers, if controls are not constructed along with the new readings. The Apocalypse,
because of its allusive nature, appears friendly to midrashic treatment,
and because of its patent use of gender codes, invites the discussion of
how such symbolism may shape reality. If our concerns rest solely with
finding our own voice, then it is likely that the symbols in the text will
be exploited, rather than heard or experienced. Such exploitation can
take the form of resisting the text's own cues as to which symbols are
interrelated, or that of going far beyond the bounds of the text in a
search for more palatable images to transform the pictures of the
Apocalypse itself. That is, the critic is faced with Scylla and Charybdis:
she or he can flatten the polyvalence, or read it idiosyncratically, or even
engage in a combination of such actions.

98.   *The Book of Revelation—Apocalypse and Empire* (Oxford University Press,
1990), p. 8. Thompson's major interest here is in the relationship of the Apocalypse
to the original situation in which the book was first produced and read. However,
since he is no 'historical positivist' (p. 3) it would seem that he would allow for a
connection between the 'whole world' of the seer and any reader's actual world,
where this is addressed by the text.

99.   Thompson, *Revelation*, p. 74.

100.   Thompson, *Revelation*, p. 87.

101.   See the combination of allegorical and flatly referential methods in the
unfinished work of the late David 'Koresh', 'The Expositions of the Seven Seals',
(unpublished, but available through Dr Philip Arnold, Reunion Institute, Houston
Texas). Koresh links the figure of the first seal to that of Ps. 45.4-6, and sees the first
seal as the key to his own identity, and the peculiar applicability of the Apocalypse to
the present day.

J. Ellul's word regarding the reading of symbols is instructive: 'It is necessary...to go back from the text to the symbol and not to study the symbol more than the text'.[102] Such a word may well be a corrective to readings which persist in seeing the woman in the desert as discarded or abandoned by God, despite the fact that this figure is connected in a network of metaphors with other pictures and figures of power.[103] Ellul's prescribed method may also lead the interpreter to notice that the pictures of divine power (which may initially smack of patriarchalism) are radicalized or inverted by unusual narrative features such as the appearance of the Lion-Lamb, or the call to battle which is never joined, or the war which is won through martyrdom rather than conflict.

If we attend to the dynamics of the text's imagery, we can detect another rhetorical agenda: the symbolism of the Apocalypse is both realistic and transformative, recognizing that a change needs to come, and yet assuring the listener that suffering itself is glory-tinged. It is through the μαρτυρίαν Ἰησοῦ Χριστοῦ (subjective and objective genitive) that preparation is being made so that God can, at the end, present the transformed community and declare everything new. Thompson tells us that '[t]he seer would draw the reader into a protean world where God alone is master of all boundary transformations'.[104] His view of the monism of the Apocalypse is a little over-reaching, and perhaps does damage to the radical distinction between the people of God and their enemies. The point of linking suffering with glory, Lion with Lamb and fleeing Mother with Bride is not to identify good with evil, but to demonstrate God's radical qualification of the latter. The beast may attempt to replicate the contour of God's actions, but is unsuccessful due to the archetypal and ongoing μαρτυρίαν Ἰησοῦ Χριστοῦ.

The symmetry of instances of the phrase 'testimony of Jesus' calls special attention to the mysterious centre and fulfilment of the

---

102. J. Ellul, *Apocalypse: The Book of Revelation* (New York: Seabury, 1977), p. 35.

103. One may cite here not only T. Pippin, but also M.J. Selvidge, 'Powerful and Powerless Women in the Apocalypse', *Neot* 26 (1992), pp. 157-67. Selvidge insists that the desert Queen posseses no armament or strategies to fight the dragon (p. 162) and that God has no more plans for her (p. 163), all the while ignoring the three and a half year period which indicates a time cut short, and which parallels the time of authority of the two witnesses in ch. 11. Nor does she deal with the embattlemented City-Bride at the climax of the book.

104. Selvidge, 'Powerful and Powerless Women', p. 201.

Apocalypse. Instances of the phrase cluster around the beginning, middle and end of the book (1.2, 5, 9; 3.14; 6.9; 11.3; 12.11, 17; 17.6; 19.10; 20.4; 22.16, 20). Such symmetry puts an accent upon the hope of the little 'epic of wrath'—the inevitable naturalization of the pilgrim Church in the larger 'epic of return'. The pursued woman is, in fact, the community of witnesses. That she is victorious already in heaven through the testimony is the burden of the little scroll; that she is bound for ultimate earthly victory is displayed gloriously in the final chapters of the Apocalypse, the resolution of the sealed scroll. In one sense, she prepares herself, and is identified as mother, warrior and witness; in the final analysis, she comes down from God, fit to be married as bride to the *Kronzeuge*, the Lamb of God. The triumph of the Apocalypse's Lady goes beyond the domestic glory of Aseneth. The figure also differs from the mysterious glory of *4 Ezra*'s Zion. In *4 Ezra*, the seer is content to offer an intimation of Zion's real status within the complexities of the central vision, but never describes the city. John presents the reader (as well as the seer) with both a portent and a revelation: the hidden mystery of the central little scroll is clear for all to see in the grand finale.

Chapter 5

REALISTIC TRANSFORMATION AND ESCHATOLOGICAL VISION
IN THE SHEPHERD OF HERMAS

A structural analysis of *The Shepherd of Hermas* within the context of
the genre apocalypse presents two immediate problems. First, the
history of criticism has not been unanimous in considering the piece an
apocalypse. Secondly, the issue of the book's unity, whether in terms of
theme, structure or authorship, must be resolved before an analysis can
be undertaken. These two preliminary questions must be settled prior to
a discussion of the transformation episodes within the structure of the
book. The curious identity of the Church as a mystery will then be
established by reference to such factors as the centrality of *Vision* 3, the
intensification of revelatory media, the transformation of the Church and
Hermas, and direct messages embedded throughout the text.

The Shepherd of Hermas as an Apocalypse

Past decisions concerning the genre of the *Shepherd* have been
connected with the evaluation of the book as literature or theology.
B.H. Streeter characterized the author as 'the White Rabbit' of the apostolic fathers, 'a timid, fussy, kindly, incompetent, middle-aged freedman,
delightfully naive', whose writing exemplified his 'pottering mediocrity'.[1]
The majority of commentators and critics, in struggling with the
paratactic arrangement which this book shares with many other ancient
pieces, have concurred: the *Shepherd* has induced 'a short attention span
and a long yawn'.[2] The book has thus suffered in comparison with the
more tightly written and theologically complex *4 Ezra* or the canonical

---

1. B.H. Streeter, *The Primitive Church* (London: Macmillan, 1929), p. 203.
2. C. Osiek, 'The Genre and Function of the Shepherd of Hermas', *Semeia* 36
(1986), p. 113. This is her assessment of the book's general reception, although not
her own sentiment.

Apocalypse. Theologians of all ages have studied it largely for its contribution to the theological question of Christian repentance;[3] church historians have been content to search it for early signs of the system of penance.

Moreover, the *Shepherd* exhibits far less interest in eschatology, especially imminent eschatology, than the traditional apocalypses. It has already been seen that 'eschatology' and 'apocalyptic' were used interchangeably by many prior to the recent in-depth study of apocalypses; hence the *Shepherd* lost the genre tag by default, rather than through a careful analysis of all the ingredients which meet together to form a genre. Martin Dibelius, in his probably unsurpassed commentary, recognizes that the book 'gibt sich als Apokalypse', but doubts that the apocalyptic structural frame includes 'einen echt prophetischen Kern'[4]— a characteristic which he considers necessary for a true apocalypse. Moreover, the earth-bound character of the *Shepherd*, that is, its preoccupation with ethics and paraenesis, is in his view decisive against it as an apocalypse. In a briefer, but slightly later discussion, Dibelius continues the same line of thought:

> Im Gegensatz zur Offenbarung des Johannes spielt also hier die Art der Übermittlung und die Figur des deutenden Interpreten eine Hauptrolle. Diese Verkünder und Deuter himmlischer Dinge sind auch das Element des Werkes, das am meisten der Apokalyptik entspricht. Denn der Zweck des Buches ist nicht ein Wissen um himmlische Dinge und kosmische Zukunftsschicksale, sondern die Predigt von der Christenbusse.[5]

> Bei der starken Anlehnung des Verfassers an Überliefertes ist es schwer zu sagen, was an eigenen visionären Erlebnissen zugrunde liegt. Jedenfalls ist es nicht viel; das eigentliche Ethos des Buches liegt in Warnung und Mahnung an die Kirche, nicht im Zusammenhang mit höheren Welten.[6]

Dibelius' decision has been followed by most until very recently, and this is not surprising considering the general definition of apocalyptic

---

3. A recent contribution to this question has been made in P. Henne, 'La pénitence et la rédaction du Pasteur d'Hermas', *RB* 98 (1991), pp. 358-97. Henne is concerned to show how the redaction of the book may have been shaped by its use in the community, mirroring stages of the believer's formation.

4. M. Dibelius, *Der Hirt des Hermas* (Tübingen: Mohr [Paul Siebeck], 1923), p. 419.

5. *Geschichte der urchristlichen Literatur* (Munich: Kaiser, 1975 [1926]), p. 88.

6. Dibelius, *Geschichte*, p. 90.

that has prevailed. With him are Franz Zeller—'Die Abhandlung ist nichts anderes als eine Mahnung zur Busse in apokalyptischer Form'[7]— and the influential P. Vielhauer. A similar division between form and content is made by the latter, when he states that 'the book is an apocalypse in its form and style, but not in its contents, since it includes no disclosures of the eschatological future or the world beyond';[8] it is therefore a 'pseudo-apocalypse'. More recently Graydon F. Snyder has analyzed the *Shepherd* alongside Jewish and Jewish-Christian apocalyptic literature, noting many similarities in form, but what he considers to be telling differences in content. Following R.M. Grant,[9] he notes that the book follows neither the Jewish 'political' model, nor the Gnostic speculative interest, nor even the later Christian homiletic practice of describing hell. In short, '*Hermas* does not fit these [apocalyptic] categories. The form is there, but the content is not.'[10] In his view, the mould is 'broken' particularly in the seer's confession of sins, 'an element impossible for the "saints" who normally receive apocalyptic visions'.[11]

An early attempt to deal with the book in terms of genre is that of Donald L. Riddle (1927), who traced a trajectory from 'Jewish apocalypses' to 'Christian Hellenistic martyrologies'. His essay is flawed by the limited information of his time (for example, 'all apocalypses were Palestinian'!).[12] However, it makes some interesting comparisons of the two genres, and some pertinent observations regarding at least one of the social functions associated with them. In all, his study does continue to drive a wedge between form and content, and he is reluctant to label the *Shepherd* a true apocalypse: the piece, due to its 'individualism' and 'Hellenism', is well on the way towards martyrology.

Recent study of the *Shepherd* has shown that it is a mistake to concentrate on content alone; moreover, apocalypses cut across 'Jewish' and 'Hellenistic' lines (if these can indeed be drawn with any real

7. F. Zeller, *Die Apostolischen Väter aus dem Griechischen Übersetzt* (Kempten: Jos. Kösel, 1918), p. 171.

8. P. Vielhauer, 'Apocalyptic in Early Christianity', in E. Hennecke (ed.), *New Testament Apocrypha* (trans. R. McL. Wilson; London: SCM Press, 1974), II, pp. 608-42 (630).

9. *Gnosticism and Early Christianity* (Columbia University Press, 1966 [1959]).

10. Snyder, *The Apostolic Fathers: A New Translation and Commentary*. VI. *The Shepherd of Hermas* (ed. R.M. Grant; London, Toronto: Nelson, 1968), p. 9.

11. *Shepherd*, p. 10.

12. 'From Apocalypse to Martyrology', *HTR* 9 (1927), p. 269.

confidence). For example, the *Shepherd* itself contains both Jewish and non-Jewish elements, the significance of which has been hotly disputed;[13] such cultural syncretism is by no means unique to this piece, and has indeed been noted in *Aseneth* and the Apocalypse in this study. Recourse to the preliminary profile of the apocalypse provided by J.J. Collins *et al.*[14] shows that the *Shepherd* is well within the bounds of the genre. Even the earlier writers recognized the formal parallels to apocalypses. In Collins's categorization, these formal characteristics would include 'manner of revelation' and 'concluding elements'. Visions, epiphanies, auditory revelation, discourse, dialogue, writing, mediators, disposition of the recipient, and reaction of the recipient, are all featured (elements 1–3).

To these formal concerns may be added a significant number of details from both the 'temporal' and 'spatial axes'. The treatment of the 'protoctist'[15] Church alongside the cosmos (*Vis.* 1.3.4-5) is certainly an example of protology (category 4). Contrary to the assertions of Vielhauer,[16] *Vision* 4 concentrates deliberately upon an 'eschatological crisis' to be faced by the Church (element 7.1); eschatological judgment (element 8) or salvation (element 9) is the premise upon which Hermas's call to repentance is based. The concentration here is on the overall judgment of the Church, an emphasis which includes but is not exhausted by 'personal salvation' (element 9.2). Little is made of the future of those outside the Church, but this is assumed in the book's moral dualism, and finds an explicit part in several of the visions and the prophecies (for example, τὸ μὲν μέλαν οὗτος ὁ κόσμος ἐστίν, *Vis.* 4.3.2).[17] Eschatological salvation (element 9) is typified by the doctrine

13. Dibelius presupposes the influence of Hellenistic traditions on the *Shepherd* in his discussion of the Sibyl and her seat at Cumae (*Der Hirt*, pp. 452ff.). More contested is the plea of R. Reitzenstein that Hermas is associated with the revealor Hermes, and hence *Similitude* 9 is associated with the legendary Arcadia. See Snyder, *Shepherd*, p. 17.

14. 'Morphology', pp. 6-8. See the chart which is Figure 1, found at the end of Chapter 1.

15. J. Danielou, *A History of Early Christian Doctrine before the Council of Nicaea. I. The Theology of Jewish Christianity* (trans. and ed. J.A. Baker; London: Darton, Longman & Todd, 1964), p. 301.

16. Vielhauer insists that 'the book is an apocalypse in its form and style, but not in its contents, since it includes no disclosures of the eschatological future or the world beyond' ('Apocalyptic', p. 630).

17. Reference will be made throughout to the Greek edition of M. Whittaker, *Die Apostolischen Vater. I. Der Hirt des Hermas* (Berlin: Akademie-Verlag, 2nd edn,

of resurrection, and the notion of 'transformation' (9.1), which will be dealt with later in detail. Although the apocalypse does not include an actual historical review, it would be inaccurate to say that the *Shepherd* has no interest in the past. Reference is made to 'events' in the book of *Eldad and Modad*, to the failure of those persecuted in the past, and to a past persecution in the *Similitudes* and *Mandates*. These references have the usual apocalyptic function of placing the message of the book in the context of knowledge of the past, although there is in the *Shepherd* an explicit paraenetic reason for this. Other apocalypses tend to use history for the purpose of inspiring confidence in the veracity of eschatological predictions; the *Shepherd* uses it for inspiring actions and attitudes consonant with repentance. The difference may only be relative, since presumably where history is used to establish credibility, the eschatological visions themselves have an implicit paraenetic purpose. This function has been recognized in the second *Semeia* volume on apocalypses, in which the definition of an apocalypse was extended to include the desired motivation of the reader or the community.[18]

With regard to the 'spatial axis', both the prominence of angelic beings and the heavenly origin of the personified Church fit category 10.2; there is no heavenly journey, but the building of the mysterious tower in both the *Vision* 3 and *Similitude* 9 is certainly an otherworldly element (10), perhaps even a heavenly region (10.1) imported to a deserted field for the benefit of Hermas. Some of the elements included under Collins's *temporal axis* or *manner of revelation* may also be properly placed in the spatial axis. Of note are the 'heavenly books' which are actual objects *within* the revelation, and the event of transformation *during* the vision rather than simply as an eschatological hope.

From the perspective of the *Semeia* group, then, the *Shepherd* is a *bona fide* apocalypse, of Type Ib ('Apocalypses with Cosmic and/or Political Eschatology, which have neither historical review nor otherworldly journey'). It shares this designation with the New Testament Apocalypse, and numerous other later non-canonical works. *Hermas*'s interest in repentance, and emphasis on the present state of the Church do not disqualify it, but simply individualize it. Neither the eschatological dimension nor the cosmic dimension have been lost from view: in fact, it is in the light of eschatological urgency and cosmic realities that the

1967 [1956]). However, the traditional referencing, rather than that suggested by Whittaker, will be adopted for the purposes of clarity and convenience.

    18. A. Yarbro Collins, 'Early Christian Apocalypticism', *Semeia* 36 (1986), p. 7.

paraenesis of the book takes place. As both Mother Church and the Shepherd emphasize, βλέπετε τὴν κρίσιν τὴν ἐπερχομένην. οἱ ὑπερέχοντες οὖν ἐκζητεῖτε τοὺς πεινῶντας ἕως οὔπω ὁ πύργος ἐτελέσθη (Vis. 3.9.5; cf. Sim. 10.4.4). In the same way, it is the cosmic reality of the Church, its special origin and its teleological place in God's creation (Vis. 1.3.4) which underscore its eventual restoration. The repentance and reformation of its members correspond to the mysterious and revealed actions of God's agents, who are 'levelling' the way for the elect (πάντα ὁμαλὰ γίνεται, Vis. 1.3.4): the earthly Church must therefore have hope and not despair, knowing that she is not alone but has a powerful ally and initiator in the hard work of perfection.

It may be seen, therefore, that the *Shepherd* not only suits the original description and profile of the *Semeia* group, but also the subsequent extension of the definition in *Semeia* 36: an apocalypse is 'intended to interpret present, earthly circumstances in light of the supernatural world and of the future, and to influence both the understanding and the behaviour of the audience by means of divine authority'.[19] Lage Pernvenden repeatedly points out the mistake of focusing exclusively on the *Shepherd*'s mundane themes, without recognizing mysteries such as the pre-existence and eschatological completion of the chief Revealer and Object of revelation, the Church: 'Just as the Church is the first thing for him, it is the last too'.[20] Hermas's revelation of the Church is no less awesome from his perspective than the heavens of *1 Enoch* or the throne room of the Apocalypse. If this is difficult to grasp in the twentieth century, that is perhaps because there has been so much discussion of the 'ideal' and 'empirical' Church that the mystery has been lost. Hermas made no such distinctions, it would seem, and so found it not inappropriate to use the apocalyptic model for content such as his own. In Carolyn Osiek's sympathetic view, the result is an interesting balance of vision and realism: 'The purpose of *The Shepherd of Hermas* is neither the proclamation of a second repentance nor the opportunity to perpetrate moralization in apocalyptic garb, but the translation of eschatological [sc. apocalyptic] vision into realistic terms'.[21]

David Aune and David Hellholm have built on the research of the

---

19. Yarbro Collins, 'Early Christian Apocalypticism'.

20. *The Concept of the Church in the Shepherd of Hermas* (Studia Theologica Ludensia 27; Lund: Gleerup, 1966), p. 297.

21. 'The Genre and Function of the Shepherd of Hermas', *Semeia* 36 (1986), pp. 113-19.

Semeia volumes to explore further dimensions of apocalypses in general and the *Shepherd* in particular. Aune's primary concern is to observe the 'literary function' of apocalypses, over against their social function.[22] Although some of his suggestions appear to be idiosyncratic, his idea of reader or hearer participation in the apocalypses has been well received. The apocalypse is intended not only as a literary record or artifice of visionary experience, but as a 'vehicle' to 'relive' the experience of the writer. Various literary devices are used both to reveal and to conceal the message of the apocalypse, into which the reader must fully enter for complete understanding. That is, the reader works through a literary puzzle or maze, and discovers the same central mysteries that were vouchsafed to the seer in the primary revelation. A weakness of his discussion is the suggestion that we can find either a dogmatic or thematic 'core' passage which overshadows the rest of the work. This was noted in reference to the centrifugal aspect of *Aseneth*,[23] and is even more problematic in the case of a paratactic work such as the *Shepherd*. Aune's intent to find such a core has been buttressed by the linguistic analysis of Hellholm.[24] It would seem too early to make a final judgment[25] concerning the value of Hellholm's research, since to date he has only applied 'text-sequential' and 'communication level' analysis to the *Visionenbuch* of the *Shepherd*, and, in a preliminary way, to the Apocalypse and the Gospel of Matthew.[26] His argument is that where the highest levels of text sequence and communication join, there is found the core 'message' of the book. His division of the books into text-sequence hierarchies is most interesting, and is based on apparently significant textual data, such as changes in scene, actor groups, renominalization, and the like. Even here, however, there remains the subjective element of choice. This subjectivity may be amplified in the case of the communication levels: it is not clear, for example, why his five grades of communication, from introductory narrative to written communication, are increasingly intense, or graded. In the case of the *Visionenbuch* (that is, *Visions* 1–4), his discovery of 2.2.5-7 as the

22. Osiek, 'Genre', p. 89.
23. Chapter 2 n. 57.
24. Hellholm, *Visionenbuch des Hermas*.
25. See, however, the provocative (if brief) critique of hierarchical levels of text in W.S. Vorster, 'Genre', *Neot* 22 (1988), pp. 113-14.
26. 'En textgrammatisk konstruktion i Matteusevangeliet', *SEÅ* 51-52 (1986–87), pp. 80-89.

central revelation may be as much influenced by the past history of the book's analysis as by mere observation. It was to be expected that a passage dealing with second repentance would be chosen. What is not obvious is why a few verses prefaced by ὤμοσεν γὰρ ὁ δεσπότης are to be considered more seriously than other passages. It may well be that other factors of intensification besides God's oath, such as the flow of the action, and repeated themes, are equally important to the book. Moreover, Yarbro Collins points out that the attempt to find a central message may run counter to the insight that 'apocalypses maximize participation of the audience in the revelatory experience'.[27] If the participatory factor is indeed important, then what is experienced by the reader, alongside the seer, as progress is made through the visions, weighs far more heavily than a discrete word of instruction given solemnity through God's oath.

The Unity of The Shepherd of Hermas

Despite these flaws, the work of Hellholm and Aune is helpful in showing the fruitfulness of treating *Visions* 1–4 as a unit. Both Aune and Hellholm feel that we can adduce historical reasons for treating the *Vision* book separately, and have adopted a generally accepted theory of the *Shepherd*'s composite background. They also argue that there are weighty internal reasons for considering the *Visionenbuch* as an aesthetic unit, regardless of its historical career. It will be helpful to look at the internal and external factors which would suggest a source theory and consider a few past solutions, before reflecting on possible evidence for the book's unity, be it historical or literary.

Internal factors do show a clear caesura between *Vision* 4 and *Vision* 5. At *Vision* 5, there is a change of mediator: the Lady Church disappears, not to return. She is supplanted by the Shepherd, who presides over both the *Mandates* and the *Similitudes*. In fact, *Vision* 5 is not in itself an extended vision, but the initial appearance of the Shepherd, and an introduction to his *Mandates*. This structural gap is underscored by the heading for the fifth *Vision* in the Codex Sinaiticus, which titles the vision *Apokalypsis* V, over against the first four ὁράσεις. The Vulgate and Palatine even more clearly recognize the division, entitling the fifth *Vision* (respectively): *Visio quinta initium pastoris* and *Incipiunt pastoris mandata duodecim*. Also absent in each version is the

27. 'Early Christian Apocalypticism', pp. 4-5.

curious *anaphora* found at *Visions* 3 and 4, which we would have expected at the subsequent fifth *Vision*; instead, the title and text are separated, as at the beginning of a new structural section. Moreover, Hermas is not named from the fifth *Vision* on, whereas he is frequently individualized in the first four by the Church and others: from *Vision* 5 on, we have the sense of an anonymous seer. Again, in the first four *Visions*, Hermas frequently addresses his recipients as 'brothers', a technique which is dropped from *Vision* 5 on. Other weaker indications of composition have been belaboured, such as different Jewish and Greek 'world views', forward-looking versus retrospective views of the persecution and different church order (perhaps more formal from 5 on).

All of these factors suggest a structural, thematic and perhaps composition-historical lack of unity, but not necessarily a difference in authorship. Even the discovery of 'theologies' in tension would not demonstrate the latter, since apocalyptic literature is well known for its synthetic and inclusive approach. Dibelius takes the lack of integrity in the *Shepherd* very seriously, but does not insist that such factors prove separate authorship for the sections.[28]

Two external factors have, however, been used to buttress several complex theories of authorship which have been considered plausible by other critics. First is the assignment of the book's authorship in the Muratorian canon to the 'brother' of Pius (ca. 150), which seems to contradict a reference in the text itself to 'Clement' as a contemporary (2.4.3). A second intimation of a complex history is the fact that *Vision* 5 to the end is found alone, without the first four visions, in the Michigan Codex and in the Sahidic version. Did this section circulate separately for a time? When these two factors are seen along with the internal indicators, plus the curious length and revisionary quality of the second tower allegory (*Sim.* 9), certain theories of re-edition, but not necessarily separate authorship, seem plausible.

Dibelius's sane suggestion is that *Visions* 1–4 and *Vision* 5 through to *Similitude* 8 existed independently, but were later fused by the addition of *Similitudes* 9 and 10. His theory, which does not exclude single authorship, is more simple than other dissection theories, such as those represented by F. Spitta, A. Hilgenfeld, and above all, Stanislas Giet.[29]

28. *Der Hirt*, p. 421.

29. *Hermas et les pasteurs: Les trois auteurs du Pasteur d'Hermas* (Paris: Presses Universaires de France, 1963). Giet rehearses the various grounds for sources, citing Hilgenfeld (who in 1881 discerned three authors on the grounds that

These authors rely on the possibility of distinguishing Jewish from Greek thought forms, and in the final analysis present different schemes which multiply authors and sources. In all, the independent cautions of Robert Joly and H. Chadwick are salutary: 'Nous ne possédons pas le moindre indice d'une existence autonome des *Visions*';[30] moreover, '[t]he textual tradition is so tenuous as not to allow any sure answer to these speculative questions'.[31] Again, certain stylistic features may be mustered on the side of a common hand, such as the consistent view of a bumbling seer, and the use of ὁμαλός throughout the entire *Shepherd*, which cuts across Giet's stages.[32] While the strength of the evidence seems to lie, then, with those who accept some sort of re-editing theory, it would seem that no real certainty is possible.

Joly's insightful and amusing commentary on Giet's hypothesis is a reminder against any doctrinaire view of the data. The question of textual history aside, it is defensible to treat *Visions* 1–4 as an interpretatively separable (although not necessarily a composition-historically separate) unit on the basis of the structure signalled internally within the *Shepherd*. The *Visionenbuch* differs from the rest of the work: it differs in the manner in which parts are enumerated, in the identity of the mediator, in its less paratactic structure, and in the presence of more numerous apocalyptic features. The unit presents itself to the reader even in an initial observation of the four ὁράσεις, which are all superintended by the Lady Church. ἀποκάλυψις έ (5) is an introduction to the Mandates, and on aesthetic, if not composition-historical grounds, belongs with the subsequent section. The discrete literary nature of *Visions* 1–4 therefore means that complicated theories of composition are not required to vindicate a separate treatment of its structure and contents. Moreover, this unit alone contains the female figure with which this study is concerned. A separate treatment of *Visions* 1–4 is not intended here to foreclose the questions of composition-historical or aesthetic unity of the entire *Shepherd*.[33] Rather, the *Visions* present an

some, but not all of the book displayed 'grec fortement marqué du judaisme', p. 66) and Spitta (who considered the book 'juive...interpolé par une maine chretienne', p. 68). His own opinion is that the *Shepherd* displays Jewish sources, but not a Jewish author.

30. R. Joly, 'Hermas et le Pasteur', *VC* 21 (1967), pp. 201-18 (204).

31. H. Chadwick, 'The New Edition of *Hermas*', *JT* NS 8 (1957), p. 275.

32. I.R. Michaels, 'The "Level Ground" in the *Shepherd of Hermas*', *ZN* 59 (1968), pp. 245-50.

33. The study of the *Shepherd* would be advanced by a serious investigation of

easily apprehended *locus* for a discussion of the transformed female figure, and references to the more paratactic *Mandates* and *Similitudes* are for the most part not helpful here. This examination will therefore be largely confined to the first four *Visions*, which shall be called *Hermas* for the purposes of brevity, while the *Shepherd* will be used for the entire *Visions–Mandates–Similitudes* complex.

The Structure of Hermas

In form, *Hermas* is itself an apocalypse within the larger whole, since it concludes with the second half of a frame. That is, the Lady Church moves from her interpretation of the final vision to a concluding paraenesis and envoi with instructions (4.3.6a). The author also deftly unifies the four *Visions* in the Church's concluding remarks when she tells Hermas, μνημονεύετε τὰ προγεγραμμένα (4.3.6c). Her speech concludes with a mysterious departure, complete with a νέφος of glory, and the seer's recollection of his attitude and actions. Aune seems correct in his assessment of the *Shepherd* as formally containing two apocalypses[34]—*Visions* 1–4, and *Vision* 5 to the end (the possible editorial nature of *Sim.* 9–10 notwithstanding). The existence of separate sets of frames around Hermas and the remainder of the *Shepherd*, plus the two different mediators, strengthens his view. The *Visionenbuch Hermas* may therefore be treated as an apocalypse in its own right along- side other examples of the genre. Its structure will be analyzed here, and the active role of the transformation motif will be demonstrated within its scheme.

Even a cursory glance at *Hermas* shows that it has an episodic style of four visions. These episodes are fairly uniform in features, although not in length. Each includes preparation and receptivity of seer, vision(s), interpretation/dialogue, often the seer's reaction, and concluding exhortation. The manuscript's own headings add to the appearance of regularity. In this respect, *Hermas* resembles *4 Ezra* more closely than it does its canonical Christian counterpart, the Johannine Apocalypse. It is therefore not necessary to discern structural units or divisions,[35] which

stylistic features, along the lines of the short study of Michaels. If such inquiries strengthen the case for aesthetic unity in the *Shepherd*, then more work may be indicated in understanding the peculiar structural features of this paratactic piece.

34. *Literary Environment*, p. 247.

35. A case is made for the diplacement of visions in *Hermas* by A. Kirkland,

are patent; rather, the discussion may proceed immediately to the
question of how these units function.

It must first be noted that each of the *'Visions'* contains more than
one revelation or visitation; these are, however, thematically and structurally integrated to form a rather complex whole. For example, the first
Vision includes a visitation by the desired wife, Rhoda, as well as a
visitation–dialogue–revelation by the Church herself. Similarly, the
second *Vision* includes the gift of a book by the Church, Hermas's
delayed knowledge of its contents, an explanation by a 'graceful' young
man (another *angelus interpres*), and an envoi by the Church. The third
Vision, which is the most lengthy and complex of all, commences with
preparatory vision, continues with an orchestrated vision of the
συμψέλιον and tower, follows with an extended quasi-allegorical
interpretation, and finishes with a supplementary interpretation by the
'young man' concerning the three forms of the Church which Hermas
has met in the three first *Visions*. This final explanation of the Church's
appearances reads as a kind of coda to the three *Visions* rather than as
simply an ending to *Vision* 3 *per se*; Hermas is in fact told that the
revelations are complete—ἀπέχεις ὁλοτελῆ τὴν ἀποκάλυψιν·
μηκέτι μηδὲν αἰτήσεις περὶ ἀποκαλύψεως (3.13.4b).

At this point, the revelatory material of the apocalypse is given a sense
of termination. The author does not return to his frame immediately,
however, but by means of a condition, builds into the idea of τήλος
qualification which allows for yet another vision—ἐάν τι δὲ δέῃ,
ἀποκαλυφθήσεταί σοι (3.13.4b). So then, the fourth *Vision* appears
to be somewhat 'detached',[36] although it is a fitting supplement to the
first three *Visions*. In conformity with the first two *Visions*, Hermas is
travelling, although not to Cumae. His meditations are interrupted by an
auditory revelation reminiscent of the *bat qôl*, although it is impossible
to say whether this feature is genuinely Jewish, a Christian recollection
of the voice which has come through tradition or gospel (cf. Mk 9.7;
Jn 12.28-29), or merely a parallel independent phenomenon. The
audition is followed by the spectre of a monster, next by a vision of the

---

'The Literary History of the *Visions* in the *Shepherd of Hermas*', *Second Century* 9
(1992), pp. 87-102. As in the case of source studies for the NT Apocalypse, perceived
aporiae in the work may be attributable to the nature of the genre apocalypse rather
than to a distruption of the original sequence. I am here concerned to analyze *Hermas*
as it stands, to see if a coherent reading emerges.

    36. Snyder, *Shepherd*, p. 55.

perfected virgin Church, and finally by her interpretation of the monster vision and a closing exhortation. Hermas's outlook has been transformed from the desire for a wife as pure as Rhoda to an inspired desire for the perfected Church. The *Visionenbuch* begins, and ends, with Rome in view, but much has changed (1.1.1-2 // 4.3.7b).

The parallel features of each vision, the substantial length of *Vision* 3, and the appendix-like appearance of *Vision* 4 become apparent when charted:

Frame 1.1.1-2

Vision 1   A   Preparation 1.1.3
                 Rhoda 1.1.4-9
                 Reaction 1.2.1
          B   Preparation 1.2.2a
                 Church 1.2.2b
                 Dialogue/Revelation 1.2.3.–1.3.4
                 Reaction 1.4.2
                 Exhortation and Conclusion 1.4.1-3

Vision 2   A   Preparation 2.1.1-2
                 Church with Book 2.1.3-4a
                 Conclusion (rapture of book) 2.1.4b
          B   Preparation 2.2.1
                 Book's contents 2.2.2–2.3.4
                 Explanation regarding Church 2.4.1
                 Exhortation and Conclusion 2.4.2-3

Vision 3   A   Preparation 3.1.1-2a
                 Visitation 3.1.2b
           B   Preparation 3.1.2-4a
                 Couch vision 3.1.4b
                 Reaction 3.1.5
                 Visitation 3.1.6
                 Explanation and exhortation 3.1.7–3.2.2
           C   Preparation 3.2.3-4a
                 Tower vision 3.2.4b–3.2.9
                 Extended interpretation/dialogue 3.3.1–3.8.11
                 Exhortation 3.9.1-10
                 Conclusion 3.10.1
                 Request for further revelation 3.10.2 and explanation of
                 request in the form of an excursus on the three appearances by
                 Hermas 3.10.3-5
          D   Preparation 3.10.6-7
                 Young man's revelation of appearances 3.10-8–3.13.4a
                 Exhortation and conclusion 3.3.4b

Vision 4   A   Preparation 4.1.1-3
                    Auditory revelation 4.1.4
                    Monster vision 4.1.5-10
              B   Introduction 4.2.1a
                    Virgin vision 4.2.1b-2
                    Interpretation of monster 4.2.3–4.3.5
                    Exhortation and Conclusion 4.3.6-7a

Frame 4.3.7b

The Centrality of Vision 3

It is immediately obvious that *Vision 3* takes the lion's share of
space, occupying thirteen chapters over against four in Vision 1, four in
Vision 2 and three in *Vision* 4. The third episode is therefore longer
than the rest of *Hermas* taken together. It is here that Hermas receives
detailed instruction regarding the divine supervision and nature of the
Church, both in her aspect as Lady and as Tower. The Tower
vision/allegory is sandwiched by the three manifestations of the Lady
Church in *Visions* 1–3, and the second description and interpretation of
these manifestations by Hermas and the young man respectively:

    Vision 1   Old Church seated   (Form 1)
    Vision 2   Middle Church standing   (Form 2)
    Vision 3   Young Church reclining   (Form 3)

    Tower vision–allegorical interpretation

    Description of Church, Forms 1, 2 and 3
    Interpretation of Church, Forms 1, 2 and 3

The return to a description and extended interpretation of the female
figure long after her appearances indicates that her various appearances
are not mere trappings for the messages which she delivers: they are the
very stuff of which the revelations are made. Both the paraenetic
messages of the Church, and her different appearances, interpreted at
various points in the text,[37] comprise the mysteries unveiled to Hermas.

37. P. Henne, 'La polysémie allégorique dans le Pasteur d'Hermas', *ETL* 65
(1989), pp. 131-35, discusses Hermas' penchant for allegorical polysemy, or
multivalence. He refers to several symbols and symbol-systems in *Hermas*, including
the different pictures of the Church. Hermas' twofold perspective—cosmological and
soteriological—is expressed by the sequential or even simultaneous adoption of
different images, which at times conflict with each other, but which are coherent within

Attention is thus called to the Church as the focus of *Hermas* as a whole, through the structuring feature of her various appearances (forms 1, 2 and 3) and her other aspect as the Tower.

Other factors make it quite clear that the primary subject matter is the Church herself. Throughout *Hermas* she is revealer, object of the vision and recipient of the vision (with Hermas as her representative). This complex of roles makes for a curious fluidity which emerges at least twice in *Hermas*. In the first case, *Vision* 4 presents the virgin Church as a separate visionary experience, but this role is then followed by her function as *angelus interpres* of the preceding monster vision. Because the epiphany of the Virgin Church is not interpreted, but leads immediately into her own interpretation of the preceding vision, she seems at first to function as a mere introduction to the real subject matter, that is, the nature of the tribulation. However, in the interpretation itself, the nature of the Church again comes to the fore, when the beast's colours, especially the golden and white parts, are explained. As the virgin says, τὸ δὲ χρυσοῦν μέρος ὑμεῖς ἐστε (4.3.4). So then, the tribulation has meaning only in reference to the Church, and in *Vision* 4 the Church takes on the roles of object, interpreter and recipient. A second case of the fusion of subject and object is even more explicit, and occurs in *Vision* 3. Here the Lady Church declares unequivocally, ὁ μὲν πύργος, ὃν βλέπεις οἰκοδομούμενον, ἐγώ εἰμι ἡ Ἐκκλησία, ἡ ὀφθεῖσά σοι καὶ νῦν καὶ τὸ πρότερον (3.3.3).

At the beginning of *Hermas*, the Church is twice described as being the very purpose of creation (1.1.6 and 1.3.4). It would seem that the Church is likewise the very purpose of *Hermas*—all of the piece moves

---

the logic of the immediate narrative. An interesting example of this technique is 'la multiplicité des fonctions assumée par la dame agée' (p. 134). Following L. Cirillo, 'Erma e l'apocallita a Roma', *Cristianesimo nella storia* 4 (1983), pp. 1-31, Henne comments on her dual function as a 'faith object' and a revealer. Cirillo has made a contrast between *4 Ezra*'s Lady who is transformed into a city, and Hermas's Lady and Tower which appear simultaneously. Henne concludes that 'un seul révélant peut symboliser plusieurs révélés' (p. 135), and he suggests that in *Similitude* 9 the process is reversed so that 'plusieurs révélants symbolisent un seul et même révélé [i.e. door, Shepherd and rock as "le Fils de Dieu"]'. In fact, the latter is also the case with the Church, which is symbolized variously and simultaneously under different aspects. It is not just that the Lady symbolizes different realities, but also that the various symbols of the Church complement each other to fill in the picture. She can be, depending on the perspective, subject, object or interpreter.

towards the revelation, description and instruction of the Church in her various aspects. It is therefore understandable why *Vision* 3 is so lengthy and complex. By the commencement of the third *Vision*, Hermas has already introduced the Lady Church in her three forms; he will now supplement this understanding with the lengthy tower episode and an explicit interpretation of her female forms. *Visions* 1 and 2 are direct words of rebuke and paraenesis, first in verbal, then in written form; *Vision* 4 presents the future tribulation and hope of the Church; *Vision* 3 explains what the Church really is, a mystery normally hidden to human eyes, while including numerous paraenetic sentences and exhortations. It would appear, then, that not only length, but focused interest come together in this third sequence. Such an understanding of the importance of *Vision* 3 was certainly shared by the author/redactor of the larger *Shepherd of Hermas*, who recapitulates his theme in *Similitude* 9 for thirty-three more chapters—a third of the book's entire length![38]

38. It is perhaps due to the length and detail of *Similitude* 9 that the entire *Shepherd* has been dismissed as tedious. In the words of Giet, this parable seems to be the work of 'un moraliste dont la manie didactique brave la monotonie et la fatigue' (p. 155). The author of the *Similitude* presents his teaching as a supplement to the tower vision of *Hermas*, intended for the more mature (*Sim.* 9.1.1-2). The building is seen against a larger context than that of the tower vision, and its message is emphasized through the parallel or complementary imagery of mountains and stones which is painstakingly decoded. The more elaborate imagery allows for details of ecclesiology to be included, which suggest a more obvious hierarchy than is seen in *Hermas* (*Vis.* 3.5.1; cf. *Sim.* 9.4.2-6). Another interesting difference is that the period for repentance is detailed as part of the *Similitude*, where twice there is a pause in the building of the tower; in the *Vision*, a short time for repentance is implied by the Lady Church (3.8.9), yet the atmosphere is one of urgency. In all, the *Vision* seems fresher, more revelatory in appearance, and more conducive to zealous action; the *Similitude* is more studied, less visionary (as its title suggests) and more at peace with the *status quo*. Whether the difference in style is due to a change in authorship, or simply a difference in genre or the author's age, is a matter of speculation. Observations of different theology or ecclesiology must also remain tenuous, since the message of the *Vision* is so much more general, and does not compare directly to the more elaborate teaching of the *Similitude*. What does seem clear is that the return to the tower theme affords the *Shepherd* a unity in its first and last parts which would be otherwise missing. The preference for the *Visions* over the *Similitude* which is common today is as much a comment on twentieth-century expectations as the inclusion of *Similitude* 9 is of the styles of an earlier age.

The Church as Mystery

To assign centrality to the subject matter of the third Vision runs counter to the suggestion of Aune and Hellholm that the 'message...is summarized in a statement by God himself in *Vision* 2.2.5-7, announcing a final opportunity for repentance to those who have denied him in the past'.[39] Their assessment of the primary function of Hermas is consistent with the traditional purpose to which church historians have put the book—an initial point along the trajectory of a developing penitential system. However, this view may reflect more the interests of scholars (how to explain Hermas's message in an era which allowed for no repentance after baptism) than the actual concern of the piece itself. Hellholm and Aune base their analysis on the first-person introduction to vv. 5 and following (where the highest text-sequential and communication levels supposedly converge). That is, the highest grade of text-sequential structure is indicated by such elements as temporal markers and renominalization, and the communication level is most intense since God 'swears' (ὤμοσεν, 2.2.5) that the declaration is true. However, it is not at all clear that the entire passage found in vv. 5-7 is a direct word of God: some or all of the message may be read as reportage (indirect speech), as in fact it is translated by both Kirsopp Lake[40] and Graydon Snyder. Secondly, we have noted other forms of intensification in *Hermas*, namely length, and repeated themes under different aspects. These may well vie with Hellholm's criteria in determining the major thrusts of *Hermas*.

While the most common view of *Hermas* has emphasized the theme of repentance, this has not been left unchallenged. Lage Pernvenden, whose dissertation concerns the concept of the Church in the whole *Shepherd*, not surprisingly asserts, 'In our opinion it is a misinterpretation to understand Hermas's essential importance as a founder figure in the history of the development of the system of penance'.[41] Likewise, L.W. Barnard says, '[I]t is a mistake to interpret him as the founder of a system of penance'.[42] Helmut Koester tries to account for what he sees as two conflicting themes by recourse to a complex history, first Jewish,

---

39. Aune, *Literary Environment*, p. 247.

40. Lake, 'The Shepherd of Hermas', in *The Apostolic Fathers* (Cambridge, MA: Harvard University Press, 1950), II, pp. 1-305.

41. L. Pernvenden, *The Concept of the Church in the Shepherd of Hermas* (Lund: Gleerup, 1976), p. 298.

42. 'The Shepherd of Hermas in Recent Study', *HeyJ* 9 (1968), p. 33.

then Christian, of the *Visions*. He tells us that *Hermas*'s view of creation and a female wisdom figure are borrowed from Jewish lore, and that a 'Christian interpretation...was secondarily attached'.[43] It is not at all clear that Hermas's Christian interests run counter to his material, traditional or otherwise. Rather, it would seem better to see the message of repentance as forming part of Hermas's overall understanding of the Church. Mystery and practical concerns come together.

Commentators have, of course, not been slow to appreciate the mystical aspect of *Hermas*, even if they have been at times hard-pressed to explain it. Joly tells us : 'Hermas conçoit l'Eglise sous deux aspects: c'est une réalité transcendante, creée avant toute chose; c'est aussi une réalité eschatologique en devenir'.[44] Joly's view of a primordial and eschatological Church must be supplemented by *Hermas*'s equally important picture of a present, imperfect, changing Church, to which the divine paraenesis is directed. Hermas holds together his pragmatic interests with a vision of the divine Church, created before all other beings, and described in terms of heavenly Wisdom. So then, to see *Vision* 3 as central is really to recognize in it the clearest expression of Hermas's vision of the Church in all her glory and with all her problems. Lightfoot recognized full well the import of Hermas's writing:

> The object of the *Visions* indeed seems to be to place before the reader the conception of the Church under the guise of an aged woman, whose features become more youthful at each successive appearance. Thus the lessons of a smitten and penitent conscience, of the Church growing and spreading (the Church militant), lastly, of the Church purified by suffering (the Church triumphant) and the terrors of judgement, occupy the four *Visions* so-called.[45]

Lightfoot's description seems perhaps a little too dogmatically-oriented to grasp the full import of the Church as a mystery, but it certainly recognizes the central focus of the writing as we have conceived it. It was not common in his day to see apocalypses as containing actual visions ('*Visions* so-called'): in fact, it was the contrived nature of

43. H. Koester, *Introduction to The New Testament: History and Literature of Early Christianity* (Philadelphia: Fortress Press; Berlin: de Gruyter, 1982), II, p. 259. Originally this was *Einfuhrung in das Neue Testament*, 1980, but the 1982 version supersedes it, being the author's own translation.

44. Joly, 'Hermas', p. 35.

45. J.B. Lightfoot *et al.*, 'The Shepherd of Hermas', in *Excluded Books of the New Testament* (London: Eveleigh, Nash & Grayson, 1927), p. 250.

apocalyptic vision which was seen to differentiate it from prophecy. The apocalypticist used a fabricated visionary format to present doctrine, and poured his instruction into visionary containers, so to speak. Critics are now more generally prepared to grant some visionary experience to apocalypticists, and do not see the incorporation of traditional material or theology as a necessary block to such a view. From such a perspective has come Aune's understanding of apocalypses as providing a vehicle for the reader to re-experience the numinous, a suggestion which many have enthusiastically embraced. If this is the case for *Hermas*, then the concept of the Church as a mystery would not be simply a theological assertion, but an experienced, and even communicable revelation. Let us turn to an actual analysis of how the four *Visions* work together in order to see whether such a dynamic—that is, the provision of a surrogate 'vision' for the reader—may be at work in *Hermas*, despite the obvious mundane concerns which run throughout it.

Thematic Frames

A feature which confirms the centrality of *Vision* 3 is the presence of two connected themes which frame the vision. Both *Vision* 2 and *Vision* 4 present the concepts of persecution and double-mindedness, often using the precise words διψυχία (and cognates) and θλῖψις, but sometimes paraphrasing the terms. Usually the themes are linked together, as at 2.2.7a and 7b, 2.3.2 and 4, and 4.2.5 and 6. Found together, the themes have two implications, the first being more obvious. Primarily, the message is, 'do not be double-minded, since persecution is coming and only with purity of heart can you escape it'. This is clearly enunciated by the maiden Church at 4.2.5, where she says: ἐὰν οὖν προετοιμάσησθε...δυνήσεσθε ἐκφυγεῖν αὐτήν (that is, the persecution). There is, however, a second and more subtle reason for the two concepts to be linked. It would seem not only that persecution may be escaped through the single heart, but that it may itself produce it. So then, Hermas prays at the commencement of *Vision* 4, ἵνα με ἰσχυροποιήσῃ (4.1.3); this prayer for spiritual strength is 'answered' (ἀπεκρίθη) by the heavenly words, μὴ διψυχήσεις (4.1.4), and the beast who is a *typos* of the persecution to come. The wording implies that the divine words are not simply an admonition or preparatory warning, but have a kind of performative function, as does the spectre of the beast. Hermas' prayer for strength, no less than his prayer to complete the visions, is answered in the audition and vision. The result of withstanding the beast is that he now sees the virgin Church. He has been 'made strong in the faith' and so has not been double-minded. The Church's interpretation makes this clear, when she says that the golden part, the faithful, must be 'tried', and so will be made pure. Once the test has been passed, there will be no need for further στενοχωρία (often a synonym for θλῖψις; see 4.3.4). Again, at 2.2.7, those who remain single-minded through the persecution are called blessed. Such a state is not the only outcome of persecution, however, since others (2.3.3) are hardened by the ordeal. The θλῖψις has the power both to purify and harden.

Visions 2 and 4, then, stress these two complementary concepts of θλῖψις and double-mindedness, and form a kind of thematic bracket around *Vision* 3. In this central vision, it has been seen that Hermas is given a mysterious revelation of the Church as she really is, in all her glory, but also in her imperfection. A further analysis of the third *Vision* will also show how the twin concepts of double-mindedness–tribulation fit into the picture of the Church given there. This can be seen in the introduction, conclusion and body of the tower vision (that is, *Vision* 3). At the commencement of the vision, Hermas desires to sit at the Lady's right hand on the συμψέλιον, but is denied, because this place is reserved for those who have 'already' (ἤδη, 3.1.9b) pleased God through suffering tribulation. He must yet be made clean along with others who are not hopelessly double-minded, before such an honour can be bestowed (3.2.2). In his present state he belongs, and shares the same 'gifts' and 'promises', only not the same δόξα (3.2.1b). He is on the συμψέλιον, only not yet on the side of glory. Similarly, in the Lady's final words to her children,[46] she warns that the leaders do not have a single heart, and

---

46. C. Osiek, 'The Social Function of Female Imagery in Second Century Prophecy', *VC* 29 (1992), pp. 55-74, argues that 'the female figure of the church...is not spousal, nor maternal, but a seemingly independent wisdom figure' (p. 60). While it is clear that the Church in *Hermas* functions primarily as a patroness conceived after the mould of Sophia, the maternal aspect is very clear at 3.9, as is the bridal aspect in *Vision* 4. It is, in my view, highly unlikely that second-century Christian readers of *Vision* 4 would hear about 'a maiden dressed in white as though coming from a bridal chamber', and simply attribute this to language from Ps. 19 (cf. Osiek, 'Social Function', p. 60), without inferring that she is the Bride of God—especially since she is pictured as escaping tribulation of an apocalyptic nature. Osiek's discussion of liminality, status dissonance and transition through imposed humiliy is, however, very helpful, and highlights the general issue of identity, as in Douglas's discussion of *Aseneth* (cf. 'Liminality and Conversion').

challenges them to accept the correction of the Lord, which is about to come (3.9.8-10). Within the vision proper, Hermas sees white stones which cannot fit into the tower, nor endure persecution until they are trimmed of earthly entanglement (3.6.5-6); presumably God's means of such 'cutting around' is the coming tribulation.

Thus Hermas learns that all things, even the beast itself, are at God's service to benefit his Church, to level the way for her. This is consonant with the idea of preparation–suffering found in the Johannine apocalypse, where the Lady's flight to the desert was also a sojourn: her place of preparation and tribulation were one. We need not be surprised, then, to find in *Hermas* the curious mixture of colours on the beast (4.1.10). What is at first glance only a spectre of horror is also under the control of the Almighty. For some, his colours are black and red; for others, gold and white. The Maiden's final words to the Church are instructive: πιστεύσατε τῷ κυρίῳ, οἱ δίψυχοι, ὅτι πάντα δύναται (4.2.6). He is even able to turn persecution into blessing.

Four Media of Revelation

Yet another interesting phenomenon in *Hermas* is the way in which the seer encounters revelation through different media. The prior discussions of *4 Ezra* and the Apocalypse have demonstrated that apocalypses are a macro-genre, containing various sorts of sub-genres, including parable, narrative, audition and vision. In *Hermas*, this encyclopaedic feature is practically schematized. The revelation of *Vision* 1 is oral—the point of the epiphanies of Rhoda and the Lady Church is to deliver a spoken message, a message both of challenge and comfort, ostensibly for Hermas himself but ultimately for the faithful group which he represents. The medium of the second *Vision* is verbal as well, but inscribed in the written form of the little book, which is first given to Hermas, then translated in full for the benefit of the reader. In *Vision* 3, Hermas (and through him, the reader) is treated to a spectacle which is explained in almost tedious detail. Finally, *Vision* 4 intrudes upon the seer and the reader as an immediate experience. It is a vision, to be sure, but linked to the narrative opening so that the line between normalcy and vision is blurred. That is, in the earlier *Visions*, we are given clear markers that the experience to come is out of the ordinary—καὶ πνεῦμά με ἔλαβεν καὶ ἀπήνεγκέν με (1.1.3); καὶ πάλιν με αἴρει πνεῦμα (2.1.1); ἐγενομην οὖν, ἀδελφοί, εἰς τὸν ἀγρὸν...καὶ ἦλθον εἰς τὸν τόπον ὅπου διεταξάμην αὐτῇ ἐλθεῖν, καὶ βλέπω...καὶ ὡσεὶ φρίκη μοι προσῆλθεν (3.1.4-5). In the final *Vision*, there are some markers that the experience is visionary: ὅρασις δ΄ (4), ὡς εἰς τὸν οὐρανόν (4.1.5) and ἰδού (4.2.1). However, elaborate preparations are not made, nor is Hermas seized from his present situation and removed to a visionary plane. Rather, the audition and vision come upon him.

We move, then, from word to text (which Hermas himself inscribes), to impressive and decidedly significant spectacle, to audition and vision impinging upon the seer's reality—the whole a progressive intensification of revelation. This line of intensification is broken somewhat by the detachment of *Vision* 4, and by the statement that with the interpretation of the Church's forms, the revelation has been given ὁλοτελῆ. *Vision* 4 is added, however, to make complete these (provisionally) finished *Visions*. It is as if Hermas were saying, 'The first three visions are sufficient for the present, but there is more to come, something which cannot be experienced except through the route of persecution and suffering, so be forewarned'. Tellingly, the Church does not appear in *Vision* 4 until *after* the spectre of tribulation: there is no virgin Church until she has been tested διὰ τοῦ πυρός (4.3.4). This is a marked departure from the sequence of the other *Visions*, where the church both arranges and interprets the revelation. That is, in the other *Visions*, she appears *prior* to the vision itself and superintends the revelation. Here in *Vision* 4 the Church appears only *after* the vision. The effect is to fix attention upon the appearance of the virgin, rather than, or at least in parallel to, the monster. Moreover, the uncharacteristic lack of interpretation of her final virginal form adds to the sense of drama and mystery. It is unlikely that Hermas has left her final shape uninterpreted simply because of its traditional nature and familiarity; this has been no impediment to near-obsessive overinterpretation throughout the *Visions* up to this point. Rather, we are left with a sense of something unfinished, something to come, both fearsome and redolent of hope.

The intensification of media or means of revelation in *Hermas*, from hearing to reading and writing, to seeing, to engagement in the vision, is therefore a powerful device of incorporation. The reader, as well as Hermas, is drawn into the revelations which he or she is reading and/or hearing. This technique is shared with all apocalypses, in that the writer of an apocalypse is never content to transmit simply the bottom line, that is, the paraenetic message, or the assurance of a future deliverance.

Rather, the visionary provides an elaborate apparatus complete with circumstances, reaction to the numinous, vision and interpretation. Techniques such as the use of pseudonymity, first-person narrative and embedment of the vision within a narrative have often been understood as providing authority: the reader/hearer should listen carefully to this message, because it is a revelation, and this is how and to whom it was given. However, the inclusion of these various elements does more than lend authority: it communicates to the reader the mysterious quality of the experience, calling attention to the worlds of the 'normal' and the 'supernatural', and showing where the lines of the two worlds converge.

In *Hermas*, this quality is accentuated by the intensification of media, and the role of closure in *Vision 4*. It is not certain whether Hermas expects his audience to have visions as well—at the very least, they are to receive the authoritative words as an 'audition' from God! He does, indeed, expect his hearers to suffer persecution, and it is only in so doing that the vision of the virgin Church may be realized. The lack of an interpretation for the final vision of the Church means that the closure of the apocalypse is only relative. Such a built-in open-endedness in the final sequence, which does itself finally come to a close in formal terms (4.3.6-7), lends both to the mystery of the revelation, and the prospect of a glorious Church through the participation of the recipient Church. The frame of the apocalypse (4.3.7b) pulls the reader back firmly into the present; when the Lady leaves, there is still the possibility, indeed the probability, of suffering for Hermas and those whom he represents. If the reader has experienced by proxy the increasingly pointed revelations communicated by Hermas, the adventure of suffering may be expected to be more direct. It is at this point that the 'mundane' pages of the *Mandates* and *Similitudes* fittingly take over, functioning as guides through this experience. Above it all, however, shines the prospect of the Bride, so far uninterpreted. The elusive quality of this vision is perhaps the one point at which *Hermas* demonstrates the centrifugal aspect found in apocalypses. The undecoded Bride retains her mystery; in *Aseneth*, there remains the secret of the heavenly visitor's name, in *4 Ezra*, the undescribed glories of the City, and in the Apocalypse, the undisclosed words of the Seven Thunders.

The Transformation of the Church and the Seer

Another clue to the function of the apocalypse as a vicarious vision is that the increasingly intense revelations are complemented by a difference in the mediatrix. In the first instance, the Lady Church is ancient, and sitting; in the second, she is middle-aged, and standing as she speaks to Hermas; in the third, she is young, and reclining upon a couch; and finally she is a virgin bride, κεκοσμημένη ὡς ἐκ νυμφῶνος ἐκπορευομένη (4.2.1; cf. Ps. 19.6; Apoc. 21.2). Each of these appearances is particularly suited to the message at hand: the solemn aspect of the ancient Church is well-suited to the oracular, serious but motherly message which she delivers; reading might well be an occupation of a middle-aged Lady; the young woman is more festive, granting privileges to sit beside her, and superintending a spectacle of enormous proportions; the virgin Church appears after a successfully completed testing.

Note again that these differences are not merely a backdrop for the relayed messages! The three appearances become themselves details of visionary significance which are inquired after and interpreted at length. Subject becomes object at the end of *Vision* 3, when the young man interprets the Lady's successive rejuvenations. In his interpretation, the aspects of the Lady are made to speak of the condition of the seer, or rather, of the whole community which he represents, since the young man uses the second- and third-person plural in his application (3.11.2– 3.13.4). The fluidity between the second-person singular and plural (for example, ὤφθη σοι and τὸ πνεῦμα ὑμῶν πρεσβύτερον, 3.11.2) is retained throughout this section; this is a strong indication that Dibelius is correct in seeing the plight of Hermas, and most of the so-called 'biographical' details in the book, as indicative of the state of the Church as a whole.[47] Hermas, no less than the Lady, is a corporate figure, and hence he is told repeatedly to stop dwelling on his own shortcomings, so that he can concentrate on the problems and glory of the Church which he represents. What Hermas experiences, we are meant to experience: what he sees reflected in the transformations of the Lady are reflections of the Church herself. As Hermas hears divine words, reads and writes divine sentences, and beholds a divine spectacle, he moves, in the words of the young man, from weakness and despair to renewal and 'manful' action (3.12.2-3). It is the visions themselves which effect the change, as well as symbolizing it. God's words and pictures are not simply illustrative of the nature of the Church, but agents of change: this is the logic of the young man's interpretation. So, then, in moving through the revelations, the Church and its members, Hermas's intended readers,

47. Dibelius, *Der Hirt*, p. 420.

may expect to be rejuvenated as well. They are informed of their identity, and, thus in-formed, are transformed.

Many have commented on the patent contradictions in *Hermas* regarding the interpretation of the ancient Lady.[48] Dibelius is representative, when he notes that during *Vision* 2, the age of the Church is explained by her similarity to the Sybil, and by her dignity (2.4.1), whereas in the later interpretation the parallel to the state of Hermas's community is drawn (3.9.1-10). His opinion is that the latter interpretation is sheer artifice: *Aber dieser Versuch erweist sich als künstlich.*[49] His reasoning is that the different appearances are not remarked upon by Hermas during the visions, but only in retrospect at 3.10.3 and following. This observation is certainly accurate. However, it may be that the conflict is inherent in the nature of the subject matter that Hermas is trying to explicate. That is, we need not explain the different interpretations in terms of traditional versus 'Christianized' symbolism, but in terms of the complex view of the Church which Hermas is announcing. There seems for the author to be no neat dividing line between the glorious pre-existent and future perfected Church on the one hand, and the feeble, present, guilt-ridden and in-process Church on the other: they are the same. Hence, the visions present both an awesome spectacle of brightness, glory and mystery (for example, λευκήν, χιονίνων, ἐν ἱματισμῷ λαμπροτάτῳ, 1.2.2) which terrify Hermas (τρόμος με ἔλαβεν, καὶ αἱ τρίχες μου ὀρθαί, 3.1.5), and a homey aspect of age, mothering, youth, sadness and cheer. Often the two atmospheres are separated by the *personae* of the Lady and Hermas, but there is a blending of these two figures which, after all, represent the same reality. That is, for the most part, Hermas plays the role of the bumbling, over-inquisitive, dejected and sinful *present* Church, whereas the role of glory is saved for the Lady. However, Hermas's relative righteousness is also emphasized (1.2.3-4), and the Lady's need for perfection comes through with the interpretation of her subsequent transformations. The Church is both mysterious and mundane. Her identity is repeatedly disclosed as one that *ought* to and can change—

---

48. See again 'La polysémie allégorique' for Henne's cogent comments on these interpretations, which are seemingly 'en tension' (p. 132). He advises: 'Le lecteur doit donc penser d'un registre d'explication à un autre pour respecter la technique interprétative d'Hermas'. Moreover, since the same technique is found throughout the work, a multiplicity of authors 'parait douteux' (p. 135).

49. Dibelius, *Der Hirt*, p. 451.

glory is the proper destination, but the present imperfection is never forgotten.

In this way, the transformations of both Hermas, who is led to repentance and a position of strength through the visions, and the Lady, who is symbolically transformed, form the framework for the entire *Visionenbuch*. We see now why *Hermas* requires the actions of a repentant, rather than heroic, seer: in *Hermas*, the genre apocalypse is put at the service of the mundane, with no sense of dissonance. It is worth noting here that although repentance for sin is a usual characteristic of the apocalypse, as Snyder underscores, it is implied in the other great Christian Apocalypse. There John's humility and solidarity with the Christian community is manifest. The churches are told repeatedly in the letters to repent. Moreover, in ch. 5 it is only the Lion, and no one else in heaven or earth, who is ἄξιος. Again, part of the meaning of the woman's sojourn in the desert is her preparation. We would not expect an explicit reference to John's own repentance, since there is little self-consciousness on the part of the seer in this panoramic Apocalypse. Nor is implicit repentance the sole property of the Christian apocalypses. *4 Ezra*, also, depends upon the attitude of contrition for its entire action: Ezra may lament, but he is also acting in solitary prayer on the behalf of Israel, for whose sin he is grieving (*4 Ezra* 5.13; 7.65). While he is told by Uriel not to compare himself with the unrighteous, and so remains in some sense the apocalyptic hero, he never attains the heights of glory experienced by one such as Enoch. His role remains that of one who leads his people in confession (14.14); part of his glory is indeed his willingness to be counted as the 'us', as one of sinful Israel. As for Aseneth, the confession element is patent, and takes up a major part of the drama, preparing for the 'apocalypse'.

It does not seem to be the case, then, that the presence of confession, repentance and contrition disqualifies a piece as an apocalypse *ipso facto*. What Snyder has observed in *Hermas* as peculiar may divide it from those Type II apocalypses which glorify the seer through his heavenly exploits; the attitude of humility is, however, shared by other apocalypses of Type I, although not always with such abandon as the theme is explored in *Hermas*. Possible reasons for this will be explored in the final chapter. At this point it is sufficient to observe that the symbolic transformations of the figures which we have observed bespeak both humility and latent glory.

The Church as Tower

This theme of humility which is so marked in *Hermas* is seen not only in the stance of the seer and the appearances of the Lady, but also in the one transformation, or supplementary vision, which has not yet been considered in detail—the Church as tower. This symbol of construction is similar to the city images in *Aseneth*, *4 Ezra* and the Apocalypse, but differs in that its import is not purely cosmic and glorious. *Hermas* presents an image with biblical echoes,[50] similar to apocalyptic cities, but more suited to his practical purpose. It might be helpful to ask at this point why *Hermas* chooses a tower image over that of the city, found in the other three works. That is, why use a partial image, and a specific one, instead of the more common one? A number of attractive responses present themselves. The image of a tower is most often used in the Old Testament to evoke ideas of God's concern for Israel (Ps. 61.3; Prov. 18.10; Mic. 4.8). Occasionally, it is the locale or image of God's watchman, or prophet (Hab. 2.1; Jer. 6.27). However, its most common use is as a counterpart to cities, or synecdoche for the temple, the former picturing human pride and the latter God's glory (Gen. 11.4; 2 Chron. 14.7; Song 4.4, and so forth). So then, the tower image is definitely related to the whole city–temple complex, and shares its ambivalence, in that it can be positive or negative.

It is most likely that *Hermas* highlights the 'watchtower' connotation, given the paraenetic atmosphere of the apocalypse. Jonathan Z. Smith points out the difference between open and closed images as views of reality. He comments that 'the walled city is a symbolic universe which serves...as an 'enclave', a 'strategic hamlet' against the threat of the boundless, chaotic desert'.[51] We have seen that the wilderness or desert is used in *4 Ezra*, the Apocalypse and *Hermas* with positive as well as negative connotations: it is threatening, but it is also the *tabula rasa* upon which God works (*4 Ezra* 9.24; Apoc. 12.14; *Herm.* 3.1.3). Assurance of God's protection is seen not only in his provision of a refuge, but also in his mastery of the wild. However, if the city is a

---

50. The exposition of the tower as shepherd's booth or *sukkah/huppah* suggested by J. Massyngberde Ford is ingenious, but wholly speculative, and based on an unprovable assumption that the direct background of *Hermas* is Jewish or Jewish Christian; see 'A Possible Liturgical Background to the Shepherd of Hermas', *RevQ* 6 (1969), pp. 531-51.

51. *Map is not Territory* (Leiden: Brill, 1978), p. 136.

symbol of refuge against the evils of the desert, then the tower is an
even more accentuated image of this. *Hermas* seeks to provide a
'strategic hamlet' against the godless world: the mysterious, divinely-
constructed Church, the tower, is his answer. The protective impulse of
this symbolism is very strong, and corresponds to the strong paraenetic
content of the apocalypse. What the Lady provides verbally and in
written form (1.3.4) is underscored visually through the tower. The
Church is the humble recipient of God's creative and sustaining power;
she must depend totally upon him.

Within the text of *Hermas*, the tower is not simply a metaphor, but
appears as a supernatural entity which can only be seen through the
quasi-magical efforts of the Lady revealer (καὶ ἐπάρασα ῥάβδον τινὰ
λαμπράν, 3.2.4b). It is God's own work, founded on water, upheld on
the mysterious foundation of his word and unseen δύναμις (3.3.5c).
Moreover, the whole purpose of its building is to reach perfection and
glory, and to this end the six protoctic (3.4.1) angels labour. Their
labour, however, meets with numerous obstacles, namely the obstinacy
and worldliness of the flawed rocks which are to be incorporated. The
'useless' must be made εὔχρηστος...καὶ ὠφέλιμος τῇ ζωῇ (3.6.7).
Thus, although the final understanding of the tower is that of a pre-
existent, perfect and glorious eschatological reality, this vision remains
off-stage. What Hermas actually sees is a reflection of the Church he
knows, albeit comfortingly superintended by the Almighty and his
agents. In *Aseneth*, the term 'City of Refuge' is one of great prestige,
honour and dignity; in *4 Ezra*, the seer is terrified by the glorious
appearance of Zion, whereas he has been able to chastise her more
humble counterpart prior to the transfiguration; the entire movement of
the Apocalypse is towards the revelation of the New Jerusalem, which
now needs no more preparation, but comes fully adorned out of heaven.
The vision of *Hermas* is more domestic, not totally void of glory, but
always aware of the imperfections which must be removed.

So, then, even where we might have expected a full-blown picture of
glory, Hermas gives us a double vision, always maintaining the tension
between the divine and the mundane, the cosmic and the pedestrian,
the pure and the tarnished. The Lady does not actually undergo a
transfiguration into a more glorious image, but is pictured in a different
vision, Tower alongside Lady. It is as though the Lady Church forfeits,
for the time being, her status as a vision, and becomes the superinten-
dent of another vision, that of the divinely-built tower. A more in-depth

view of the Church is given, but not really a more glorified one. We wait until the final bride sequence to get a hint of what the τέλος might be, and receive there only an intimation, not an intense description. Hermas's final word is one of paraenesis and warning, although this is not his only word.

The 'Messages' Embedded in the Action

We have seen a movement from verbal through to experiential revelation in the four episodes of *Hermas*. However, embedded in every episode there are various direct messages, which put in propositional form the themes that have been enacted in the drama. The Lady's encouraging βιβλίον in *Vision* 1 reinforces God's action, later pictured in *Vision* 3: God has created; he is preparing; he is levelling the way for his elect (1.3.4). The chastising βιβλαρίδιον which is delivered to Hermas in *Vision* 2 and which he later deciphers looks forward to the flaws of the stones and the spectre of the monster. Its message: Repent quickly! If you do, you will receive. Endure the coming persecution (2.2.2-8). In *Vision* 3, Mother Church speaks directly to her children, with words that are from God as much as from her: I nurtured you. Be at peace; share with the poor; you leaders, turn around (3.9.1-10). Hermas's voice in *Vision* 4 warns him not to be double-minded (4.1.4), and the Bride instructs him to tell the elect, yet again: Be prepared, keep pure, and do not fear (4.2.5-6). As if all this instruction were not enough, the final instruction is to remember what has been written, that is, the whole book, words, pictures, experiences, glimpses of the eternal, assurance and warning.

These embedded messages, directed as they are to the elect, recall the major themes of mysterious Church in her many aspects, the meaning of persecution for her purification, and the promise of God's direction of her building. In the structure of the piece, which highlights the third *Vision*, in the thematic frames of persecution and double-mindedness, and in the four media of increasingly intensified revelation, the common denominator is the question of the identity of the Church. How is it that this imperfect, tired and dispirited body of which Hermas is the representative can be the glorious building, the stately and noble Lady, which Hermas sees before him? This is the question which troubles the seer, and which is addressed in detail through a number of different methods, both literary and propositional. In the course of the answer, both the inherent nobility of the Church, the fact that she is the creation of God, and her ultimate goal, the fact that she is destined for glory, are acknowledged. However, the focus of the seer remains upon the present changing Church, and upon the belief that the Almighty is overseeing her ongoing transformation. That transformation is envisioned as being furthered by the very visions that Hermas has viewed and has, upon divine instruction and with due comment and interpretation, passed on to others of the elect. The identity of the Church is that of the work of God which must, can and will change: one of the vehicles of transformation is the book of *Hermas* itself.

Praise without Reason

It would seem, then, that *Hermas* does not have one core message, as suggested by Hellholm and Aune, but several, delivered both in propositional and in visionary form. What many have seen to be the main thrust of the book is both its best feature and its worst: for Carolyn Osiek, the paraenesis of *Hermas* 'translates' the apocalyptic vision into 'realistic terms'.[52] For others, the realism works against the vision to produce a pedantic, rather boring homily which may have been helpful at the time of its writing but has little enduring value. It may well be that part of the problem is that *Hermas* itself represents the stance of the 'tired Church' pictured in *Vision* 1.9.12, an 'old man' with 'no hope', much 'grief', and great need of rejuvenation. Walter Brüggemann, in his provocative *Israel's Praise*,[53] speaks of the dangers of those biblical passages which call for praise without reason. Inevitably, in such pieces, the reasons for praise remain offstage, and a sheer call to adulation of God is given to the faithful. Often in such works, the political or social *status quo* is justified; all is seen as part of God's plan. It has been seen in *Hermas* that reasons are given for praise. God is creator, preserver, nurturer, builder, and so on. However, the reasons are nearly pre-empted by the paraenetic thrust of the piece: despite glimpses of glory, it is the preaching tone that predominates. Moreover, at 3.5.1, Hermas comes perilously close to using his vision in a propagandistic manner, establishing the *status quo*. Here, the apostles are seen as near-perfect, and the tension between glory and the Church-in-process is lost. Again, in

52. Osiek, 'Genre', p. 119.

53. *Israel's Praise: Doxology against Idolatry and Ideology* (Philadelphia: Fortress Press, 1988).

Vision 4, the monster does not actually touch Hermas—it is as though the realities of life are kept at one remove at the critical point. The envoy of the entire *Shepherd of Hermas* instructs the seer, and through him, the entire Church, to 'tell everyone about the wonders of God' (*Sim.* 10.4.1). Hermas discharges his responsibility, but keeps most of these wonders in the realm of the unseen. Moderate or realistic transformation is his concrete dream for the present Church; the vision of final transfiguration must remain an article of faith.

Chapter 6

TRANSFORMATION AND IDENTITY

The Perspective of Apocalyptic Transformation

The aim of the analysis of each of our four texts has been to read their actual lines, specifically the passages of transformation, rather than to read *between* them in an effort to discover theologies, or *behind* them, in an effort to discover historical milieu, or even *against* them, in an ideological deconstruction. The apocalypse genre is particularly interesting because of its reveal–conceal dialectic. There is, within each of the pieces, a centripetal force around a central idea or mystery which is explained, at least in part; there is also a centrifugal force, which spins off from this revelation, hinting at further mysteries for the wise, intimating further glories yet to be experienced, and so on. These four apocalypses, probably because they do not contain tours of heaven or hell, are less diffuse, less centrifugal than other of the more 'esoteric' apocalypses, such as the *Enoch* corpus. This lack of esoterica may account for the fact that, with the exception of *Aseneth* (which is popular literature, and not intended as sacred), these apocalypses were not suppressed, but enjoyed great popularity in the Church, so that the *Shepherd* was considered canonical in the East, *4 Ezra* was appended to the Vulgate, and the Apocalypse was canonized outright. Concentration on certain matters of 'theological' or 'ecclesiological' concern ensured, perhaps, that their mysterious aspects were not considered prominent enough to be dangerous. At any rate, all four texts do seem to centre on certain problems or questions that are solved or revealed by travelling through the apocalypse. John J. Collins, in the *Apocalyptic Imagination*, comments,

> The generic framework…of apocalypse… is important because it invokes a conceptual structure or view of the world…Specifically, the world is mysterious…human life is bounded in the present by the supernatural

> world of angels and demons and in the future by the inevitability of a final
> judgment. This conceptual structure...provides a framework for viewing
> the problems of life.[1]

The notion of a divine 'framework' or 'perspective' is certainly one that has emerged during this analysis of structure in *Aseneth, 4 Ezra*, the Apocalypse and *Hermas*. In each one of these pieces, a problem or problems are overcome, answered or contained by reference to the mysteries included in the apocalypse. There is a change of perspective on the part of the seer, hence (ideally) on the part of the hearer/reader, whereby the problem finds its resolution. This is not to say that we can reduce each work to a statement of its question or purpose, nor to suggest that we can necessarily get a hold on its original writer and audience, and thereby decode the message. However, it seems clear that the stance of the seer in each apocalypse is that of a questioner, and the patent purpose of a revelation is to make something clear. Because *Aseneth* is a story, the 'problem' is a dramatic one: how can the unclean Aseneth become the bride of the pure and godly Joseph? In *4 Ezra*, the questions are more philosophical, and stated clearly throughout the dialogue sections: why is judgment the lot of Israel and of humanity? In the Apocalypse, John laments greatly because he believes that no one can 'open the seals' and look into the scroll (5.4). And in *Hermas*, the practical problems of a fatigued Church and repentance come to the fore. The change in perspective is marked by Aseneth's repentance and admission to the heavenly mysteries, Ezra's consolation and sight of Zion, John's view of the Lion who is a Lamb and the persecuted woman who is a Bride, and Hermas's multiple vision of the human but mysterious Church in the process of being built.

John J. Collins has argued that all apocalypses involve the presentation of an apocalyptic perspective which may serve as an alternative basis for the problems addressed. It is as though the seer were inviting the reader to change vantage points and look at life from *here*—from the locales of heaven, hell, the past and the future. What is different about our apocalypses is that the movement from one perspective to another is illustrated through the event of transformation. The seer does not simply call on his or her hearer to change, but actually traces the steps for us. This change is pictured in a symbolic transformation.

In *Aseneth*, the seer herself undergoes a radical transfiguration, one

---

1. Collins, *Apocalyptic Imagination*, p. 7.

which confirms her internal change, and which heralds the retelling
of the story in chiasmic reversals. Because the transfiguration is
confirmatory, it is placed just after the central angelic visitation and
revelation, and announces the 'de-complication' of the plot. Aseneth, the
heroine, is transformed and gives hope to the reader that others outside
of Israel may likewise be changed into a state of purity before the
Almighty. She is, symbolically, their mother and 'City of Refuge'.
Although Aseneth is a romantic heroine who 'steals the stage', so to
speak, there is no suggestion that she *alone* is to be transformed because
of her own piety and great wisdom. All along it has been the effort of
God's servant, Joseph, who has provided the initiative for the improved
status of his bride-to-be. Aseneth is exemplary, and sounds a call to
courage for others in her situation. There is no sense that she is an
especially endowed mystic rewarded for her esoteric adventures: her
story is the story of the penitent *par excellence*. Whether or not her
children may expect to see angels or undergo physical transfiguration is
unclear—after all, this is a story.[2] However, they may certainly expect to
be changed so as to please God. We may depict the function of
Aseneth's transformation in the sentence, *This confirms that. This* transformation confirms the spiritual transformation that has taken place
through prayer, repentance and revelation; it also confirms the transformation promised to those who follow the pioneer heroine. The
transformation takes a confirmatory role within the plot and within the
conceptual framework of the whole piece. Extended structural chiasmus
is the vehicle through which the outworking of the transformation is
expressed in dramatic form.

The situation in *4 Ezra* is somewhat different: the transformation here
is in fact the *peripeteia* of the apocalypse. The most obvious transformation is that of the lamenting woman into the glorified Zion. The
seer is confronted with a symbolic transformation and is required to
respond to it. However, the symbol is itself a complex one; Zion is not
simply a symbol seen in a vision, but a dramatic actor with whom Ezra
has to do. The structure of *4 Ezra* is artfully composed so that the
lamenting sections lead up to the appearance of the lamenting Zion;
similarly, the three revelatory visions follow her revelation in glory.

2.   If one subscribes to such views as those presented by Philonenko concerning
the relationship between *Aseneth* and mysticism, perhaps such expectations might be
seen as involved. The likelihood of such cultic aspects is minimal, however, given the
popular appearance of the romance.

Ezra's own experience is therefore mirrored in the central symbolic transfiguration. Moreover, his own change occurs at the episode of Zion's dual appearance. This is all the more successful because Ezra actually enters into conversation with the woman, reversing his earlier role of lamenter, and after viewing her splendour, enters into it— although what he actually sees within the gates of Zion is not described! The transformations of Zion and Ezra *enable* the further revelations to be grasped, and are in themselves revelations. The lamenting–glorified Zion is the figure that provides a perspective by which Ezra can understand both his complaints (visions 1, 2 and 3) and the mysterious visions which follow (5, 6 and 7). The lamenting and divinely visited Ezra serves in his turn as an example to his community (ch. 14), and holds out the lamp in a dark place. Within the structure of *4 Ezra*, transfiguration occurs so that one can say, *This is that. This* lamenting one *is* the glorified one. This weeping one *is* the one with a future. Both visually and verbally the transformation serves to enable the action to proceed, identifying the distressed with the glorious.

In the Apocalypse, the structure is less patent, but still clear enough in broad outline. Change is a key theme throughout the book. It is called for in the letters, suggested symbolically in the Lion who is a Lamb, and its results are seen in ch. 21 when the glorified Bride arrives, finally adorned for her husband. Transformation has occurred as a result of the conquest of evil (chs. 17–19), and so the glorified Zion is presented at the climax of the apocalypse, when the battle has finally been won. However, the story is not a simple linear progression; it has been previewed, particularly in the central sections of the little scroll, chs. 10–14. Here we are also presented with a glorious woman (12.1), albeit a figure who must run to the desert in exile. Her stay in the desert seems to be the result of persecution but is really God's own preparation. So then, 12.1-7 presents the reader with a mystery: the suffering Church who is really Queen of Heaven, just as the Lamb is really the Lion. The witnessing and the blood of suffering are necessary for the glory (12.11); they are the means of preparing the transformed New Jerusalem. Bride and Lion are hidden under the aspect of the woman and the Lamb. Structurally, the central section of chs. 10–14 previews the final victory at the end of the Apocalypse. To adopt the terminology of Northrop Frye, a miniature 'epic of wrath' (the little scroll) is found within the larger 'epic of return'[3] (the Apocalypse as a whole). The perspective

3.   Frye, 'Theory of Genres', pp. 316-24.

offered is: *This comes from that. This* victory, this conquest, this glorification, comes from that persecution, humility and suffering. Proleptically, the kingdom 'has been given'—this is clear because suffering and wrath are now doing their work. There is a continuity between the present situation and what will come, despite their radically different outward appearances. What is now implicit and hidden will finally be revealed. Further, what is hidden to the world is in fact revealed now to the faithful who understand the outcome of suffering.

Transformation in *Hermas* is not a singular occurrence at one key point of the plot, as is the case in *Aseneth, 4 Ezra* and the Apocalypse. Rather, multiple transformations or aspects of the Church form the very structure of the *Visionenbuch*, marking the four visions off from each other and intensifying the message. A major focus seems to be placed upon the third lengthy vision, where the ancient Lady, the interpretation of her metamorphoses, and the picture of the Tower appear together. Transformation, then, structures the book and shapes the teaching. The phrase, *This means that*, would seem to characterize the whole thrust of *Hermas*. *This* form of the ancient Lady means that the Church, and you, Hermas, are spiritually weak, though honourable; *this* form of the Tower shows that a divinely superintended process of preparation is under way; *this* form of the young Church means that repentance has done her work and single-mindedness has been accomplished, and so on. At almost every turn, the transformations are decoded for the benefit of the seer and his listeners. As in *4 Ezra*, the seer's spiritual pilgrimage is pictured in the symbolic aspects of the woman and Tower: *Hermas* draws the lessons explicitly, whereas in *4 Ezra* the effort is more subtle, and more amenable to modern tastes. Only the final transformation remains undecoded, perhaps because it is a future and tantalizing hope rather than a desired and urged present reality. Whereas the seer fades in the Apocalypse, in *Hermas* the visionary is self-advertising through his very self-deprecation. The perspective offered is multiple, but coherent and extremely explicit. To the reader who considers himself or herself a child of the Church, the message is: You now know, like Hermas, that this means that, so act accordingly; ensure that you enter the Tower by the gate, and are renewed like the Lady, since you have seen that a Tower and a rejuvenating Lady are mysteries that apply to you. The expectation of transformation is rather modest for the present, but Hermas does hold out for his reader a shining eschatological hope in the undecoded figure of the joyful Bride.

So then, in *Aseneth* the transformation is confirmatory, and set just past the turning point of the apocalypse, heralding chiasmic reversals. In *4 Ezra* the dual transformation of the central episode, verbal and visual, facilitates the action, and contains the laments of the seer and his community. In the Apocalypse, there is continuity between the exiled woman and her glorious transfigured reappearance as the New Jerusalem, just as the little scroll previews the events of the last chapters. And in *Hermas*, the multiple transformations structure the visions and the didactic message, urging moderate transformation, but intimating a future glory that goes beyond mere paraenesis. In each piece, an alternate perspective is offered, and symbolized in the dramatic transformations that speak to the situation of both the seer and her or his 'community'. The change of Aseneth confirms that converts can see themselves as accepted by God; the change of the woman and Ezra shows that the faithful can see lament and glory as part of the same reality; the change of exile into Bride indicates that suffering is to be seen as necessary to triumph; and the changes of the Ancient Lady and built Tower teach that the weak Church is to be seen as a shining work of God, a mystery. The paraenetic function, implicit or explicit, of the apocalyptic genre, comes strongly to the fore in these female figures of solidarity, which mirror the plight and experience of the seer, and stand for the experience and hope of the faithful as a whole.

What is remarkable is how many similarities mark the four pieces, despite their patent differences. Only *4 Ezra*, after all, begins with a stated philosophical question to be answered. *Aseneth* is a story, or perhaps a religious myth, rather than the romantic formation of a problem, if seen in its own terms. The Apocalypse is more a proclamation of triumph than a response to difficulties, although critics have persisted in labelling it 'persecution literature'. And *Hermas* is essentially a teaching or series of teachings on the Church rather than an answer to the problem of second repentance. Because each one of these different literary entities shares a visionary stance and apocalyptic form, they do have many generic characteristics in common. This has become apparent through comparison of each work to the *Semeia* profile, comparisons which have demonstrated, even in the unusual case of *Aseneth*, the appropriateness of considering these texts as apocalypses. Each of the apocalypses includes a narrative framework, vision or visions mediated by an otherworldly figure, and numerous elements in the spatial and temporal axis. These parallels are heightened by the use of the symbolic female figure who is transfigured. The story, philosophical problem, proclamation and teaching are themselves transformed into the revelation of a mystery or mysteries to which the transformed woman is related.

Transformation and Identity

As a result of this common figure, similar or parallel themes emerge in each book. The most obvious theme which the four works share is that of identity. Who is Aseneth—a pitiable unclean woman, or the Bride of Joseph and the City of Refuge (and who is the angel—mystery of mysteries!)? Who is the lamenting woman—one who requires consolation and correction, or the messenger of hope for the prophet himself? Who is Ezra—one of the lost or a lamp to his community? Who is the Apocalypse's Lady in the desert—the Queen of heaven or a refugee at the mercy of the serpent? Who is Hermas's Ancient Lady—Sibyl or Church, fatigued or honourable? The theme of identity is informative since it makes explicit the function of the transformations, and provides a link between the literary world and the world of the author/reader/community. Identity is one of the themes proper to the apocalyptic genre, since it is a revelatory theme corresponding to the question, 'Who?' It would seem that the pieces considered here are particularly directed to this end, in contrast to other apocalypses which answer to the question, 'What?', or 'When?' The *Enoch* literature, for example, and other apocalypses with heavenly or infernal journeys, tend to dwell upon the furniture or workings of these realms. The mysteries described in such apocalypses (Type II in Collins's scheme) fall into the category of esoteric phenomena, and cluster into the section which Collins labels 'spatial axis'. In these apocalypses, even questions of identity are answered in terms of filling in the pictures of heaven or hell, rather than explaining in any depth about the personality described. That is, the names of angels and spirits are recited as part of the description of the places visited, and they augment the vision of the mysterious realm, rather than being probed for their own sake (for example, *1 En.* 6; *2 En.* 4; *Mart. Isa.* 7.9).

In the *Semeia* paradigm, the alternate to these spatial apocalypses are those apocalypses along the 'temporal axis', especially Type Ia. There are indeed some apocalypses which seem to emphasize questions of history and eschatology, that is, they respond to the question, 'When?'

Of the apocalypses analyzed here, probably *4 Ezra* would fit most readily into this category, followed by the Apocalypse. However, the heavy emphasis upon identity, the answering of the question, 'Who?', is at least as important as matters of history or eschatology, even in these pieces. It would seem that this analysis of transformation has uncovered another key component of apocalypses which could only be fitted into the 'spatial axis' in the *Semeia* grid and not the temporal. This is because we cannot say that the transformations of either the seer or the Lady/building symbol are for the most part eschatological occurrences. That is, in *Aseneth* the transformation envisaged is present and most probably an inner one, in *4 Ezra* it is a present revelation of a hidden present reality, and in *Hermas* it is an ongoing process extending into the future—only the Apocalypse views transformation as an eschatological event. To chart such transformations using Collins's scheme, it would seem that 'otherworldly elements', specifically 'otherworldly beings' (10.2), is the closest category. However, the category is neither accurate in describing a this-worldly figure which is transfigured, nor sufficient to point to an ongoing discussion of identity. The category could, however, be expanded to allow for revelatory material answering to questions of identity. This would be a salutary balance to the heavy amount of material documented on the 'temporal axis' (five categories with sub-sections, over against only one). The comments of Martha Himmelfarb are instructive: 'Greater attention to these elements would allow a more helpful categorization'.[4] Her specific concern is to allow for a fuller definition of the apocalypses with heavenly (or infernal) journeys, since the *Semeia* paradigm is at present better suited to describing eschatological or historical apocalypses.[5] What is interesting is

4. 'The Experience of the Visionary', *Semeia* 36 (1986), p. 98.
5. Even a cursory glance at the *Semeia* paradigm and chart demonstrates the strong influence of the 'historical' apocalypses on generic description—even in a volume which attempted to break away from this. That is, under the 'temporal axis', there are numerous categories and subcategories, whereas the spatial axis admits of only two: otherworldly realms and otherworldly beings. The detail in the temporal category parallels the attention that has been given to the historical apocalypses, an attention due mostly to the canonical status of Daniel and its subsequent use as a prototype or model for the genre, despite the earlier dating of some of the *Enoch* corpus (e.g. the *Astronomical Book*). Martha Himmelfarb has called attention to the inadequacy of this analysis, particularly in relation to the cosmological apocalypses, that is, those which have little historical or eschatological matter. She has ably demonstrated the need for a further breakdown of categories under the spatial axis,

that our pieces do not fall, as do those discussed by Himmelfarb, within Type II. They should, accordingly, be easier to categorize than the heavenly journey apocalypses which Himmelfarb feels have been neglected. *4 Ezra*, *Aseneth*, the Apocalypse and *Hermas* nevertheless contain even within them characteristic features which are not easily identified in the present system.

Himmelfarb's diagnosis of the inadequacies of the master paradigm is

especially in her discussion of 'tours of hell' as a sub-genre, discernible through formal analysis. Other important additions to the spatial axis might include such features as 'astronomical' or 'cosmological' mysteries (cf. *1 Enoch* or *Jubilees*), and the differentiation of 'otherworldly beings' as demonic, angelic or divine. In the four pieces discussed here, the existence of 'heavenly books' and 'heavenly writing' is actually a feature of the otherworldly mysteries, and not simply a mode of revelation, as charted by Collins (1.4). That is, books are introduced not merely as a means of revelation (although they do function in this way, especially in *Hermas*), but as an element of the divine world. At times, in fact, the content of the book or writing is *withheld*, preventing revelation. Its bare existence stands as a reminder of God's action and authority. Hence, in the Apocalypse, the believer is promised a 'stone with a name known only to himself', just as in 10.4, John is told to seal what the thunders have uttered, although we are told that they have sounded. When revelation occurs through writing, the actual image of the book is often as important as the message it contains. It is *in itself* a solemn sign of God's authority, confirmation, judgment or salvation, and not a simple vehicle for some proposition or teaching. We might make reference here to the *performative* function of language. In Aseneth, the angel's decla-ration was not simply confirmatory, but accomplished her acceptance (*pace* Chesnutt). God's word of declaration enacts its message, rather than simply announcing intention. The power of the word is even more acute in the case of a written declaration which purports to encode the will of the Almighty. This function of writing is particularly congenial to the ancient view, 'What I have written, I have written', a high attitude towards the written word which is at home in the world of the written revelation, the apocalypse. Acknowledgment of this feature may well be an important key to our understanding of the genre apocalypse in contrast to that of prophecy, since the prophetic word and the scribal action consistently come together in a way not found in other revelatory literature. The written word assumes a special authority within the world of the apocalypse, where seer and scribe unite. At any rate, it is clear that there is a need for an augmentation of what Collins calls 'the spatial axis', based on careful observation of the apocalypses themselves. Although it is wise to beware simple methods of discerning meaning, the suggestions of Aune and Hellholm concerning hierarchical statements and the importance of vowed or written divine words should not be taken lightly. At any rate, the self-consciousness of the written word is a factor in the genre apocalypse that should be reflected in any breakdown of recurring features. This is particularly so when the written quality of the word is hedged about with sanctions, as in the closing verses of the Apocalypse (22.18-19).

in fact more radical than a simple suggestion to augment the spatial axis. Her analysis of the apocalypses containing a 'tour of hell' suggests that 'the absence or presence of...eschatology is of minor importance [here]...[hence] not a useful criterion for categorization'.[6] In fact, a criticism of the eschatological criterion of the *Semeia* paradigm has far-reaching consequences. It is on the basis of history and eschatology (the temporal axis) that sub-types a, b and c of both Types I and II are to be discerned. Hence, although the spatial axis is especially illustrated in Type II apocalypses, the setup of the grid ensures that the temporal axis cuts across these categories. That is, sub-types a, b and c depend on history and eschatology, and are used to categorize every apocalypse. There remains, therefore, a tyranny of the temporal axis in the paradigm currently used, although this paradigm has significantly modified the traditional view of apocalyptic which went so far as to equate apocalyptic with eschatology.

We have considered here four examples of Type I apocalypses with a common narrative component of symbolic transformation. *Aseneth*, because of its affinities with the romance genre, may seem an unpromising place to start for a study of the genre apocalypse, and because of the way that its inner 'apocalypse' is so firmly embedded within the overall narrative. The visionary sequence of chs. 14–17 is nevertheless helpful because of its links with the personal transformation of seers, a phenomenon found commonly in type II apocalypses. Moreover, the 'apocalypse' of *Aseneth* is in other respects not an atypical example of Ic works, and demonstrates the extension of the envelope structure of the genre apocalypse (which always has a narrative framework)[7] into the body of the work itself. The other three apocalypses considered here bear even more significance for reflections upon the genre as a whole. If two major examples of a Ib apocalypse (the New Testament Apocalypse and *Hermas*) and one prominent example of Ia (*4 Ezra*) show a previously unnoted concentration upon the issue of identity, then this at least requires consideration. In our sampling, identity was emphasized through the events of transformation—is the issue also joined in other apocalypses, and by what means?

It would seem that sub-types a, b and c ('historical', 'cosmic and/or political eschatology' and 'only personal eschatology') do not adequately

6.   Himmelfarb, 'Experience', p. 97.
7.   It may be that structural parallelism is a common enough feature in apocalypses to warrant its inclusion under possible 'formal' features.

distinguish or contain these four apocalypses of Type I much better than they do the Type II apocalypses described by Himmelfarb. That is, the question of identity clearly overshadows questions of time in all four of our pieces, which are spread over sub-types a, b and c. Perhaps a grid which encompasses space and time, although complex enough, excludes by its very nature other essential elements of this comprehensive genre. If other apocalypses prove to answer the question 'who' as readily as 'when' or 'what', then some reformulation of the model may be indicated. How such a problem might be remedied is a difficult issue, and one that lies beyond the scope of this discussion. Any remodelling must take into account the flexibility of the genre, and the fact that eschatology, although present in most, if not virtually all apocalypses, does take a subordinate role to other concerns in at least some of them. At first glance, the question of identity may seem more a matter of the *function* of the apocalypse than of its content. We have seen, however, in all four pieces, that identity is touched upon as part of the very stuff of revelation. To have an inspired insight into God's 'who' may direct the reading (or listening) community along certain lines—but so, too, does an insight into the 'whats' and 'whens'. Content and function are bound up together.

It may be, then, that a third axis, one related to the question of 'Who?', is in order. Apocalypses could then be analyzed by reference to three axes, the temporal, the spatial, and the 'identical'.[8] Such an addition would probably make a chart impractical, but it would do justice to the element of identity which may well be integral to the genre. The apocalyptic perspective urges the reader to consider life from a different stance in time (temporal), and in space (spatial); it also suggests that the reader may adopt a transformed perspective by becoming, as it were, *someone else*, someone more in tune with the mysteries he or she is viewing (the 'identical'). This is suggested explicitly in the Apocalypse: just as there is a New Jerusalem, there is also a 'new name' provided for its inhabitants. Connected to this question of 'Who?' would also be the concept of the identity of God, and the relationship of God to the

8.   The term 'identical' is used here to refer to one thing viewed at different times so as to express an identity. This is the first application noted in the *Oxford Dictionary*, although 'identical' is used more frequently in common speech to refer to two objects alike in every detail. 'Identical' used in the first manner is consonant with the primary meaning of the noun 'identity', that is, 'individuality; personality; the condition of being a specified person'.

community, to the seer, to the other beings detailed in the apocalypse, wherever such questions are explicitly entertained by the author.

Transformation and Humility

Related to the question of identity is another theme, one which is found in all four of the pieces under discussion. This is the element of humility— the sober evaluation of the role of the seer and humankind in relation to the divine and the angelic. Martha Himmelfarb's discussion of the experience of the visionary highlights the idea of transcendence, and suggests that if transcendence is a key issue in apocalypses, '[W]e still need to ask, what kind of transcendence?'[9] Her contrast of the *Martyrdom of Isaiah* and the *Apocalypse of Paul*, the first of which employs the motif of the seer's transformation, and the second of which rejects this, is instructive in our discussion of transformation and humility. She suggests that in the *Apocalypse of Paul* such a transformation is rejected because the work is a third-century one which allows for the sinfulness of the righteous; the corresponding view of heaven is one which allows for various levels and rewards. Hence, '[f]or people who believe that the righteous sometimes sin, the boundary between human beings and angels is likely to be well defined'.[10] In the *Apocalypse of Paul*, humans keep their place even in heaven, and the transformation is not described for the seer nor the righteous in general. Such a tendency reminds us that in three of our pieces, the actual physical transformation of the seer is not envisioned, either as a reward for special righteousness, or as an example for the faithful as a whole. In *4 Ezra*, the whole concept of ascending to the council of God is explicitly rejected (4.5), and speculation about the heavenly realms is kept to a minimum (4.23). Moreover, Ezra continues to identify himself with imperfect humanity, although he is forbidden by Uriel to do so (8.47); the approval of Ezra's lamentation makes the simple adoption of Uriel's view simplistic. Similarly, in the Apocalypse, there is no one found innately 'worthy' except for the Lamb himself, even though there is a radical dualism between good and evil, a scheme into which the faithful are fitted. John may be invited up to heaven as a vantage point for the subsequent visions, but he is not himself transformed, nor does he join in the songs of either the angels or the multitudes in white. In *Hermas*, the self-

9. Himmelfarb, 'Experience', p. 109.
10. Himmelfarb, 'Experience', p. 106.

deprecation of the seer is obvious, and he is continually scolded by the Lady or an *angelus interpres* for prying into matters beyond his understanding. At 3.4.3, the theme of humility is linked explicitly with that of God's glory. The Church tells us,

Οὐχ ὅτι σὺ ἐκ πάντων ἀξιώτερος εἶ ἵνα σοι ἀποκαλυφθῇ·
ἄλλοι γάρ σου πρότεροί εἰσιν καὶ βελτίονές σου, οἷς
ἔδει ἀποκαλυφθῆναι τὰ ὁράματα ταῦτα· ἀλλ' ἵνα δοξασθῇ
τὸ ὄνομα τοῦ θεοῦ, σοὶ ἀπεκαλύφθη καὶ ἀποκαλυφθήσεται
διὰ τοὺς διψύχους, τοὺς διαλογιζομένους ἐν ταῖς
καρδίαις αὐτῶν εἰ ἄρα ἔστιν ταῦτα ἢ οὐκ ἔστιν·

Here, then, we have an explicit reflection upon the relationship between humble humanity and glorious divinity. The implication is that humility is both a prerequisite and a necessary reaction to God's glory. It might be said that there is in our apocalypses an ambivalence concerning the righteousness of the seer and of the faithful, an ambivalence that is reflected in the reserve with which the experience of transcendence is treated.

Aseneth provides a link with those other apocalypses in which the transcendence of the seer is described. In the *Enoch* literature, the seer is singled out especially for transfiguration during his mystical 'experience', although the righteous as a whole are promised such a transformation only after death. This is also the case in the *Martyrdom of Isaiah*, as Himmelfarb has indicated. Aseneth, although not ascending to the heavens, is transformed as a special case. Her description, coupled with the ostentatious description of Joseph, and the similarities between Joseph and the mysterious angel, does not suggest a clear dividing line between the angelic and the faithful. Even here, however, repentance, meekness and humility are seen as quintessential virtues, and play key roles in the drama. The romantic nature of the piece makes such extravagant descriptions of transcended humanity less theologically suggestive than if they were to occur in a more serious piece, accompanied by warnings and assertions of divine superintendence. Thus in *Aseneth*, even though the heroine herself is transformed, the romantic nature of the book and its popular appearance argue against an interpretation that Aseneth's physical transformation might be repeated by the individual proselyte with mystical leanings. She is a symbolic heroine: the faithful convert would expect to appropriate her amazing transfiguration no more than he or she would anticipate a natural Jew to demonstrate the physical radiance of Joseph (*Aseneth* 5.5; 6.2-6).

This stance of humility, evident in all four of our pieces, distinguishes them from both *merkavah* mysticism and Gnostic texts, in which ascent and transformation are common themes. Just as the 'historical apocalypses' such as Daniel and *2 Apocalypse of Baruch* provide an answer or response to the more 'cosmological' approach of the esoteric apocalypses,[11] so too do the apocalypses of identity provide their own response. Such a response may be the product of time and provenance, rather than the result of a self-conscious polemic. Nevertheless, it is probably no accident that the later mystical writings took their point of departure from *1 Enoch* rather than from *4 Ezra*, the Apocalypse or *Hermas*—despite their intimations of mystery, the latter apocalypses offer no real grist for the mystical mill. Standing in the place of the vacancy provided by 'no otherworldly journey' is a marked stance of humility, a stance that is consonant with the questions of identity raised by the transformation theme. The humble aspect of the seer ensures that the interpretation of the symbolic transformation does not veer off in the direction of identifying the faithful too closely with God. Hence, the transformations and the closely connected question of identity function largely in the realm of paraenesis and encouragement, rather than opening up a philosophical discussion or mystical exploration of ontology *per se*.

Transformation and Suffering

Another motif which adheres to the transformation episodes is that of suffering, and concomitant issues such as lamentation, repentance and prayer. Since *Aseneth* is a conversion story, the whole dimension of repentance and prayer takes precedence. The chiastic arrangement of the plot balances Aseneth's repentance and humiliation (H, I, 10.1–13.15) against her transformation and adoption of bridal attire (I′, H′, 18.5-11), both sections enclosing the apocalyptic vision. Similarly, the ἥμαρτον psalm (21.11-21) emphasizes the movement from sin and pride to adoration and transformation, through the vehicle of confession.

In contrast, but with certain parallels, *4 Ezra*'s very plot moves from lamentation to consolation, and it has been seen that the suffering itself is very likely the means by which transformation occurs—both the cry of the Lady and the most vivid lament of Ezra herald their changes. It might also be noted that the lament of the community at 12.45 indicates

11. Collins, 'Jewish Apocalypses', p. 22.

that they are prepared to hear Ezra and receive his later teaching as
their 'lamp'.

Suffering and lamentation are key themes in the Apocalypse, since it
is through μαρτύριον that the kingdom has become the kingdom of
God (12.11), it is the very casting down of Satan that means the tribulation of the saints, it is in exile that the Bride is prepared, and it is in the
glorified City that every tear will be wiped away. It might even be said
that the prime identifying mark of the community is the θλῖψις which
John says he 'shares' (1.9) with the churches, along with more positive
possessions. As in *4 Ezra*, sorrow is to be transcended, but is not
belittled.

Finally, in *Hermas*, repentance is a catalyst for the visions (1.1.3),
invokes the presence of the Ancient Lady (2.1.3), is enjoined throughout
the messages, and plays a key part in the Tower vision (3.5.5). The
prominence of confession and repentance in *Hermas* does not count
against its apocalyptic form, but simply means that the issues of corporate salvation and humility found in other apocalypses have been taken
to their logical conclusion. In concert with the Apocalypse and *4 Ezra*,
the order of the monster–Bride vision in *Hermas* makes it clear that
tribulation begets purity. These connected themes of suffering–
repentance–lamentation–tribulation fill in the picture of the community
whose identity is revealed by the visions. Who is this one who suffers?—
the glorified Lady, the Mother of the faithful, the Bride of the Almighty!

The Allusive Symbol

The issue of identity is, in a special way, illustrative of the allusive nature
of symbolic language. Each of our pieces presents a symbolic figure of
the woman/building which is rich in allusive power, but which functions
in a unique way. Because of the long history behind the use of a female
figure to portray Israel, and the traditional understanding of Zion as the
special *locus* of God, these pieces can call upon such concepts implicitly.
Each of the works assumes an interest and knowledge of the biblical
material, and places itself in continuity with this corpus when it uses,
often unexplained, such images as Bride and mother. The interpreting
angel or mediator does clarify visionary material, but in apocalypses,
very often traditional material is left uninterpreted, and image is piled
upon image to produce an effect. Thus, in the Apocalypse we read of
'the dragon...that ancient serpent, who is called the Devil and Satan, the

deceiver' (12.9), and of the harlot, Babylon, the great City (that is, Jerusalem) who sits on seven hills (that is, Rome, ch. 17 *passim*).

Such allusiveness in the genre apocalypse very seriously qualifies the view of many, enunciated most clearly by Norman Perrin, that apocalypses use inferior 'steno'[12] rather than 'tensive' symbolism. Such charges may be true of certain passages within apocalypses (for example, the *Animal Apocalypse, 1 En.* 85–90), but do not do justice to the many other passages in which symbols, without or despite their interpretations, call up a multitude of images. The best testimony to this is the ability of each of our pieces to have meaning outside of its original setting. This allusive quality of symbol is so vital that the symbols gain for themselves a life of their own.

In *Aseneth*, the characters assume symbolic proportions, so that some critics have been tempted to read the romance as a *roman à clef* or the work of a mystery cult (Philonenko, Kuhn, Kee, Kohler). Such allegorical approaches, however, are demonstrably tenuous by virtue of their very discrepancies and number. A better explanation for the symbolism of *Aseneth* is to see it as a means of communication with a biblically literate readership. Careful analysis of the text would yield numerous extended systems of allusion,[13] a venture not possible here. However, we might see as exemplary the creation imagery called up by Aseneth's overtures to the Almighty at ch. 12, or the use of symbolism from Psalm 19 throughout the work.[14] This heavy symbolic atmosphere surrounds Aseneth as the heroine of the romance. It is created, as has been seen, through extravagant description which employs traditional symbolism such as light and dark, death and life, virginity and fecundity. The poetic passages, notably the prayers, advance this symbolic aim, and Aseneth is depicted as the virgin (8.11), the persecuted (12.9), the suppliant (12.3), the orphan (12.13), and so on. By the point of her transformation, her recreation in symbolic proportions is complete, so that both her 'foster-father' (18.11b) and Joseph himself (12.5) exclaim at her beauty, and

---

12. See Chapter 3, p. 72 n. 58.

13. P. Slater, *The Dynamics of Religion: Meaning and Change in Religious Tradition* (New York: Harper & Row, 1978), p. 30, points out the phenomenon of a symbolic network attached to a key symbol. This allusive aspect of symbolism is explored in relation to the Zion symbol by Ollenburger, *Zion, the City of the Great King*, pp. 19-20.

14. See 'Excursus: Aseneth and Wisdom Literature, with Special Reference to Psalm 18 (LXX)', in my original dissertation, 'The Ladies and the Cities', pp. 44-48.

enquire as to her identity. They take up the question which the reader has been encouraged to pose throughout these striking descriptions, descriptions which are redolent of biblical phraseology: Who is this glorious one? Her 'blessed' identity is confirmed by the 'son of God', Joseph, who crowns the descriptions by recognizing her as the 'City of Refuge' (19.9). She is the 'chaste virgin' who will be the mother of many.

In *4 Ezra*, the female symbol enters into actual conversation with the seer, drawing him into the vision, and obscuring the line between vision and the book's 'reality'. Without this obscurity, in fact, the *peripeteia* of the apocalypse could not be enacted, since it is Ezra's ignorance which calls him to adopt a different stance, moving from lamenter to comforter. The change in Ezra mirrors the transformation of the 'surprise' Zion symbol; Ezra himself functions as more than a representative of his community. He indeed functions as a quasi-symbol. His is a 'lamp', a light showing the promise of God to his people. His people's identity and future are potently symbolized by his own transformation and that of the weeping–glorious Woman–City, Zion. The *angelus interpres*, in accord with apocalyptic tradition and for the sake of clarity, makes the woman's identity clear at the point of her transformation. However, for the reader of the apocalypse, the Woman–City symbolism will have already evoked ideas of Israel as the Bride of Yahweh, with promises of fruition (cf. Isa. 54.1-14).

Interestingly, in the Apocalypse the seer almost vanishes from view. He presents the problem, the need for change through the transmission of the letters and through his own response at 5.1, but is almost entirely absorbed into the visions which take centre stage for the rest of the work. Except for vision markers such as 'I saw', 'I heard', and the occasional intrusion at key points (10.8; 22.8), the seer who identifies himself as John reminds us of the modern convention of omniscient narrator. Without his constant intrusion, the drama is rendered more immediate. The effect is that the reader/hearer is drawn into the panorama, and is immediately confronted by the portents of exiled woman, dragon and New Jerusalem: these are not only John's symbols, but the believer's symbols, speaking to the faithful directly, despite the mediated method of apocalypse.[15] Aune and Hellholm have intimated

15. This mediated quality is, it would seem, more qualified in the Johannine Apocalypse than in other examples of the genre. The book is noted for its departure from certain apocalyptic norms, one of these being its 'open' rather than 'closed'

how the very 'digressive' and integrative structure of the book, and the use of repetition, function to include the reader in this way. The reader is moved by a benign manipulation to see himself as one of the 'blessed' with washed garments who may enter the City by the gates.

Hermas follows the same symbolic method as *4 Ezra* in that the seer has actual concourse with the symbolic Lady, so that the plane of vision and the plane of the book's 'reality' merge. The apocalypse evokes a wealth of traditional symbolism both biblical and Hellenistic[16] in depicting the various aspects of the Church, who is transformed both relatively, as she is progressively rejuvenated, and radically, when she appears as a Tower. Despite the sometimes wooden appearance of the symbolism, a certain polyvalence and vitality are retained, as may be seen in the dual explanation for her aged appearance, or the free re-writing (expansion?) of the Tower vision in *Similitude* 9. The use of the Tower image recalls God's provision for the Church in the chaotic desert, and reinforces the direct messages of divine superintendence found throughout the visions. While the mysterious status and glory of the Church aids the paraenesis, it nevertheless does retain a sort of life of its own. *Hermas* (if not the whole of the *Shepherd*) is at least partially rescued from sheer dogmatism or ethical concern, through its network of symbolism which has been set into a captivating line of action. The dynamic movement of the symbolism from ancient Lady to Bride, coupled with the intriguing juxtaposition of images (Lady and Tower in *Vision* 3) evokes a richer understanding of the 'Who?' of the faithful, and does not descend into mere pedantry, despite a certain taming of the images.

Each of the pieces uses the natural allusive property of symbolism in different ways, then. It might be judged that with *Aseneth* and the Apocalypse, the symbolism is 'wilder', being allowed, so to speak, to 'take over' the text. *Aseneth* thus assumes, through its symbolic complex, of which the female symbolism is a part, an appearance more significant than that of mere popular 'romance'. Such a situation, however, may not

revelation. Such characteristics are indicative of a work by an author who is familiar with a form, and can depart from what is expected, i.e., Fowler's final stage in the development of a genre ('Life and Death', pp. 199-216).

16. Dibelius gives ample evidence for awareness of Hellenistic traditions in his discussion of the Sibyl and her seat at Cumae (*Der Hirt*, pp. 452-54). Less clear is the common plea that Hermas is associated with the revealer Hermes, and hence *Sim.* 9 is associated with the legendary Arcadia; for the debate, see Snyder, *Shepherd*, p. 17.

be so very unique, given its time of writing. As Bickerman reminds us, 'the genre of historical fiction' in the Jewish Hellenistic age required the creation of a 'parabiblical book'.[17] In the Apocalypse, the untamed quality of the symbols is accentuated through the seer's lack of inter- ference, and the noticeable lack of interpretation at various obscure stages of the visions. This 'untamed' quality, of course, may be delibe- rate, rather than simply naïve, as has been argued in recent treatments of the Apocalypse.[18] In *4 Ezra*, the symbolism is more controlled, perhaps because of the consistent use of the *angelus interpres*, but perhaps also because of the centripetal focus of the work. Finally, in *Hermas*, the symbols are all but tamed, making the 'message' of the book its main burden. Despite the different methods, each of the four draws upon the traditional stock of biblical imagery (and some may indeed draw upon one or more of the other—definite dating would make this more ascertainable) in order to call attention to the glorious Lady who is transformed and who is identified with the community of the faithful. From the most centrifugal, *Aseneth*, to the most centripetal, *Hermas*, these apocalypses highlight the question of identity through special attention to the female figure.

Transformation and the Lady

One of the questions which emerges from such a study concerns the reason for the *femaleness* of the transformed figure. In our own time, such a question is of particular interest, but may be more a function of our interest in feminist studies than a problem which arises naturally in the texts. It is certain that the female figure of Israel, later transposed into Church, was a dominant one in a corpus which saw the community as the Spouse of Yahweh, and later of Christ. Perhaps later ecclesiastical reflection did a disservice to the breadth and fruitfulness of the image by concentrating on the bridal to the near-exclusion of the wifely and

17. E.J. Bickerman, *The Jews in the Greek Age* (Cambridge: Harvard University Press, 1988), pp. 203-204.
18. Such deliberate 'naïveté' is consonant with the views of Lohmeyer and Kraft. See Chapter 4, p. 86 n. 10 above. It should be noted also, however, that the openness of the imagery is not absolute, and that the analyst need to remain sensitive to the cues given in the text, it the text is not to become a pretext for a foreign agenda. The serpent, or dragon of Rev. 12, for example, is firmly placed within the logic of the symbolism *against* the woman, not as a possible ally, *pace* Keller, 'Die Frau', p. 424.

motherly aspects. That is, Wife and Mother are more tested relationships and hence may be more useful images in informing our ideas of these on a human level. The Bride is a shining hope, but a more remote and static symbol by its very nature: no one stays a bride for long. It may be that the position of women in later church ages would have been very different if the female imagery had been retained in its complexity, without an undue preference for the bridal aspect.

Some have indeed argued that the damage has already begun with the material considered in this study. Schüssler Fiorenza, for example, speaks of the danger of 'surrender[ing] our imaginations' to the 'dramatic action' of the Apocalypse, where 'both the oppressive and eschatologically redemptive communities are female because cities were personified as women'.[19] The difficulty which she sees is a change in rhetorical situation, so that the response enjoined by a reading today is no longer completely 'fitting'. Her way of reclaiming the text is to call attention to the persecution setting of the original writing/reading, and to understand the rhetoric in this light. Catherine Keller, working from a postmodernist stance, reclaims the inherently misogynistic Apocalypse by means of a creative midrash upon the work. She plays 'with and against'[20] the imagery, in order to deconstruct the primary patriarchal-messianic-prophetic tradition, and in order to allow its latent and submerged life-nurturing wisdom tradition to come forth. A third vocal respondent to the Apocalypse, Tina Pippin, insists that the book is, in its gender codes, unreclaimable, and 'not a safe space for woman';[21] nevertheless, it retains a certain value for liberation, for 'united action' and 'apocalyptic thunders'. It is certain that the problems encountered by these critics with the New Testament Apocalypse would be multiplied were they to do parallel readings of *Aseneth, 4 Ezra* and *Hermas*—all of which encode female imagery in terms of marginalization, humility and suffering. The books, after all, are addressed to communities for whom such stances were a reality, either in social or perspectival terms. Moreover, the texts set forth *seeming* weakness as a means of

---

19. 'Visionary Rhetoric and Social-Political Situation', p. 199.

20. 'Die Frau', p. 415.

21. *Death and Desire*, p. 80. See also the more moderate criticism of A. Yarbro Collins in 'Feminine Symbolism in the Book of Revelation', *Biblical Interpretation* 1 (1993), pp. 20-33. Here she considers the Apocalypse's feminine symbols to be 'limited and limiting for women' because 'mother, prostitute and bride are relational terms with the male at the centre' (p. 33).

strength—they had the history of Israel or the pattern of the Lamb as backdrop to their own drama.

I have engaged in this study with the presupposition that these works have a life beyond their original *Sitze im Leben*, and not necessarily a sinister one. By speaking of this ongoing power, I do not intend to argue for an essentialist reading, but to recognize that the communities addressed are not temporally limited. This is true simply in terms of the human experience: *humani nil a me alienum puto*. It is especially true of two of these apocalypses because of their enshrinement within, or adjacent to, a 'canon'. Moreover, to qualify the violent or subjugating language by ascribing to them a persecution mentality, or by expanding their meaning through creative midrash, or by rejecting such symbolism outright, is not to understand these works, but to neutralize them.

Before the modern reader can hope to begin a nuanced critique of any piece of ancient literature, she or he must engage in a more-or-less sympathetic reading. It is evident that such a reading will proceed from certain social, political and religious presuppositions, but an attempt to waive these must at least be made so that the text may be heard, and not simply reacted against. We may, reading in a certain direction, discover that 'Rev. engages the imagination of the contemporary reader to perceive *women* in terms of good or evil, pure or impure, heavenly or destructive, helpless or powerful, bride or temptress, wife or whore';[22] we may even read the climactic entry into the New Jerusalem as a picture of 'mass intercourse' (!) with the Bride by 144,000 'virginal males'.[23] If we stay with such readings, then perhaps we have forgotten that the Apocalypse paints its pictures not only for women, but also for men—indeed for both together as a group, and not separately. To read the symbol backwards is a defensive and emotional response similar to the capitalist who would enthusiastically champion usury on the basis of the Parable of the Talents. While symbols do shape reality, and sometimes shape it contrary to our desires, we will do well to note when misappropriation has occurred. The subordination of the female figure in these pieces is first of all a reflection of the supreme status of the Almighty, not a commendation of a 'chain of being'. The careful reader of *Aseneth* will note that she is not only handmaiden but also scribe (20.5) and mystic; similarly, the lament of *4 Ezra*'s woman is the powerful catalyst for change, the Apocalypse's Lady is mother, martyr,

22. *Death and Desire*, p. 80.
23. *Death and Desire*, p. 80.

warrior and Bride, and *Hermas*'s Church is similarly many-faceted. Although in three of these pieces the final state is that of Bride, we have seen that the other images are not abandoned, but subsumed or taken up into the final one. The identity of Bride in relation to God does not detract from the rich identity of the female figures in the world in which they move. Moreover, the identification of the female symbols with that of City or Tower is a continuous reminder of the power of the Lady. As she is subordinate to God, she retains strength over against her detractors through the symbol of the fortress/tower/city/temple. And in the Apocalypse, at any rate, the ratios of power and humility undergo a thorough reversal: readerly assumptions about the seat of human power are challenged. Amidst all this narrative and symbolic activity, the image remains a rich and vital one.

The symbol is in no way peculiar to apocalypses, however, and so remains only tangential to a discussion of apocalypse *per se*. What may be said is that, given the milieu, the use of a female figure is particularly apt in apocalypses which stress the theme of humility, and related themes of suffering, repentance and meekness. The glory intimated by the transformations is always qualified by virtue of the subordination of the figure. This is an action which we should not be surprised to find in four works from the Judaeo-Christian tradition.

Alongside this subordination goes a certain idealization of the community of God through the female figure. While the female imagery retains a certain complexity, including notions of wife, mother and Bride, she is never depicted in derogatory terms, as in the prophetic view of Israel 'playing the harlot' or being ignobly born (Hos. 1–3; Ezek. 16; Jer. 2.20, 3.1-3; Isa. 1.21).[24] The transformed women in *Aseneth*, *4 Ezra*, the Apocalypse and *Hermas* are 'ladies', born to divine glory. The pagan Aseneth is a virtuous woman, even though her very virtue leads

---

24. J. Fekkes, '"His Bride has Prepared herself": Revelation 19–21 and Isaian Nuptial Imagery', *JBL* (1990), pp. 272-73, indicates the more likely background of Isaiah over against Ezek. 16 (so H. Kraft) for the bride of the Apocalypse. Her description of the Isaianic marriage imagery as 'consistently positive' is a slight exaggeration (see Isa. 1.8, 18-21; 3.16–4.1); even in the closing chapters of Isaiah, the spouse's restoration is seen against the backdrop of Yahweh's previous anger (54.8). Even though the faithful city can be described as 'playing the harlot' (1.21), the closing vision is one of complete transformation. Fekkes's point that the ideal imagery of the closing chapters of Isaiah informs the Apocalypse, rather than Ezekiel's portrait, is well taken. It would seem that the four apocalypses discussed here go even beyond the Isaianic vision in idealization.

to pride which must be purged: a harlot would never have done as Bride for the divine son Joseph. Her name was written in the book from eternity: glorious though her transfiguration is, it does not come as a shock to anyone except the players in the drama. In *4 Ezra*, where we might have expected reference to Zion's unfaithfulness as an explanation for her suffering, a wedge is driven between righteous Zion and her sinful inhabitants. That is, although sin is attributed to the community both by Uriel and Ezra, the sinfulness is not associated with the ideal woman who depicts the community as she should be. She herself is always described in positive terms, so that she is a barren woman who has been faithful to her husband for 30 years, and who has been over-taken by misfortune (10.48). This distinction is recognized, and taken to the extreme in the Christian introduction to the piece, where mother Zion disowns her wilful children (2.1-4). In the Apocalypse, the perse-cuted woman starts out as a Queen (in relation to the cosmos), and ends as a Bride (in relation to God). The aspect of impurity is pictured in her foil, Babylon, out of which the people of God are called. While sinfulness is acknowledged in the letters to the churches, it is not presented as part of the profile of the pure Lady. This is equally true of the Sibyl-like Church in *Hermas*, whose transformations emphasize the need for change, but who always retains her nobility and her white hair.

There is an ideal quality to these figures, then, even at the point where they are connected with repentance, suffering, punishment and humility. Unlike the harlot Israel of the Old Testament, the figure is never deposed in the eyes of God, even as a prelude to reinstatement. This is a radical departure from the dramatic pictures of such prophets as Hosea, Ezekiel and Jeremiah. Mary Joan Leith makes some fruitful observations concerning the initiation pattern of Israel's redemption in Hosea 1–3, where Israel 'becomes a woman who must suffer the cosmic conse-quences of her wickedness but who ultimately enjoys the equally cosmic blessings of redemption and recreation'.[25] Leith points to the themes of identity, wilderness, transformation and new creation in this passage as she traces a tripartite initiation pattern of accusation, punishment and restoration in the career of Hosea's Israel. What is missing in our pieces is the harshness of accusation evident in Hosea. Aseneth may be initially rejected by Joseph, but the rejection is tempered by his prayer; she may

25. 'Verse and Reverse: The Transformation of the Woman, Israel, in Hosea 1–3', in P.L. Day (ed.), *Gender and Difference in Ancient Israel* (Minneapolis: Fortress Press, 1989), pp. 95-108.

repent in ashes, but she is not stripped naked as in the day when she was born. In *4 Ezra*, Zion is desolate, but never pictured as 'weltering in [her] blood' (Ezek. 16.6). She is the chosen lily of the Almighty, not the daughter of an Amorite father and Hittite mother! In the letters of the Apocalypse, the people are called to repentance, but there is only the *faintest* suggestion that she might not be reinstated (Laodicea): the Lady is bound for glory. Finally, in *Hermas*, the seer is initially comforted concerning his standing, and although the warnings are grave, the ongoing presence of the Lady Church is a reminder of divine blessing and providence. Our ladies sojourn, so to speak, in the desert, undergo transformation, and are finally united with God or given their rightful place. They do not—except for Aseneth—have to be 'initiated', since they are already in the care of God. Aseneth does undergo an initiation which includes abasement, but this is a self-imposed, rather than external humiliation, itself indicative of her righteous nature.

Part of the difference between the ladies and the restored harlot may be the choice of Zion rather than *eretz Israel* as the figure to be personified, although certainly the image of the City and of Jerusalem in particular have had a chequered career (cf. Lam. 1.8, 15, where Zion is both a virgin daughter *and* filthy). The notion of a heavenly or ideal Zion seems, then, to indicate an idea of the people of God over against the world,[26] an assurance of standing even where present imperfection is recognized. The focus in our pieces is on the people of God *as they should be*, or perhaps, as they are seen by God. Moreover, the thrust of the prophets seems in general to have been to undercut false assurance. Our authors have more need, or more confidence and inclination, to offer comfort—even where that comfort is coupled with a realistic warning. Such a difference may be vital in discerning the possible self-identity of communities reflected by, or utilizing, the apocalypses discussed here. At any rate, the transformed figures of *Aseneth, 4 Ezra*, the Apocalypse and *Hermas* are not merely *female*, they are, in the particular sense of the word, *ladies*. Although such imagery may appear

---

26. For an idea of the implications of this idealization in diaspora Judaism, see J.N. Lightstone, *The Commerce of the Sacred: Mediation of the Divine among Jews in the Graeco-Roman Diaspora* (BJS 59; Chico, CA: Scholars Press, 1984), pp. 7-16. Lightstone shows how the concentric view of the sacred, from the most holy (inside) to the profane (outside) lost its concreteness in the diaspora; the scattered Jews could no longer be a literal *'am levadon yiskon*, and saw instead 'a world studded with "colonies" of that mother of all sacred space, Jerusalem'.

quaint to today's reader, the imaginative power of their transformations, and the rich variation of the theme from work to work should make us sensitive to the issue of identity which has emerged from this study: 'What is this, my mistress, and what is this great and wonderful beauty? At last the Lord God of heaven has chosen you as a bride...' (*Aseneth* 18.10).

Prospect

This study has focused upon the structure of *Aseneth*, *4 Ezra*, the Apocalypse and *Hermas*, and the place of the transformed Lady in each of these, so as to demonstrate that the 'identical' mysteries feature alongside the 'temporal' and 'spatial' as key concerns in the genre apocalypse. However, the examination of the 'Lady/City' motif, the event of 'transformation', and the issue of 'identity' may well open up other courses of investigation. An obvious study would be to consider the function of symbols as models for social transformation, a discussion pursued by Jonathan Z. Smith in *Map is not Territory*, and commenced in connection with the Apocalypse by David L. Barr. The latter comments briefly but poignantly on the possible social effect of the Apocalypse's potent and world-overturning imagery,

> They no longer suffer helplessly at the hands of Rome; they are now in charge of their own destiny and by their voluntary suffering they participate in the overthrow of evil and the establishment of God's kingdom. They now see themselves as actors in charge of their own destiny. And that is perhaps more of a victory than most folks achieved in first century Asia Minor.[27]

The limits of viewing the Apocalypse primarily as persecution literature have already been suggested; however, whenever literature evokes a change of paradigm or perspective on the part of its readers (that is, suffering Lady = glorious City), there is certainly the possibility of fruitful study for the sociologist or social historian.[28] Those interested in the

27. Barr, *Symbolic Transformation*, p. 50.

28. In his forthcoming *Who are the People of God?* (New Haven: Yale University Press, 1995), Howard Clark Kee has made a recent overture to socio-cultural exploration, in which he considers 'the city-community where God dwells' as a primary image of identity among five community models which he finds in post-exilic, early Jewish and early Christian literature. In his scheme, the Apocalypse is categorized as expressing its identity through the image of the 'community where God dwells among his people', whereas *4 Ezra* is treated under another model—'the

possible outward effect of imagery which combines victory with humility, and which also maintains a strong distinction between the chosen people of God and the world, may find an *entrée* here.

Within the area of comparative religion, the transformations observed here may certainly be compared and contrasted to those found in the whole corpus of Hellenistic *metamorphoses*, within the mystery religions, within the cult of heroic or imperial apotheosis, and within the *merkavah* writings. It would seem, for example, that there are certain formal parallels to the notion of the initiate being transformed through a vision of divine mysteries, but that there are enormous material differences. Behm has already made observations to this effect in comparing the Pauline 2 Cor. 3.18 and Rom. 12.2 to the Hellenistic mysteries;[29] the issues are strikingly reminiscent of those suggested by the apocalypses discussed here. Such comparisons would be possible in connection with *Aseneth*, but even more fruitful with other Type II apocalypses, however, since the transformations in the pieces treated here are not actually the result of mystical experience, and are symbolic, thus not the special prerogative of an individual seer. The themes of corporate identity and humility, added to the careful distinction between the human and the divine, act as a constant guard against the actual notion of divinization both in Paul and in our four texts. Reference to the *Aseneth*, *4 Ezra*, the Apocalypse and *Hermas* may provide either background or parallels to the Pauline conception of transfiguration, and may also help to demonstrate the establishment of early Jewish and Christian self-identities over against contemporary religion.

Finally, the establishment of identity as an important concern for the apocalypse should have some impact on those New Testament passages often considered 'apocalyptic'. Alongside obvious eschatological passages

community of the wise'. Kee does not here discuss the special juxtapositions of women–city–community imagery found variously in both works, although he does suggest that the 'five community models' were often 'blended...with each other' (p. 227). It would seem that an analysis of the *particular* configuration of images (which takes into account both similarities and differences) might provide the best starting point for a more explicit socio-cultural study. What actual community might be reflected in any one piece using such imagery? Alternatively, what socio-cultural effects could a particular model or blending of models have on the self-awareness of the community or communities that used this body of literature? (I would like to express my thanks to Dr Kee and Yale University Press for making the page proofs of this book available to me prior to publication.)

29. 'μεταμορφόω', *TDNT*, IV, pp. 755-59.

such as the so-called synoptic 'little apocalypses' and 2 Thess. 2.1-12 should be placed passages with notable configurations of 'apocalyptic' interest, such as 2 Cor. 12.1-10, or the transfiguration of Jesus passages (especially Lk. 9.28-36). Both of these detail numerous motifs and concepts which are best understood by reference to the apocalypses proper, including the perception of heavenly mysteries, the idea of glory, an interpretative word, the theme of humility, and the problem of identity. In 2 Corinthians 12, the use of apocalyptic themes is certainly ironic, whereas in the transfiguration episodes it is more direct. Once the breadth of the genre apocalypse has been recognized, other New Testament passages such as these may be rightfully and fruitfully seen as being informed by the genre. Eschatology may be prominent in the apocalypses, but it is not the last word. In the corpus of a movement which has been perceived as the offspring of 'apocalyptic' we should not be surprised to see many and various points of contact. These may come as either direct or inverse comparisons. That is, the οἰκονόμοι μυστηρίων θεοῦ (1 Cor. 4.1) may equally display indebtedness or reaction to a type of literature which claims unveiled access to divine 'mysteries' of space, time and identity.

BIBLIOGRAPHY

I. General Works: Background, Genre, Literary Criticism, Symbolism

Alter, R., *The Art of Biblical Narrative* (New York: Basic Books, 1981).

Attridge, H.W., 'Greek and Latin Apocalypses', *Semeia* 14 (1979), pp. 159-86.

Aune, D.E., *The New Testament in its Literary Environment* (Library of Early Christianity; Philadelphia: Westminster Press, 1987).

Bal, M., *Narratology: Introduction to the Theory of Narrative* (trans. C. van Boheemen; Toronto: University of Toronto Press, 1985).

Behm, J., 'μεταμοφόω', *TDNT*, IV, pp. 755-59.

Berger, K., *Formgeschichte des Neuen Testaments* (Heidelberg: Quelle & Meyer, 1984).

Bickerman, E., *The Jews in the Greek Age* (Cambridge, MA: Harvard University Press, 1988).

Böcher, O., 'Wilderness', in C. Brown (ed.), *Dictionary of New Testament Theology* (Grand Rapids: Zondervan, 1978), III, pp. 1004-1008.

Brüggeman, W., *Israel's Praise: Doxology against Idolatry and Ideology* (Philadelphia: Fortress Press, 1988).

Caird, G.B., *The Language and Imagery of the Bible* (Philadelphia: Westminster Press, 1981).

Collins, J.J., *The Apocalyptic Imagination: An Introduction to the Jewish Matrix of Christianity* (New York: Crossroad, 1987).

—*Between Athens and Jerusalem: Jewish Identity in the Hellenistic Diaspora* (New York: Crossroad, 1983).

—'Introduction: Towards the Morphology of a Genre', *Semeia* 14 (1979), pp. 1-20.

—'The Jewish Apocalypses', *Semeia* 14 (1979), pp. 21-59.

Culley, R., *Studies in the Structure of Hebrew Narrative* (Semeia Supplements 3; Philadelphia: Fortress Press, 1976).

Culpepper, R.A., *Anatomy of the Fourth Gospel: A Study in Literary Design* (Philadelphia: Fortress Press, 1983).

Fallon, F.T., 'The Gnostic Apocalypses', *Semeia* 14 (1979), pp. 123-58.

Fischer, U., *Eschatologie und Jenseitserwartung im hellenistischen Diasporajudentum* (BZNW 44; Berlin: de Gruyter, 1978).

Fohrer, G., 'Σιών, Ἰερουσαλήμ, Ἰεροσόλυμα, Ἰεροσολυμίτης', *TDNT*, VII, pp. 292-319.

Fokkelman, J.P., *Narrative Art in Genesis: Specimens of Stylistic and Structural Analysis* (trans. P. Visser-Hagedoorn; Assen: Van Gorcum, 1975).

Fowler, A., 'The Life and Death of Literary Forms', *NLH* 2 (1971), pp. 199-216.

Frost, S.B., *Old Testament Apocalyptic* (London: Epworth, 1952).

Frye, N., *Anatomy of Criticism: Four Essays* (New York: Atheneum, 1969 [1957]).

Gammie, J.G., 'The Classification, Stages of Growth and Changing Intentions in the Book of Daniel', *JBL* 95 (1976), pp. 191-204.

Ginzberg, L., *The Legends of the Jews* (6 vols.; Philadelphia: JPS, 1928).

Grant, R.M., *Gnosticism and Early Christianity* (New York: Columbia University Press, 2nd edn, 1966).

Gruenwald, I., *Apocalyptic and Merkavah Mysticism* (Leiden: Brill, 1980).

Hanson, J.S., 'Dreams and Visions in the Greco-Roman World and Early Christianity', in *ANRW* II.23.2, pp. 1395-1427.

Hanson, P.D., 'Old Testament Apocalyptic Re-Examined', *Int* 25 (1979), pp. 454-79.

Hellholm, D., 'The Problem of Apocalyptic Genre and the Apocalypse of John', *Semeia* 36 (1986), pp. 13-64.

Hellholm, D. (ed.), *Apocalypticism in the Mediterranean World and the Near East: Proceedings of the International Colloquium on Apocalypticism, Uppsala, August 12–17, 1979* (Tübingen: Mohr, 1983).

—'En textgrammatisk konstruktion i Matteusevangeliet', *SEÅ* 51-52 (1986–87), pp. 80-89.

Himmelfarb, M., *Tours of Hell: An Apocalyptic Form in Jewish and Christian Literature* (Philadelphia: Fortress Press, 1983).

—'The Experience of the Visionary and Genre in the Ascension of Isaiah 6–11 and the Apocalypse of Paul', *Semeia* 36 (1986), pp. 97-111.

Kee, H.C., *Who are the People of God?* (New Haven, CT: Yale University Press, 1995).

Kennedy, G.A., *New Testament Interpretation through Rhetorical Criticism* (Chapel Hill: University of North Carolina Press, 1984).

Koch, K., *The Rediscovery of Apocalyptic: A Polemical Work on a Neglected Area of Biblical Studies and its Damaging Effects on Theology and Philosophy* (trans. M. Kohl; London: SCM Press, 1972).

Koester, H., *Introduction to the New Testament: History and Literature of Early Christianity* (2 vols.; ET; Philadelphia: Fortress Press; Berlin: de Gruyter, 1982).

Kraemer, R., 'Hellenistic Jewish Women: The Epigraphical Evidence', *SBLSP 1986* (ed. K.H. Richards; Atlanta, GA: Scholars Press, 1986):

Leith, M.J., 'Verse and Reverse: The Transformation of the Woman, Israel, in Hosea 1–3', in P.L. Day (ed.), *Gender and Difference in Ancient Israel* (Minneapolis: Fortress Press, 1989), pp. 95-108.

Lightstone, J.N., *The Commerce of the Sacred: Mediation of the Divine among Jews in the Graeco-Roman Diaspora* (BJS 59; Chico, CA: Scholars Press, 1984).

Lohse, E., 'Σιών, Ἰερουσαλήμ κτλ', *TDNT*, VII, pp. 319-38.

Lurker, M., *The Gods and Symbols of Ancient Egypt* (trans. B. Cummings; London: Thames & Hudson, 1980 [German original: Wilhelm Barth Verlag, 1974]).

Muilenburg, J., 'Form Criticism and Beyond', *JBL* 88 (1969), pp. 1-18.

Ollenburger, B., *Zion, the City of the Great King: A Theological Symbol of the Jerusalem Cult* (JSOTSup 41; Sheffield: JSOT Press, 1987).

Pannenberg, W. 'Appearance as the Arrival of the Future', *JAAR* 35 (1967), pp. 107-18.

Perrin, N., *Jesus and the Language of the Kingdom* (Philadelphia: Fortress Press, 1976).

Plöger, O., *Theokratie und Eschatologie* (WMANT 2; Neukirchen–Moers: Neukirchener Verlag, 1959).

Polzin, R., 'The Framework of the Book of Job', *Int* 28 (1974), pp. 183-200.

Porteous, N.W., 'Jerusalem-Zion: The Growth of a Symbol', in *idem* (ed.), *Living the Mystery: Collected Essays* (Oxford: Basil Blackwell, 1967), pp. 93-111.

Rad, G. von, *Theologie des Alten Testaments* (2 vols.; Munich: Kaiser, 4th edn, 1965 [1957]).

Ransome, H.M., *The Sacred Bee in Ancient Times and Folklore* (London: George Allen & Unwin, 1937).

Ricoeur, P., 'Biblical Hermeneutics', *Semeia* 4 (1975), pp. 27-148.

Rössler, D., *Gesetz und Geschichte* (Neukirchen–Vluyn: Neukirchener Verlag, 1960).

Rowland, C., *The Open Heaven* (New York: Crossroad, 1982).

—'The Visions of God in Apocalyptic Literature', *JSJ* 10 (1979), pp. 137-54.

Rowley, H.H., *The Relevance of Apocalyptic* (London: Lutterworth, 1944).

Russell, D.S., *The Method and Message of Apocalyptic* (London: SCM Press, 1964).

Sanders, E.P., 'The Genre of Palestinian Jewish Apocalypses', in D. Hellholm (ed.), *Apocalypticism in the Mediterranean World and the Near East: Proceedings of the International Colloquium on Apocalypticism, Uppsala, August 12–17, 1979* (Tübingen: Mohr, 1983), pp. 447-59.

Scholem, G., *Major Trends in Jewish Mysticism* (New York: Schocken Books, 3rd rev. edn, 1961 [1949]).

Slater, P., *The Dynamics of Religion: Meaning and Change in Religious Tradition* (New York: Harper & Row, 1978).

Smith, J.Z., *Map is not Territory* (Leiden: Brill, 1978).

Stauffer, E., 'γαμέω, γάμος', *TDNT*, I, pp. 648-57.

Stroll, A., 'Identity', in P. Edwards (ed.), *The Encyclopaedia of Philosophy* (New York: MacMillan and the Free Press; London: Collier MacMillan, 1967), IV, pp. 121-24.

Strotmann, A., *Mein Vater Bist Du! (Sir 51,10): Zur Bedeutung der Vaterschaft Gottes in kanonischen und nichtkanonischen frühjüdischen Schriften* (Frankfurter Theologische Studien 39; Frankfurt am Main: Knecht, 1991).

Telfer, W., '"Bees" in Clement of Alexandria', *JTS* 28 (1926–27), pp. 167-78.

Trible, P., *God and the Rhetoric of Sexuality* (Overtures to Biblical Theology; Philadelphia: Fortress Press, 1978).

Webb, B.G., 'Zion in Transformation: A Literary Approach to Isaiah', in D.J.A. Clines, S.E. Fowl and S.E. Porter (eds.), *The Bible in Three Dimensions* (JSOTSup 87; Sheffield: JSOT Press, 1990), pp. 64-84.

Welch, John W. (ed.), *Chiasmus in Antiquity* (Hildesheim: Gerstenberg, 1981).

Yarbro Collins, A., 'Introduction: Early Christian Apocalypticism', *Semeia* 36 (1986), pp. 1-11.

II. *The Apocalypse*

Allo, E.-B., *Saint Jean: L'Apocalypse* (EBib; Paris: Gabalda, 4th edn, 1933).

Aune, D.E., 'The Apocalypse of John and the Problem of Genre', *Semeia* 36 (1986), pp. 65-96.

Barr, D.L., 'The Apocalypse as a Symbolic Transformation of the World: A Literary Analysis', *Int* 38 (1984), pp. 39-50.

Beagley, A.J., *The 'Sitz im Leben' of the Apocalypse with Particular Reference to the Role of the Church's Enemies* (Berlin: de Gruyter, 1987).

Boismard, M.E., '"L'Apocalypse", ou "les apocalypses" de S. Jean', *RB* (1949), pp. 507-27.

Bornkamm, G., 'Die Komposition der apokalyptischen Visionen in der Offenbarung

Johannis', *ZNW* 36 (1937), pp. 132-49; repr. in *Studien zu Antike und Urchristentum: Gesammelte Aufsätze Band II* (BEvt 28; Munich: Chr. Kaiser, 1959), pp. 204-22.

Bowman, J.W., 'The Revelation to John: Its Dramatic Structure and Message', *Int* 9 (1955), pp. 436-53.

Brewer, R.R., 'The Influence of Greek Drama on the Apocalypse of John', *ATR* 18 (1936), pp. 74-92.

Charles, R.H., *A Critical and Exegetical Commentary on the Revelation of St John* (2 vols.; ICC; New York: Scribner's, 1920).

—*Studies in the Apocalypse* (Edinburgh: T. & T. Clark, 1913).

du Rand, J.A., 'The Imagery of the Heavenly Jerusalem (Revelation 21.9–22.5', *Neot* 22 (1988), pp. 65-86.

Ellul, J., *Apocalypse: The Book of Revelation* (New York: Seabury, 1977).

Farrer, A., *A Rebirth of Images* (Westminster: Dacre, 1949; repr. Boston: Beacon, 1964).

—*The Revelation of St John the Divine* (Oxford: Clarendon, 1964).

Fekkes, J., '"His Bride Has Prepared Herself": Revelation 19–21 and Isaian Nuptial Imagery', *JBL* 109 (1990), pp. 272-73.

Ford, J. Massyngberde, *The Revelation of John* (AB 38; New York: Doubleday, 1975).

Gager, J.G., 'The Attainment of Millennial Bliss through Myth and the Book of Revelation', in P.D. Hanson (ed.), *Visionaries and their Apocalypses* (Philadelphia: Fortress Press, 1983), pp. 146-55.

Hellholm, D., 'The Problem of Apocalyptic Genre and the Apocalypse of John', *Semeia* 36 (1986), pp. 13-64.

Isaac, J., *L'Apocalypse du Jésus Christ: Les épreuves de l'alliance et le sens de l'histoire* (Paris: Cerf, 1991).

Keller, C., 'Die Frau in der Wüste: Ein feministlisch-theologischer Midrasch zur Offb 12', *EvT* 50 (1990), pp. 414-32.

Kiddle, M., *The Revelation of St John* (assisted by M.K. Ross; MNTC; London: Hodder & Stoughton, 1940).

Kraft, H., *Das Offenbarung des Johannes* (HNT 16a; Tübingen: Mohr, 1974).

Loenertz, R.J., *The Apocalypse of St John* (London: Sheed & Ward, 1947).

Lohmeyer, E., *Die Offenbarung des Johannes* (HNT 16; Tübingen: Mohr, 2nd edn, 1953 [1927]).

Minear, P.S., 'Far as the Curse is Found: The Point of Rev. 12.15-16', *NovT* 33 (1991), pp. 71-77.

—'Ontology and Ecclesiology in the Apocalypse', *NTS* 12 (1965), pp. 89-105.

Palmer, F., *The Drama of the Apocalypse* (New York, 1903).

Pippin, T., *Death and Desire: The Rhetoric of Gender in the Apocalypse of John* (Literary Currents in Biblical Interpretation; Louisville, KY: Westminster/John Knox Press, 1992).

Rissi, M., *Zeit und Geschichte in der Offenbarung des Johannes* (Zürich: Zwingli Verlag, 1952).

Rousseau, F., *L'Apocalypse et le milieu prophétique du Nouveau Testament: Structure et préhistoire du texte* (Tournai: Desclée & Cie; Montreal: Bellarmin, 1971).

Schüssler Fiorenza, E., 'The Composition and Structure of the Book of Revelation', in E.S. Fiorenza (ed.), *The Book of Revelation: Justice and Judgment* (Philadelphia: Fortress Press, 1985), pp. 159-80.

—'Followers of the Lamb: Visionary Rhetoric and Social-Political Situation', in

E.S. Fiorenza (ed.), *The Book of Revelation: Justice and Judgment* (Philadelphia: Fortress Press, 1985), pp. 181-203.

—*Revelation: Vision of a Just World* (Proclamation Commentaries; Minneapolis: Fortress Press, 1991).

Selvidge, M.J., 'Powerful and Powerless Women in the Apocalypse', *Neot* 26 (1992), pp. 157-67.

Spinks, L.C., 'A Critical Examination of J.W. Bowman's Proposed Structure of the Revelation', *EvQ* 50 (1978), pp. 211-22.

Sweet, J.P.M., *Revelation* (Philadelphia: Westminster Press, 1979).

Swete, H.B., *The Apocalypse of John* (London: Macmillan, 1922).

Thompson, L.L., *The Book of Revelation—Apocalypse and Empire* (Oxford: Oxford University Press, 1990).

Wall, R.W., *Revelation* (New International Bible Commentary 18; Peabody, MA: Hendrikson, 1991).

Wilcock, M., *I Saw Heaven Opened: The Message of Revelation* (London: Inter-Varsity, 1975).

Yarbro Collins, A., *The Apocalypse* (NTM 22; Wilmington: Glazier, 1979).

—*The Combat Myth in the Book of Revelation* (HDR 9; Missoula: Scholars Press, 1976).

—'Feminine Symbolism in the Book of Revelation', *Biblical Interpretation* 1 (1973), pp. 20-23.

Vorster, W.S., '"Genre" in the Revelation of John. A Study in Text, Context and Intertext', *Neot* 22 (1988), pp. 103-23.

III. *4 Ezra*

Bensly, R.L., *The Missing Fragment of the Latin Translation of the Fourth Book of Ezra* (Cambridge: Cambridge University Press, 1875).

Bensley, R.L. (ed.), *The Fourth Book of Ezra: The Latin Version Edited from the MSS* (Texts and Studies 3.2; Cambridge: Cambridge University Press, 1895).

Box, G.H., 'General Introduction' to 'IV Ezra', in R.H. Charles (ed.), *The Apocrypha and Pseudepigrapha of the Old Testament* (Oxford: Clarendon, 1913), II, pp. 542-60.

Brandenburger, E., *Adam und Christus: Exegetische-religionsgeschichtliche Untersuchung zu Röm. 5.12-21* (WMANT 7; Neukirchen–Vluyn: Neukirchener Verlag, 1962).

—*Die Verborgenheit Gottes im Weltgeschehen: Das literarische und theologische Problem des 4 Esrabuches* (ATANT 68; Zürich: Theologischer Verlag, 1981).

Breech, E., 'These Fragments I have Shored against my Ruins: The Form and Function of 4 Ezra', *JBL* 92 (1973), pp. 267-74.

Desjardins, M., 'Law in 2 Baruch and 4 Ezra', *SR* 14 (1985), pp. 25-37.

Esler, P.F., 'The Social Function of 4 Ezra', *JSNT* 53 (1994), pp. 99-123.

Gunkel, H., Review of R. Kabisch, *Das vierte Buch Esra auf seine Quellen untersucht*, *TLZ* 16 (1891), pp. 5-11.

Harnisch, W., *Verhängnis und Verheissung der Geschichte: Untersuchungen zum Zeit- und Geschichtsverständnis im 4. Buch Esra und in der syr. Baruch-apokalypse* (FRLANT 97; Göttingen: Vandenhoeck & Ruprecht, 1969).

—'Die Ironie der Offenbarung: Exegetische Erwägungen zur Zionvision im 4. Buch Esra', *ZAW* 95 (1983), pp. 74-95.

Hayman, A.P., 'The Problem of Pseudonymity in the Ezra Apocalypse', *JSJ* 6 (1975), pp. 47-56.
Harrelson, W., 'Ezra among the Wicked in 2 Esdras 3–10', in J.L. Crenshaw and S. Sandmel (eds.), *The Divine Helmsman: Studies on God's Control of Human Events Presented to Lou H. Silberman* (New York: KTAV, 1980), pp. 21-40.
James, M.R., 'Salathiel qui et Esdras', *JTS* 19 (1918), pp. 347-49.
Kabisch, R., *Das vierte Buch Ezra auf seine Quellen untersucht* (Göttingen: Vandenhoeck & Ruprecht, 1889).
Kirschner, R., 'Apocalyptic and Rabbinic Responses to the Destruction of 70', *HTR* 78 (1985), pp. 27-46.
Longenecker, B.W., *Eschatology and Covenant: A Comparison of 4 Ezra and Romans 1–11* (JSNTSup 57; Sheffield: JSOT Press, 1991).
Metzger, B.M., 'The Fourth Book of Ezra: A New Translation and Introduction', in *OTP*, I, pp. 516-59.
—'The "Lost" Section of II Esdras (= 4 Ezra)', *JBL* 76 (1957), pp. 153-57.
Myers, J., *I and II Esdras* (AB 42; Garden City, NY: Doubleday, 1974).
Rowland, C., 'The Parting of the Ways: The Evidence of Jewish and Christian Apocalyptic and Mystical Material', in J.D.G. Dunn (ed.), *Jews and Christians: the Parting of the Ways, AD 70–135* (WUNT 66; Tübingen: Mohr, 1992), pp. 213-37.
Stone, M.E., 'Apocalyptic Literature', in M.E. Stone (ed.), *Jewish Writings of the Second Temple Period* (Philadelphia: Fortress Press, 1984).
—'Coherence and Inconsistency in the Apocalypses: The Case of the End in 4 Ezra', *JBL* 102 (1983), pp. 229-43.
—*Features of the Eschatology of IV Ezra* (Atlanta: Scholars Press, 1989).
—*Fourth Ezra: A Commentary on the Book of Fourth Ezra* (Hermeneia; Minneapolis: Fortress Press, 1990).
—'On Reading an Apocalypse', in J.J. Collins and J.H. Charlesworth (eds.), *Mysteries and Revelations: Apocalyptic Studies since the Uppsala Conference* (JSPSup 9; Sheffield: JSOT Press, 1991).
Thompson, A.L., *Responsibility for Evil in the Theodicy of IV Ezra* (SBLDS 29; Missoula, MT: Scholars Press, 1977).
Violet, B., *Die Esra-Apokalypse (IV Esra)*. I. *Die Überlieferung* (GCS 18; Leipzig: Hinrichs, 1910).
Volz, P., *Eschatologie der jüdischen Gemeinde* (Tübingen: Mohr, 1934).
Westermann, C., 'Struktur und Geschichte der Klage im Alten Testament', *ZAW* 66 (1954), pp. 44-80.

IV. *Joseph and Aseneth*

Aptowitzer, V., 'Asenath, the Wife of Joseph: A Haggadic Literary-Historical Study', *HUCA* 1 (1924), pp. 239-306.
Beckwith, R.T., 'The Solar Calendar of *Joseph and Aseneth*: A Suggestion', *JSJ* 15 (1984), pp. 90-100.
Bohak, G., 'Aseneth's Honeycomb and Onias' Temple: The Key to Joseph and Aseneth?', in *Proceedings of the Eleventh World Congress of Jewish Studies, Jerusalem, June 22–29, 1993* (Jerusalem: World Union of Jewish Studies, 1994), pp. 163-70.

—'Joseph and Aseneth and the Jewish Temple in Heliopolis' (PhD dissertation, Princeton University, 1994).

Burchard, C., 'Ein vorläufiger griechischer Text von Joseph und Aseneth', *DBAT* 14 (1979), pp. 2-53.

—'The Importance of Joseph and Aseneth for the Study of the New Testament', *NTS* 33 (1987), pp. 102-34.

—'The Present State of Research on Joseph and Aseneth', in J. Neusner, P. Borgen, E.S. Frerichs and R. Horsley (eds.), *New Perspectives on Ancient Judaism* (Lanham, MD: University Press of America, 1987), II, pp. 31-52.

—'Joseph and Aseneth—A New Translation and Introduction', in *OTP*, II, pp. 176-247.

—'Verbesserungen zum vorläufigen Text von Joseph und Aseneth', *DBAT* 16 (1982), pp. 37-39.

—'Zum Text von "Joseph und Aseneth"', *JSJ* 1 (1970), pp. 3-34.

Chesnutt, R.D., *Conversion in Joseph and Aseneth* (JSPSup 16; Sheffield Academic Press, 1995).

—'The Social Setting and Purpose of Joseph and Aseneth', *JSP* 2 (1988), pp. 121-48.

Denis, A.M., OP (ed.), *Concordance Grecque des Pseudépigraphes d'Ancien Testament* (Louvain-la-Neuve: Université Catholique de Louvain Institut Orientaliste, 1987).

Douglas, R.C., 'Liminality and Conversion in Joseph and Aseneth', *JSP* 3 (1988), pp. 1-42.

Holz, T., 'Christliche Interpolationem in Joseph und Aseneth', *NTS* 14 (1968), pp. 482-97.

James, M.R., 'Le livre de la prière d'Aséneth', in P. Batiffol (ed.), *Studia Patristica*, I (Paris: Leroux, 1889), pp. 1-80.

Kee, H.C., 'The Socio-Cultural Setting of *Joseph and Aseneth*', *NTS* 29 (1983), pp. 393-413.

—'The Socio-Religious Setting and the Aims of Joseph and Aseneth', in G. Macrae (ed.), *SBLSP 1976* (Missoula, MT: Scholars Press, 1976), pp. 183-92.

Kilpatrick, G.D., 'The Last Supper', *ExpTim* 64 (1952), pp. 4-8.

Kohler, K., 'Aseneth, Life and Confession or Prayer of', *JewEnc*, II, pp. 172-76.

Kuhn, K.G., 'The Lord's Supper and the Communal Meal at Qumran', in K. Stendahl (ed.), *The Scrolls and the New Testament* (New York: Harper & Bros., 1957), pp. 75-77.

Pervo, R.I., 'Joseph and Asenath and the Greek Novel', in G. Macrae (ed.), *SBLSP 1976* (Missoula, MT: Scholars Press, 1976), pp. 171-82.

Philonenko, M., *Joseph et Aséneth: Introduction, text critique, traduction, et notes* (SPB 13; Leiden: Brill, 1968).

Riessler, P., 'Joseph und Asenath: Eine altjüdische Erzählung', *TQ* 103 (1922), pp. 1-22, 145-83.

Sänger, D., 'Bekehrung und Exodos: Zum jüdischen Traditionshintergrund von "Joseph und Aseneth"', *JSJ* 10 (1979), pp. 11-36.

—'Jüdisch-hellenistische Missionsliteratur und die Weisheit', *Kairos* 23 (1981), pp. 231-42.

Smith, E.W., '"Joseph and Aseneth" and Early Christian Literature: A Contribution to the Corpus Hellenisticum Novi Testamenti' (PhD dissertation, Claremont Graduate School, 1974).

West, S., 'Joseph and Aseneth: A Neglected Greek Romance', *Classical Quarterly* NS 24 (1974), pp. 70-81.

V. *The Shepherd of Hermas*

Die Apostolischen Väter: Die griechischen christlichen Schriftsteller der ersten Jahrhunderte. I. *Der Hirt des Hermas* (ed. and trans. M. Whittaker; Berlin: Akademie-Verlag, 2nd edn, 1967 [1956]).

Barnard, L.W., 'The Shepherd of Hermas in Recent Study', *HeyJ* 9 (1968), pp. 29-36.

Chadwick, H., 'The New Edition of *Hermas*', *JTS* NS 8 (1957), pp. 274-80.

Cirillo, L., 'Erma e l'apocallita a Roma', *Cristianesimo nella storia* 4 (1983), pp. 1-31.

Daniélou, J., *Geschichte der urchristlischen Literatur* (Munich: Chr. Kaiser, 1975 [1926]).

—*A History of Early Christian Doctrine Before the Council of Nicaea.* I. *Theology of Jewish Christianity* (trans. and ed. J.A. Baker; London: Darton, Longman & Todd, 1964).

Dibelius, M., *Die Apostolischen Väter.* IV. *Der Hirt des Hermas* (HNT; Tübingen: Mohr [Paul Siebeck], 1923).

Ford, J.M., 'A Possible Liturgical Background to the Shepherd of Hermas', *RevQ* 6 (1969), pp. 531-51.

Giet, S., *Hermas et les Pasteurs: Les Trois Auteurs du Pasteur d'Hermas* (Paris: Presses Universaires de France, 1963).

Hellholm, D., *Das Visionenbuch des Hermas als Apokalypse: Formgeschichtliche und texttheoretische Studien zu einer literarischen Gattung*, I (ConBNT 13.1; Lund: Gleerup, 1980).

Henne, P., 'La penitence et la rédaction du Pasteur d'Hermas', *RB* 98 (1991), pp. 358-97.

—'La polysémie allégorique dans le Pasteur d'Hermas', *ETL* 65 (1989), pp. 131-35.

Hennecke, E. (ed.), *New Testament Apocrypha* (2 vols.; trans. R.McL. Wilson; London: SCM Press, 1974 [1965]).

Joly, R., 'Hermas et le Pasteur', *VigChr* 21 (1967), pp. 201-18.

Kirkland, A., 'The Literary History of the *Visions* in the *Shepherd of Hermas*', *Second Century* 9 (1992), pp. 87-102.

Lake, K. (trans.), 'The Shepherd of Hermas', in *The Apostolic Fathers* (LCL; Cambridge, MA: Harvard University Press, 1950 [1913]), II, pp. 1-305.

Lightfoot, J.B., 'The Shepherd of Hermas', in *Excluded Books of the New Testament* (London: Eveleigh Nash & Grayson, 1927), pp. 1-403.

Michaels, J.R., 'The "Level Ground" in the *Shepherd of Hermas*', *ZNW* 59 (1968), pp. 245-50.

Osiek, C., 'The Genre and Function of the Shepherd of Hermas', *Semeia* 36 (1986), pp. 113-21.

—'The Social Function of Female Imagery in Second Century Prophecy', *Vetera Christianorum* 29 (1992), pp. 55-74.

Pernvenden, L., *The Concept of the Church in the Shepherd of Hermas* (Lund: Gleerup, 1966).

Riddle, D.L., 'From Apocalypse to Martyrology', *HTR* 9 (1927), pp. 260-80.

Snyder, G.F., *The Shepherd of Hermas* (ed. R.M. Grant; Cambden, NJ: Thos Nelson, 1968).

Streeter, B.H., *The Primitive Church* (London: Macmillan, 1929).

Zeller, F., *Die apostolischen Väter aus dem Griechischen übersetzt* (Kempten: Kösel Verlag, 1918).

INDEXES

INDEX OF REFERENCES

OLD TESTAMENT

CHRISTIAN AUTHORS

Made in the USA
Middletown, DE
18 February 2020

84989010R00108